7.31

SAPscript

SAPscript

Michaelson Buchanan

McGraw-Hill

New York   San Francisco   Washington, D.C.
Auckland   Bogotá   Caracas   Lisbon   London
Madrid   Mexico City   Milan   Montreal   New Delhi
San Juan   Singapore   Sydney   Tokyo   Toronto

Library of Congress Cataloging-in-Publication Data

Buchanan, Michaelson.
    SAPscript / Michaelson Buchanan.
        p. cm.
    ISBN 0-07-134618-X
    1. SAPScript. 2. Business—Computer programs. 3. Client/server
computing. 4. ABAP/4 (Computer program language) I. Title.
HF5548.4.R2B826 1999
650'.0285'53769—dc21

                                      98-55122
                                        CIP

SAP is a registered trademark of SAP Aktiengesellschaft, Systems, Applications and Products in Data Processing, Neurottstrasse 16, 69190 Walldorf, Germany. The publisher gratefully acknowledges SAP's kind permission to use its trademark in this publication. SAP AG is not the publisher of this book and is not responsible for it under any aspect of press law.

McGraw-Hill

A Division of The McGraw·Hill Companies

The views expressed in this book are solely those of the author, and do not represent the views of any other party or parties.

1 2 3 4 5 6 7 8 9 0 DOC/DOC 9 0 4 3 2 1 0 9

P/N 134619-8
PART OF ISBN 0-07-134618-X

The sponsoring editor for this book was Simon Yates and the production supervisor was Sherri Souffrance. It was set in Life by Patricia Wallenburg.

Printed and bound by R. R. Donnelley & Sons Company.

McGraw-Hill books are available at special quantity discounts to use as premiums and sales promotions, or for use in corporate training programs. For more information, please write to the Director of Special Sales, McGraw-Hill, 11 West 19th Street, New York, NY 10011. Or contact your local bookstore.

 This book is printed on recycled, acid-free paper containing a minimum of 50% recycled, de-inked fiber.

Dedication

For Lissa and Alex

Acknowledgments

The author would like to thank the following individuals for their significant contributions to the completion of this book: Lissa Buchanan, Bill Hofford, Ed Swarbrick, Kathy Balentine and John Duram.

The author would also like to thank the following persons for their guidance and mentorship: Ted Hoffman, Jay Smith, Lance Bellamy, Jim Thomas, "Chief" Blackwell (deceased), Cecil Saunders, and the management and staff at DeCA Central Region.

Contents

Contents

CHAPTER 3 **Calling Layout Sets Directly from an ABAP Program**

CHAPTER 4 **Building Blocks**

Foreword

As SAP proliferates throughout the globe, and more and more businesses become dependent on SAP, massive amounts of information are being compiled in large databases throughout the world. If information is in a database, eventually someone is going to want to see it. Managers are going to want to view that information in a format easily understood and pleasant to the eye. Customers will need an invoice that shows all materials and the cost for each item they have purchased.

Creative formatting will become a growing need in the world of SAP R/3 development. As competitive pressures grow in the global economy, companies will need to send more e-mails, faxes and customized reports to their customers and end users. Mike Buchanan's book will help the ABAP programmer start their trek to becoming a more valuable asset to their client or company.

Too many technical books are written without step-by-step instructions of how to build something useful. Mr. Buchanan has taken the time to show an ABAP programmer how to construct powerful templates for their documents and reports.

As a SAP R/3 instructor I am always looking for tools to help my students expand their knowledge in SAP R/3 quickly and effectively. When students take educational classes there are only so many notes that one can take and only so much information a student can absorb. Students are always looking for a beneficial reference tool to utilize after the training class.

As I travel around the country training consultants and employees of companies in SAP R/3 and ABAP/4 I am always asked "Where can I get a good book about ABAP or SAP R/3?" or "Can you recommend a valuable resource about Basis". Many of the students are at a loss due to the dearth of educational materials available for many SAP subjects. This book will eliminate SAPscript from that list.

The preliminary sections of this book provide a basic understanding of SAPscript and its integration into ABAP/4 source code beginning with an introduction to SAPscript, its uses and components and when and where to use SAPscript. This book also covers the architecture and building blocks of SAPscript.

Once the fundamental concepts are covered, the author walks the reader through tutorials covering creating layout sets and creating the ABAP/4 code for enhanced document creation. A very useful command reference, at the conclusion of the tutorials, provides that "Comprehensive Resource" that most students are looking for.

This book will fill that gap and familiarize ABAP/4 programmers with the knowledge that they need to make themselves just a little more valuable to their client or employer.

Best of luck to all as you expand your knowledge in the world of SAP R/3.

Rick Chalkley
Vice President Consulting Services
e-Integrators, Inc.
Boca Raton, Florida

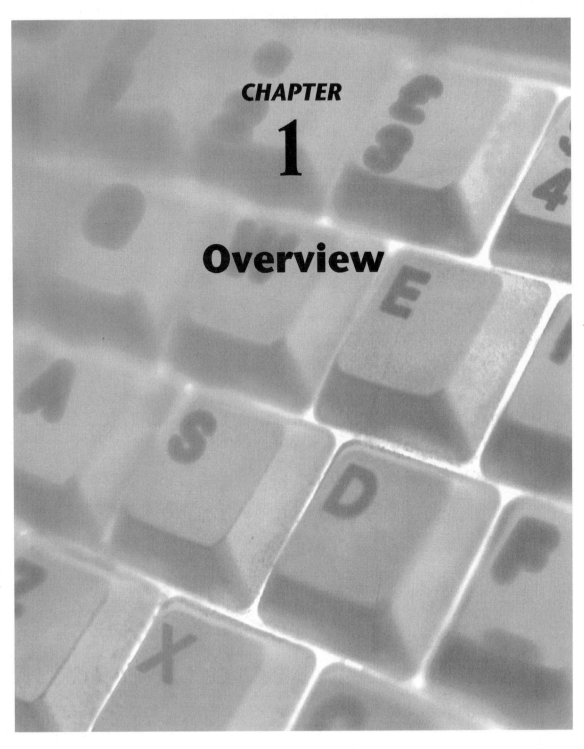

CHAPTER

1

Overview

What Is SAPscript™?

Definition

SAPscript refers to SAP's word processing system. In its simplest form, SAPscript is the editor used to create text documents in SAP. SAPscript text is the text created by the SAP script editor. A layout set defines how page outputs are formatted and contain text elements, *blocks* of text created with the SAPscript editor. Often the term SAPscript is loosely used to describe the combination of layout sets and text elements used to render printed or viewed documents. It is this loose definition which is largely the topic of this book.

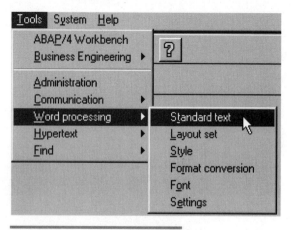

FIGURE 1.1   SAPscript path
Copyright by SAP AG

Introduction to the Concepts

To get to the SAPscript editor, the path (Figure 1.1) from the main menu is: **Tools → Word processing → Standard text** (transaction code SO10). **Tools → Word processing → Layout set** will arrive at the Layout Set: Request menu where layout sets are created, modified and viewed (transaction code SE71). (See also Figure 1.2.)

Standard texts are used for many other things besides layout sets. Basically, any time free form text is needed, the information is stored as standard text. If header text is typed in an application document, SAPscript is used. If documentation is created for an ABAP program (in SE38), it is done using SAPscript. As we will see in Chapter 3, standard text can be created with reference to specific layout sets, and layout sets can include standard text as necessary.

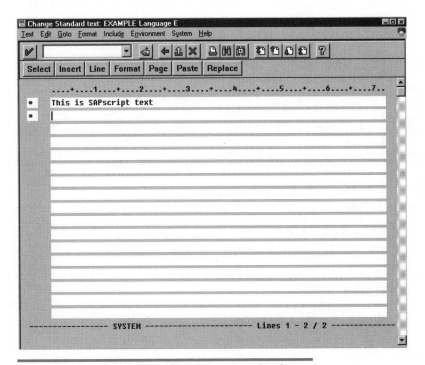

FIGURE 1.2   SAPscript editor for standard text
Copyright by SAP AG

How to Use This Book

The primary purpose of this book is to provide developers and consultants with a reference for completing SAPscript projects. To that end, there is a comprehensive index for looking up key terms, a command reference and tutorials. For the most part, the information is "how-to" in nature.

Icons

NOTE

The note is used throughout to designate "information" of particular interest. This is information that is relevant but would disrupt the flow of the topic if placed in the body of the text. The note might contain information that is important but not directly related to the topic, for example a helpful hint about a special use of a SAPscript command pertinent to a specific scenario. Information contained in notes is included in the index.

WARNING

Warnings provide information about possible problem areas. The icon is followed by a narrative that describes the warning. Information contained in warning sections is also accounted for in the index.

CD-ROM

This symbol will generally appear next to code examples and will be followed by a name. On the CD-ROM, the code example by this name can be used to cut and paste into running code. To cut and paste into the SAPscript editor first paste the upload text into the editor clipboard. See the section called "How Standard Texts are Used", in Chapter 2, for information on pasting text into the SAPscript editor.

Major Segments

The chapters are grouped into four segments:

▲ Introduction
▲ Layout Set Components
▲ Tutorials
▲ Command Reference

The *Introduction* provides a higher-level discussion for those who do not need all the details and gives the technical reader a grounding in the terms and concepts before moving on to the particulars. This segment should provide a reader with enough information to make a rough order-of-magnitude estimate. It will answer such questions as: Do we need to use SAPscript or can we satisfy the business requirements with an ABAP report? If SAPscript customization is necessary, can we get by with making changes to existing reports?

The Architecture chapter in the first segment discusses how things work—in more detail it describes how the layout set components are related. This provides a road map before jumping into the more technical discussions of components and tutorials.

The *layout set components* section provides a detailed analysis of each layout set component. These components are the tools that will be used create SAPscript outputs. A thorough grounding in the components is essential. This section is cumulative, so it is important to read through all the information unless more advanced solutions are required.

The *Tutorial* segment: When a new type of programming requirement arises, I usually go the easy route first and look for similar programs or examples to model from. Here are two examples for that purpose. I tried to pick tutorials that represent typical requirements.

> **How to Modify an Existing SAP Layout Set**—The easiest of the two, this tutorial walks you through how to change the company name on the printed output. It could be used for any simple modification to a layout set where neither the calling ABAP needs to be changed nor the overall structure of the report (altering detail record grouping and so on). To change the way the form processes look at the next tutorial.
>
> **Creating Custom Layout Sets For ABAP Report**—For when a client or employer says, "your ABAP report looks great, just change the font on the header line and we'll be all set." This tutorial is good if an existing ABAP report exists and it must be printed out using SAPscript.

The last segment, **Command Reference**, provides an alphabetical listing of each of the commands. Formatting options and control commands are grouped separately. Each command includes a description, syntax statement, and examples. An example of a command reference is shown here:

CASE   *(name of a valid command as recognized by the SAPscript editor)*

Description: This works the same way as the case statement in ABAP, except we use symbols instead of fields (see the Define command for more information on symbols). Lines between the When statements are processed when the value of the first When statement equals the symbol value. If there is no match then the lines between WHEN OTHERS and ENDCASE will be processed. WHEN OTHERS is optional, so if it is not used and none of the When statements matches the symbol then the whole Case statement will be ignored.

Syntax:

/:	CASE	*symbol*	
	...		
/:	WHEN	*value1*	
	...		
/:	WHEN	*value2*	*(Dynamic values are shown in lower*
	...		*case italic.)*
/:	WHEN	*value3*	
	...		
/:	WHEN	*value n ...*	
[/:	WHEN	OTHERS.]	*(Optional components are shown*
/:	ENDCASE		*in brackets.)*

Symbol is any valid symbol at runtime and *value* is a literal of choice. Symbols must be surrounded by &.

The Case statement must be concluded with the ENDCASE command.

EXAMPLE:

The following example shows the case statement used within an IF command.

```
/: IF &VBDKL-LAND1_AG& = 'AR'
/: CASE &VBDKL-LFART(2)&
/: WHEN 'NL'
H1 Country is Argentina, Delivery type is NL
/: WHEN 'FD'
H1 Country is Argentina, Delivery type is FD
/: WHEN 'KB'
H1 Country is Argentina, Delivery type is KB
/: WHEN OTHERS
H1 Delivery type is unknown
/: ENDCASE
/: ENDIF
```

CD-ROM

Case Statement CE001

In this example we are checking for a specific condition where the country is Argentina and the delivery type is NL, FD or KB. Depending on the delivery type we print a different message. If the country is not Argentina we print nothing. In this case VBDKL-LAND1_AG is the ship-to country taken from the document header record and VBDKL-LFART(2) is the first two characters of the delivery type, taken from the document header.

Why Use SAPscript?

Basically, layout sets will be used for any report that will go outside the enterprise organization. ABAP reports do not lend themselves to printing in multiple fonts so reports generated by ABAP programs alone will be printed in a single font. While these reports are fine for internal information, they do not look professional enough for external communications.

SAPscript and ABAP Examples

Here is an example of a report printed two ways, first with SAPscript (Figure 1.3) then with an ABAP program alone (Figure 1.4).

The two reports look vastly different. The SAPscript report makes use of boxes, multiple fonts and shading. If any of these properties is necessary in a report then the report must be created using a SAPscript layout set.

When to Use SAPscript

If there is a multi-lingual requirement it will probably be necessary to use SAPscript. Although a combination of ABAP and language-dependent standard text could be used to create a multilingual report, it would be better to use SAPscript for this purpose as languages in different reports may have slightly different formatting characteristics; they would be easy to handle in the layout set. Code for this an ABAP report, would be rather cumbersome.

To create a custom version of any SAP report that currently uses SAPscript to generate the output, SAPscript must be used. To generate a different version of a report depending on the output printer, SAPscript would be the best bet. It is entirely possible to have a report look different on two different printers depending on the characteristics of the printers. Layout sets can be copied and altered slightly to allow for the characteristics of each particular printer. The particular layout sets can be matched with the printer and output type in output determination to provide a seamless way of altering the printouts to account for the varying abilities of each printer. Typical ABAP list reports will not have this problem but complex reports that require specific outputs on each page might. The Unearned Discount Report in Figures 1.3 and 1.4, might look drastically different if there were not enough line width to complete the box containing the detail records.

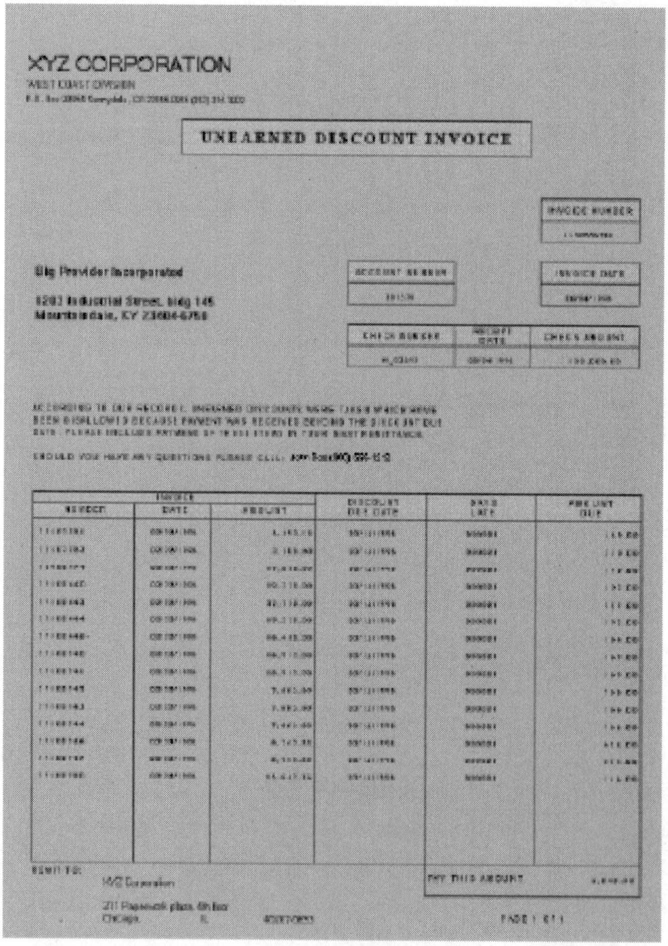
XYZ CORPORATION

UNEARNED DISCOUNT INVOICE

FIGURE 1.3 Unearned discount report using ABAP and SAPscript

Layout sets can also be used to print labels. Particularly if the labels are aligned in more than one column on a page, the layout set can be very helpful in handling this task. See the New-Window command for more information about labels.

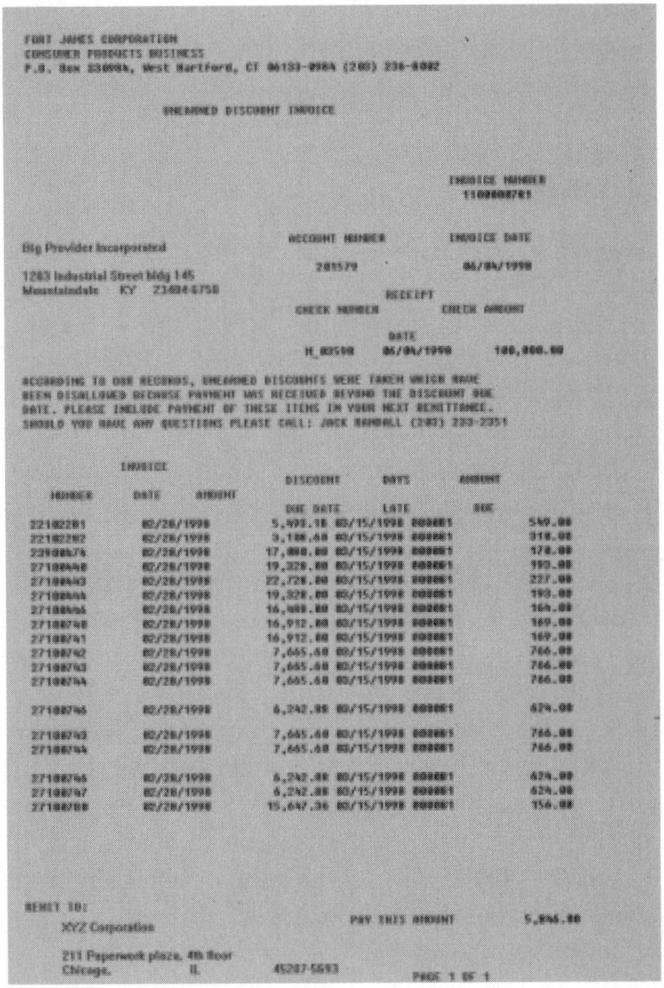

FIGURE 1.4   Unearned discount report using ABAP alone

Use SAPscript when:

▲ The outputs will be sent to an outside entity
▲ Shaded and/or outlined boxes are desired
▲ Specific and/or multiple fonts are desired
▲ Multilingual outputs are required
▲ Creating a custom version of a report that currently uses a layout set (do not change a SAPscript report to a standard ABAP report)
▲ Printing labels with multiple columns on a page

▲ Creating mailing labels
▲ Barcodes are required.

Layout Sets Defined

What Are Layout Sets?

Layout sets are essentially very powerful page layouts. In one respect they are similar to output from a typical word processor. Paragraph attributes and character string attributes can be defined, grouped, and recalled as needed. As with a word processor, page attributes such as page size and default fonts can be defined, but the similarities stop there. Layout sets include page windows, containing text elements. Within the text element it is possible to process SAPscript code and and/or print text. A special type of window called the Main window handles text that will appear in a recurring manner, such as the detail records of a report. Much like the Attributes screen in ABAP, layout sets have a Header screen which describes the key features of the layout set. Like ABAP program objects, layout set objects are unique by name.

There is always a primary language associated with a layout set. If another layout set is created by the same name in a different language, it will become a derivative of the layout set with the primary language but not a new, unique layout set. Only the text elements can be manipulated. To rearrange the format of the layout set go back to the layout set with the original language. This will be easier to visualize after seeing a few examples.

A Layout Set in Use

Figure 1.5 shows an output from a layout set capable of printing multiple pages. This is from the same layout set shown in Figure 1.3 but in this example data fill two pages.

The key to understanding the layout set is understanding the *Main window*. When the Main window on the first page fills up it will go to the Main window on the next page and fill it up; when that page is full, it will continue to the next page and fill it up and so on. The number of pages printed is driven by filling up the Main window on each consecutive page. If the Main window on the first page will hold 15 records, then the 16th record will be printed at the top of the Main window on the second page.

Details on filling up the Main window are in Chapter 4 under the section "Main Window."

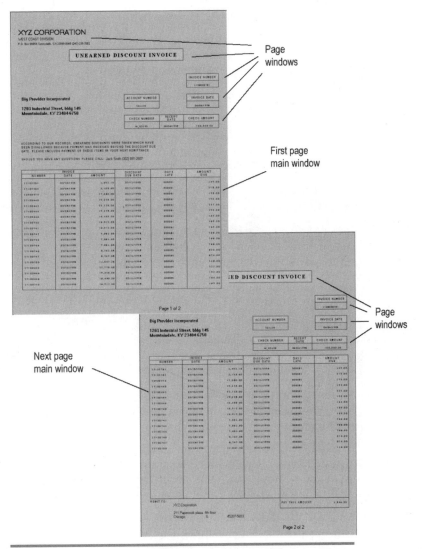

FIGURE 1.5   Unearned discount report with two pages

Page windows are windows for placing text. When a Page window is full, text that cannot fit in the Page window does not appear. The Page window needs to be large enough to contain all the intended text. The primary characteristic of the Page window is the size and location. Find more on Page windows in Chapter 4 under the section "Page Windows."

All the text on a page is contained in either a Main window or a Page window. The text contained in both types of windows can be dynamic or static.

Figure 1.6 shows the layout set header for Figures 1.3 and 1.5. The header contains the basic attributes of the layout set.

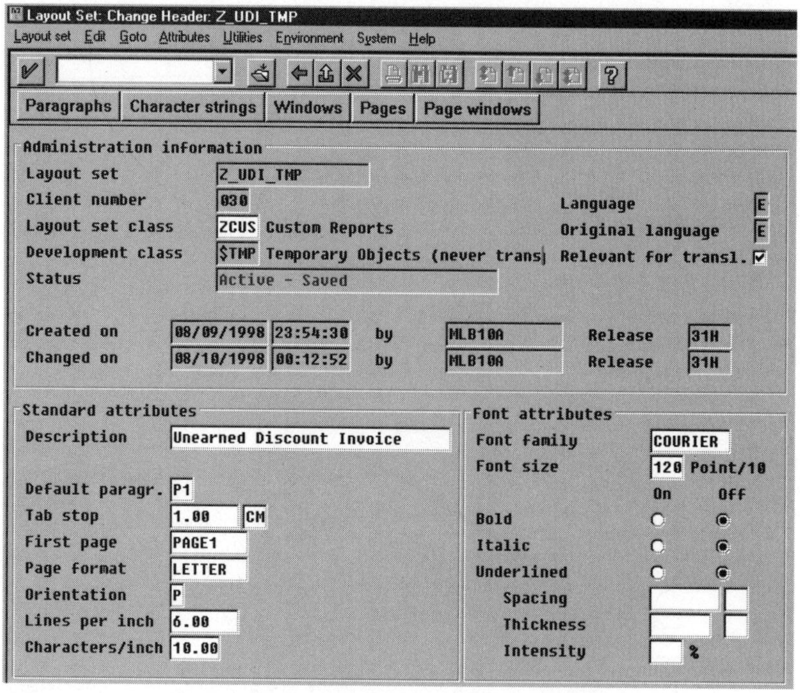

FIGURE 1.6   Layout set header
Copyright by SAP AG

The section on Building Blocks details all the necessary entries, but here is the basic idea. Layout sets are objects, so some of the administration information should look familiar. Unless otherwise specified the standard attributes and font attributes are used throughout the layout set.

The first page is critical because it tells the layout set where to start. The first page and default paragraph must be defined and then entered in the header.

What Are Text Elements?

Text Elements Defined

In the simplest form, a text element is the text that goes in a Page window or Main window. The text is typed in using the SAPscript editor. Windows can be defined to hold or place text of varying fonts and characteristics. From the previous example, what follows in Figure 1.7 is the text element that holds the large note at the top of the first page.

Q1 is the name of the default paragraph to use for the text. The text on each line will use the attributes that have been assigned to paragraph Q1. The line with a Q1 in the tag column, but nothing entered for text, will print a blank line. The tag column is where to tell SAPscript what type of line to expect. In this case all the lines are text and use the attributes of paragraph Q1. Text elements can also contain commands or a combination of text and commands. The following text element (Figure 1.8) is more complex and contains the commands that create the grid pattern on page 1 of the report in Figure 1.5.

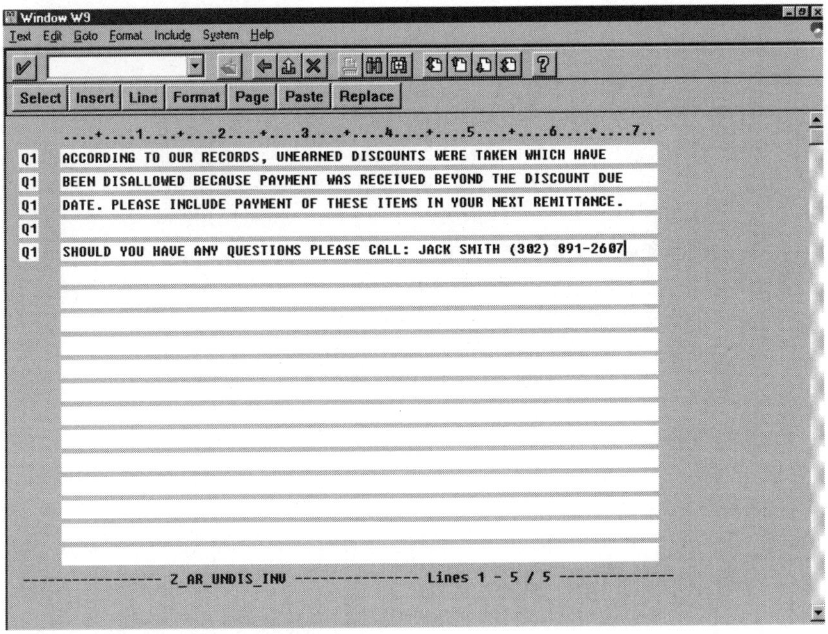

FIGURE 1.7   Simple text element
Copyright by SAP AG

```
Window X2                                                          _|8|x
Text  Edit  Goto  Format  Include  System  Help

 ✔ |          ▼| ◄| ←|⏏|✗| |🔍🔍| |⏣⏣⏣⏣| |❓|
 Select | Insert | Line | Format | Page | Paste | Replace |

    ....+....1....+....2....+....3....+....4....+....5....+....6....+....7..
/*    Grid for FIRST page item details
/:    POSITION WINDOW
/:    BOX FRAME 20 TW
/:    POSITION WINDOW
/:    SIZE WIDTH '18.1' CM HEIGHT '7.5' MM
/:    BOX FRAME 20 TW INTENSITY 20
/:    SIZE WIDTH '8.5' CM HEIGHT '3.5' MM
/:    BOX HEIGHT '3.5' MM FRAME 10 TW
/:    SIZE WIDTH '18.10' CM HEIGHT '7.5' MM
/:    BOX HEIGHT '7.5' MM FRAME 10 TW
/:    SIZE WIDTH '8.5' CM HEIGHT '10.75' CM
/:    BOX FRAME 10 TW
/:    SIZE WIDTH '11.75' CM HEIGHT '10.75' CM
/:    BOX FRAME 10 TW
/:    SIZE WIDTH '15' CM HEIGHT '10.75' CM
/:    BOX FRAME 10 TW
/:    POSITION WINDOW
/:    POSITION YORIGIN '+3.5' MM
--------------- Z_UDI_TMP --------------- Lines 1 - 18 / 24 ---------------
```

FIGURE 1.8   Text element with commands
Copyright by SAP AG

CD-ROM

Grid Pattern CE002

The tag column in this example contains "/:" which tells SAPscript to expect a command in the line that follows. In this example a combination of boxes is used to create a grid structure. Only part of the code appears in the figure, to provide an example for reference. The entire text element is provided on the CD-ROM. Text and commands cannot be used on the same line.

Symbols

Dynamic values are referred to in SAPscript as symbols. Symbols can be passed to the layout set by the calling ABAP program or defined within the text element. Symbols are passed from the calling ABAP via structures. There is no single structure or format that must be used, any valid structure will do. To create a symbol using SAPscript within the text element, the Define command is used. Typically this is used to concatenate several values from structure fields to create a new value needed for printing.

In Figure 1.9, symbols are passed from a structure called ZUDI. In this case each symbol of the customer address is passed as a field value in a structure. Each symbol is printed in the order shown within the Page window. The font and attributes for paragraph Q3 are used when it is rendered.

```
Window V9                                                    _ □ X
Text  Edit  Goto  Format  Include  System  Help
┌──┐ ┌─────────────┬─┐  ┌─┐ ┌─┬─┬─┬─┐ ┌─┐ ┌─┬─┬─┬─┐ ┌─┐
│ ✔│ │             │▼│  │ ◁│ │←│⇧│X│  │▤│▥│▦│ │▧│▨│▩│ │?│
└──┘ └─────────────┴─┘  └─┘ └─┴─┴─┘   └─┴─┘   └─┴─┴─┴─┘
┌──────┬──────┬──────┬────────┬──────┬───────┬─────────┐
│Select│Insert│ Line │ Format │ Page │ Paste │ Replace │
└──────┴──────┴──────┴────────┴──────┴───────┴─────────┘
     ....+....1....+....2....+....3....+....4....+....5....+....6....+....7..
 Q3  &ZUDI-NAME1&
 Q3  &ZUDI-NAME2&
 Q3  &ZUDI-NAME3&
 Q3  &ZUDI-NAME3&
 Q3  &ZUDI-STREET&
 Q3  &ZUDI-CITY(20)& &ZUDI-STATE& &ZUDI-ZIP&




---------------- Z_UDI_TMP ---------------- Lines 1 - 6 / 6 ----------
```

The font always stays the same during inspection of the SAPscript editor (whatever the user default). When the image is previewed or printed, then the font and other attributes are applied to the output.

NOTE

A formatting option is used to limit the number of characters shown for the "city" name. See the section on formatting options for more ways to substring symbols.

Estimating Work Requirements

As with ABAP programs, some changes are relatively minor while others are more complex. Things to consider when estimating the number of hours needed to complete an SAPscript project include:

▲ Does the calling ABAP program need to be modified or created?
▲ Will the report be a top-down list (like a list of materials) or will the entire report need to be calculated (like financial statements)?
▲ Are multiple languages required?
▲ How many symbols will be required?

The Calling ABAP Program

Layout sets must be called by an *ABAP program* to be initiated. If the request only involves changing the layout set, then a substantial piece of work need not be undertaken. If, however, the main processing loop of the report needs to be altered, then the request will probably involve changing the ABAP program associated with the layout set.

NOTE Never actually change an SAP program or layout set. Follow the standard practice of copying and renaming. If a new custom ABAP object is created from a standard SAP report, the new ABAP program can be addressed in output determination. See the section called "Output Determination and Layout Sets."

For instance, if the company name changes and the name on an outgoing report must reflect the new name, this would only involve changing the layout set. The ABAP program is already sending the necessary information. Adding batch breakouts to the detail records of a delivery order, would involve changing both the ABAP program and the layout set. The ABAP program would have to be changed to gather the new information, move it to a structure and trigger the output (via `write_form`) at the appropriate place in the processing loop. Chapter 3 "Calling Layout Sets Directly from an ABAP Program", walks through the ABAP to Layout set connection.

Top-down Lists

A *top-down list* will be easier to create than a report where every element is calculated. In a top-down list, the line item segment is defined and then repeated. This is the way typical reports are structured. In contrast, a balance sheet is made up of many individual calculations. There is no list per se.

Multiple Languages

If *multiple languages* are required, they may not take as much time as expected. If the report is structured the same way, and only the language components are different, then the task of adding the additional languages to any SAPscript report is not so complex. The layout set will be created in an initial language and then copied to other sets with the appropriate language designator. The new version of the layout set is translated by replacing the text components with those of the new language.

Number of Symbols

Knowing the number of *symbols* required in a layout set will permit a rough order-of-magnitude guess at the complexity of the task. Each symbol takes time to resolve in the ABAP and then display in the layout set. Symbols take more time than just typing in text. Text does not change. Finding the necessary data in SAP that are needed in a program can be half the task. If there are more things to find, that will take more time.

Time estimates per report are not possible because there are many other external factors to consider, like, whether test data will be provided or must be created, and a functional counterpart's level of experience with the module. Once a user has experience with SAPscript, creating reports involving SAPscript will not take considerably longer than a standard ABAP report of the same level of complexity.

Key Terms and Abbreviations

Term or Abbreviation	Description
ABAP	Advanced Business Application Programming language
Access key	The key to enter in order to change objects in SAP
Basis	Foundation upon which the application modules reside
Character string	Formatting characteristics that can be applied to a string of characters
ITF	Interchange Text Format; the format used by the SAPscript editor (tag columns and text lines)
Layout set	Predefined layout for pages
Page	With respect to layout set definitions, unique name for the characteristics of a page in a layout set
Page window	An area of the page where the text element is to be placed
Paragraph	With respect to layout set definitions, a unique name for characteristics of a paragraph
OTF	Output Text Format; format for outgoing documents
SAP	Systeme, Anwendungen, Produkte in der Datenverarbeitung (German); [Systems, Applications & Products in Data Processing]
SAPscript	Text and script generated with the SAPscript editor; used in conjunction with layout sets
SAPscript editor	The editor used to create standard text or to create text elements within layout sets
Standard text	Predefined text messages (see transaction SO10)

Assumptions

▲ A working knowledge of ABAP
▲ Basic screen navigation skills
▲ CTS support
▲ Security support

ABAP

Familiarity with the ABAP language is assumed. Although ABAP topics and examples are explored in depth in some sections, they are not the subject of this book. Other books can offer a thorough treatment on the topic. Our use of ABAP is limited to those areas which have a direct bearing on SAPscript principles.

Screen Navigation

Paths and transaction codes are given but screen navigation and general GUI principles are not covered. Readers familiar with ABAP, probably have experience with such things, unless their ABAP experience is entirely from an R/2 system. Menu navigation, shortcut keys, ABAP workbench, and windows should all be familiar.

Corrections and Transports

Corrections and transports (CTS) are an integral part of any development activity. Mature development organizations are more rigorous in their practice of baseline control and configuration management. Although topics of interest are explored that directly relate to SAPscript objects, CTS is not the subject of this book.

Security

It will be necessary for a *security* profile be set up so it is possible to access all the transactions and tables that the work requires. This is a discipline of basis that is typically administered by a central authority. If necessary, provide the security specialist with a list of transactions for which access will be required. Depending on the work at hand, these may include:

SE71	*Layout Set: Request*
SO10	*Standard Text: Request*
SE75	*SAPscript Settings*
SE38	*ABAP/IV Editor*
SE11	*Data Dictionary*

Required access to other transactions and tables will depend on the task. This list is only partial. Access to the application transactions will typically be necessary in order to run tests.

Overview in Review

1. SAPscript is used throughout SAP. External correspondence documents evoke SAPscript objects through the layout set.
2. Layout sets are generally used to print out external documents that require multiple fonts and characteristics not available with ABAP alone.
3. Familiarity with SAP and ABAP is advisable.
4. As with ABAP customizations, SAPscript customization estimates can vary widely depending on the level of complexity and the amount of rework required.

CHAPTER

2

Architecture

How Layout Sets Work—A Process Description

Triggering

Layout sets are objects called forms. Form objects are generally triggered in one of two ways. One way is for the layout set to be used by a standard text. When this happens the standard text is automatically included in the Main window. (When creating a standard text and opting to use a custom layout set, notice that the text shows up in the Main window of the layout set by default when print preview of the standard text is used.) In this scenario the layout set is being used like a *style*.

A style is a layout set that has only paragraph and character definitions. It is located next to layout sets in the path (transaction code: SE72).

NOTE

The second way that layout sets are generally triggered is by calling an ABAP program. The ABAP program tells the layout set which parts of the form to print and what the values for the symbols are. This is the way all the SAP standard report layout sets are triggered. We are really only concerned with this more rigorous use of the layout set (Figure 2.1).

The Print Program

The ABAP program uses a series of Function modules to communicate with the layout set. It gathers information from various sources to prepare what it needs to call the layout set. SAP standard ABAP print programs get printer information and various other settings from the output determination. Here we have already defined things like the printer name and timing preferences.

If the ABAP program is a custom report program that does not use output determination, the printer information must be requested of the user during processing. (These function modules are described in detail in Chapter 3.)

As in ABAP report programs, the Write command is issued once for each detail record in a loop. A simplistic use of the Loop and Write commands would look like this in a standard ABAP report:

Th ABAP program gathers data about the print job from user inputs and/or configuration settings, resolves any necessary computations and calls the layout set as it's ready to print each piece.

SAPscript is told which layout set to use and which parts of it to print. The layout set knows where to print each piece and how the attributes should look because of the page window, paragraph and character string settings.

Knowing the capabilities of the printer and the information from above, SAPscript renders a print preview or prints the document.

FIGURE 2.1   Process description

```
LOOP AT itab.
WRITE: / itab-field1, itab-field2.
ENDLOOP.
```

The statement would be structured essentially the same way when calling the layout set; the major difference being that instead of issuing the Write command we call the layout set and tell it to print one line of the detail record.

```
LOOP AT itab.
   CALL FUNCTION  'WRITE_FORM'
      EXPORTING WINDOW     =      'MAIN'
ENDLOOP.
```

In this example, 'MAIN' refers to the Main window in the layout set. We are telling the layout set to print only what is in the Main window. To print the two fields shown above, the script for the Main window would look like Figure 2.2.

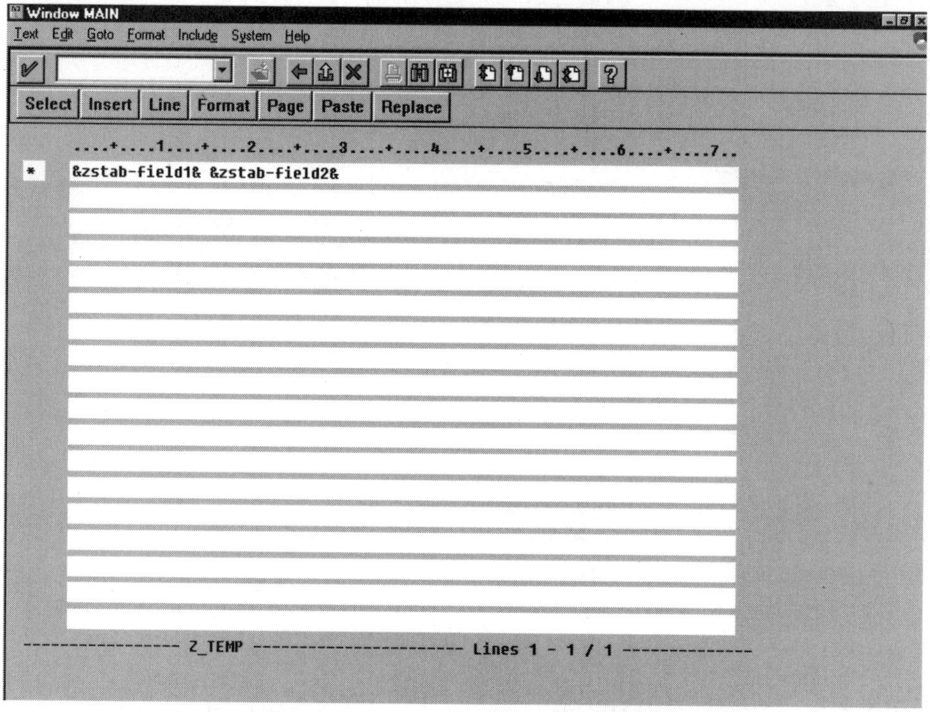

FIGURE 2.2   Simple detail record in a Main window
Copyright by SAP AG

Notice in Figure 2.2 that we have used `zstab` instead of `itab`. This is because all fields to be used in a layout set should be passed in a structure. When the function `WRITE_FORM` is called, SAPscript will use whatever values are populated in these structure fields at that time. Note that, we need to move the internal table values over to structure fields before calling the layout set. The program would take the basic form:

```
LOOP AT itab.
   MOVE itab-field1 to zstab-field1.
   MOVE itab-field2 to zstab-field2.
   CALL FUNCTION  'WRITE_FORM'
      EXPORTING WINDOW      =      'MAIN'
ENDLOOP.
```

(itab is an internal table and zstab is a structure with the same format as itab.)

NOTE

Keep in mind that this is a simplified view. The data and select statements are omitted to allow us to concentrate on those sections related to SAPscript. A more complete example can be found in Chapter 3.

Notice that nowhere in the example did the ABAP program tell SAPscript which layout set to use. This is done with the function module OPEN_FORM. The layout set must be open before the function module WRITE_FORM can be called. Once the layout set is open then WRITE_FORM can be called as many times as is necessary. CLOSE_FORM is used to close the layout set. Adding this to our previous example we get:

```
CALL FUNCTION 'OPEN_FORM'
    EXPORTING FORM       =       'Z_TEMP'
    language  =   'E'
    device =   'PRINTER'.
LOOP AT itab.
    MOVE itab-field1 to zstab-field1.
    MOVE itab-field2 to zstab-field2.
    CALL FUNCTION 'WRITE_FORM'
        EXPORTING WINDOW      =       'MAIN'
ENDLOOP.
CALL FUNCTION 'CLOSE_FORM'.
```

The basic process steps are:

1. Open the layout set (OPEN_FORM)
2. Loop through the internal table
3. Move dynamic values to structures and call WRITE_FORM at each pass
4. Close layout set (CLOSE_FORM).

Notice that the form is not opened inside the loop statement. If had been, the form would get opened and closed once for every line in the internal table. If there were five lines in itab, there would be five reports of one line each.

NOTE

This is how the basic print program works. In other derivatives, START_FORM can be used to provide the layout set name. Refer to Chapter 3 to explore more options.

WARNING

If you use START_FORM, you must use END_FORM. CLOSE_FORM must always be used regardless.

Print Options

Figure 2.1 illustrates that the ABAP program gathers data about the print job from user inputs and/or configuration settings. User inputs will be something the user types online and configuration settings are table inputs that remain.

```
Print:                                                                    ☒

   Output device      prn1 Basis Support dummy printer
   Number of copies   1
   Page selection     [                                              ]

  ┌─Spool request────────────────────────────────────────────────────┐
   Name               SCRIPT prn1 MLB10A
   Title              [                                              ]
   Authorization      [         ]
  └───────────────────────────────────────────────────────────────────┘

  ┌─Output options──────────────────┐  ┌─Cover sheet──────────────────┐
   ☑ Print immediately
   ☐ Delete after print                   ☐  SAP cover sheet
   ☑ New spool request
   Spool retention per. 8 Day(s)          Recipient   [            ]
   Archiving mode       1 Print only      Department  [            ]
  └─────────────────────────────────┘  └──────────────────────────────┘

  ┌──────────────┬───────┬────────┐
   Print preview │ Print │ Cancel
  └──────────────┴───────┴────────┘
```

FIGURE 2.3   Print parameters
Copyright by SAP AG

If the program is not triggered by output determination, then the ABAP program and thus the layout set must have some way of knowing which printer to print to, how many copies to print and so on. One option might be to provide parameters for the user to enter the information when the program starts. This is not necessary, since the OPEN_FORM will initiate the necessary user dialog to capture the print options. This is engaged in the function module by setting the Import parameter called *dialog* to "X." The Print Parameters dialog screen, shown in Figure 2.3, is engaged by OPEN_FORM and is similar to the screen visible whenever a list is printed.

If the print program is triggered by output determination, then the Print parameters for that layout set are taken from output determination settings. Depending on the module, output determination may have a different look and feel but the process is basically the same. There are criteria for determining which output should be employed under which circumstances. The output is then related to a processing program and a layout set (and any other application-specific parameters).

The High-Level Process

When layout sets are triggered by output determination, as standard SAP layout sets are, the process looks essentially like the diagram in Figure 2.4.

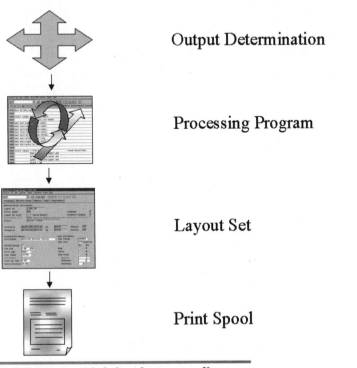

Output Determination

Processing Program

Layout Set

Print Spool

FIGURE 2.4   High-level process diagram

Output Determination and Layout Sets

Although output determination configuration is beyond the scope of this book, it is important to understand how it works and how it is related to business correspondence. We will explore output determination in two specific areas, Financial Accounting–Correspondence and Sales and Distribution–Outputs. Other flavors of the output determination concept are used throughout SAP, but the same basic framework is used in all.

NOTE Usually these configuration items are maintained by those responsible for configuring the application module.

Financial Accounting Correspondence Documents Overview

Financial accounting correspondence documents can be found in the IMG with **Financial Accounting → Financial Accounting Global Settings → Correspondence → Define Correspondence Types** (transaction code OB77). This will show the different types of documents defined as correspondence. Depending on the business need, it may be necessary to change the layout set and/or processing program associated with the standard correspondence type or to create a new correspondence type. This is not as confusing as it sounds. Look at the correspondence type Open Item List in Figure 2.5. The "official name" or "key" is SAP08 and Open Item List is the text name associated with it.

Correspondence Types

Figure 2.5 defines correspondence types. To add a new one, we add it here. The details for each item contain characteristics of the correspondence type. The specific characteristics are not significant for our purposes. The characteristics are referred to in the print program. This allows the configure to set processing options relevant to the application without having to change the ABAP program. How does the correspondence type know which print program to start?

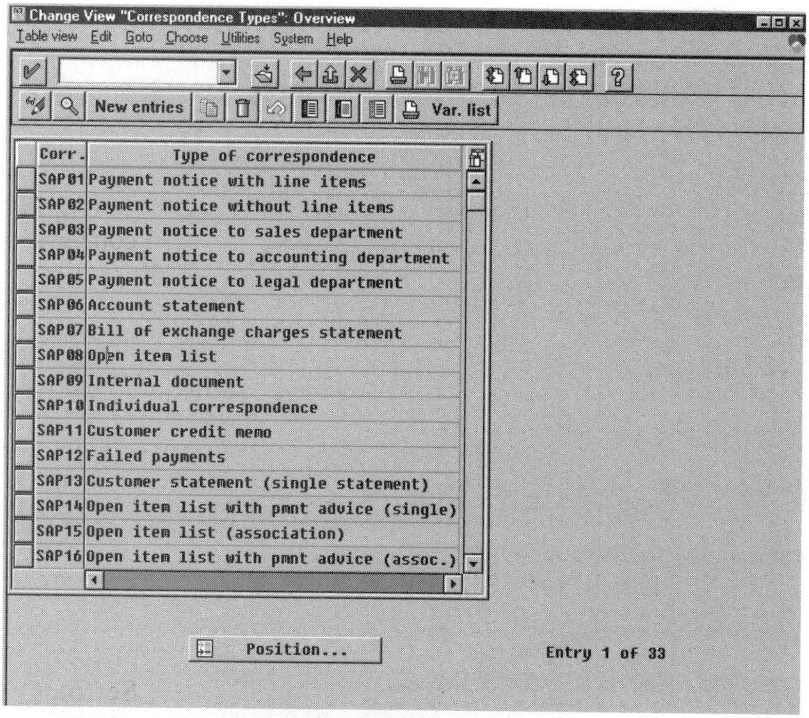

FIGURE 2.5   Correspondence types
Copyright by SAP AG

The Print Program for Correspondence Types

The screen in Figure 2.6 shows how the correspondence type is related to the print program. This is where to type the name of the new print program if it must be changed. In this case use a variant in the print program and enter it here. Not all modules associate variants with their print programs. The screen in Figure 2.6 is retrieved from the IMG with **Financial Accounting → Financial Accounting Global Settings → Correspondence → Define Form Names for Correspondence Print** (transaction OB78). Finally the print program needs to know what layout set (form) to use.

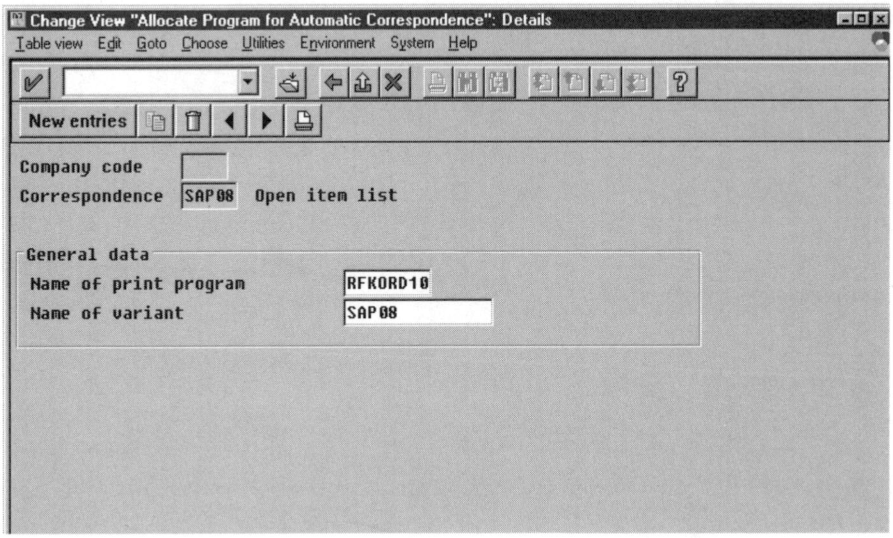

FIGURE 2.6   Correspondence types
Copyright by SAP AG

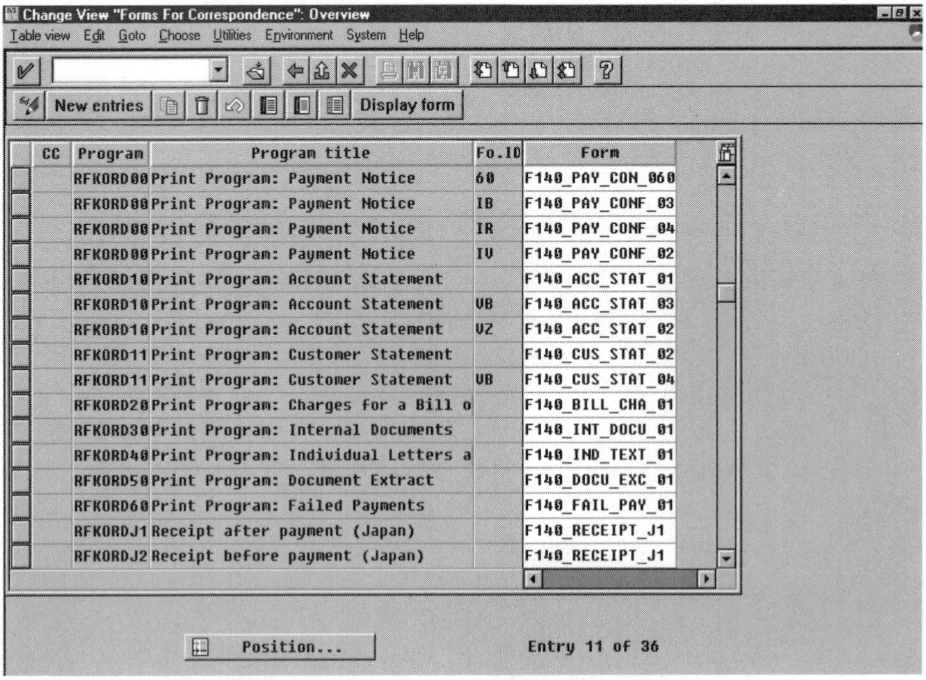

FIGURE 2.7   Print programs and layout sets
Copyright by SAP AG

Form Names and Correspondence Types

The screen in Figure 2.7 relates the print program to the layout set (form). The path for this screen in the IMG is: **Financial Accounting → Financial Accounting Global Settings → Correspondence → Define Form Names for Correspondence Print**. From Figure 2.6, correspondence type SAP08 was related to print program RFKORD10 and variant SAP08. In Figure 2.7 this print program is attached to layout set F140_ACC_STAT_01. It is not shown in this screen, but the variant SAP08 has a blank for the FO.ID which tells the program to use the first of the three forms associated with this print program. Notice the entries are company code-dependent for Accounting–correspondence documents.

Accounting–correspondence documents are triggered manually at various locations within the application or scheduled in the "periodic processing" menu. To look at the periodic processing menu, the path is: **Accounting → Financial accounting → Accounts receivable → Periodic processing**.

To wrap it all up, here is the basic connection: Periodic processing or manual requests are associated with correspondence types. The correspondence type is linked to a processing program and variant. The variant is linked to a form ID. The program and form ID are linked to a layout set. This is how a particular output for the application documents is associated with its respective processing program and layout set.

Sales and Distribution (SD) Outputs Overview

Sales and distribution outputs fundamentals are similar. Using the delivery note as an example, we begin with an *output type*. The output type is initially defined in transaction V/34, called output type overview and the path in the IMG is: **Sales and Distribution → Basic Functions → Output → Output determination → Output proposal using the condition technique → Maintain output determination for deliveries → Maintain output types**.

Output Types

The screen in Figure 2.8 looks similar to the one used to define correspondence types in Figure 2.5. As before, double clicking to open an entry will produce a screen where characteristics of the output type are added. In this case there is a link to transaction NACW, the transaction where the output type is connected to the processing program and layout set. The path in the IMG is: **Sales and Distribution → Basic Functions → Output → Output determination → Process output and forms**.

Print Programs, Layout Sets and Output Types

Figure 2.9 looks similar to the corresponding screen in the Figure 2.7. Here we can see that our delivery note printout is set to use processing program RVADDN01 and layout set RVDELNOTE. In the Figure 2.6 the print program was set up in one screen and the layout set was in turn associated with the print program (Figure 2.8) in another screen.

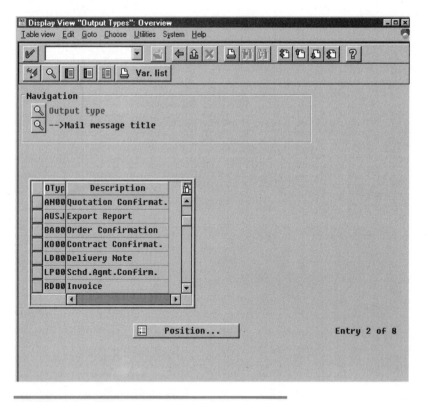

FIGURE 2.8   Print programs and layout sets
Copyright by SAP AG

Change View "Output: Processing Programs": Overview

Table view   Edit   Goto   Choose   Utilities   System   Help

Output: Processing Programs

Out.	Name	Med	Program	FORM routine	Layout set
KRML	Credit Processing	7	RSNASTSO	POFFICE_AUFRUF_VX	
LALE	ShipNotifctn to SP	6	RSNASTED	EDI_PROCESSING	
LALE	ShipNotifctn to SP	A	RSNASTED	ALE_PROCESSING	
LAVA	Outg. ship.notifica.	6	RSNASTED	EDI_PROCESSING	
LAVA	Outg. ship.notifica.	A	RSNASTED	ALE_PROCESSING	
LD00	Delivery Note	1	RVADDN01	ENTRY	RVDELNOTE
LD00	Delivery Note	2	RVADDN01	ENTRY	RVDELNOTE
LD01	Delivr Note DIN4994	1	SDADDN02	ENTRY	SD_DELNOTE_SUPPL
LQCA	Q cert. goods recip.	1	RQCAAP00	ENTRY	
LQCA	Q cert. goods recip.	2	RQCAAP00	ENTRY	
LQCB	Q cert. sold-to par.	1	RQCAAP00	ENTRY	
LQCB	Q cert. sold-to par.	2	RQCAAP00	ENTRY	
LRUE	Decentr.Confirmation	8	RULRUE00	ENTRY	
MAIL	Mail	7	RSNASTSO	SAPOFFICE_AUFRUF_VX	

Display form   Position...   Entry 1 of 19

FIGURE 2.9   Print programs and layout sets
Copyright by SAP AG

The Essentials of Standard Outputs

We can see how these examples take the same basic form. Essentially we always have a processing program and a layout set. The associations are made in various definable outputs. The processing program and layout set make it all happen once an output has been chosen.

NOTE   Other areas of output determination: access sequences and condition tables are not necessary to explore for our purposes. The primary purpose of these areas is to determine under what conditions specific outputs are suggested or chosen, while we are chiefly concerned with what happens after the output is selected.

How Standard Texts Are Used

Getting Started

As the name implies, a standard text is a piece of text that has been predefined. Once defined it can be interjected into a layout set as necessary. It works like a text symbol in an ABAP program. In this section, we will create a standard text, include it in a layout set and then print preview the layout set.

Suppose that we want to print the following phrase on a page:

```
Should you have any questions please contact Mr. Brackett at
        (301) 555-1234.
```

Since this phrase is subject to change, we want to make it easier for the customer to maintain without going into the layout set or processing program. Also, if we use this same phrase on multiple reports, we only have to maintain it in one place if Mr. Brackett leaves the company. Some customers like being able to maintain the text. This can be particularly helpful when building multilingual reports. (The text gets changed often during the project life cycle and this format is helpful because a space for the text can be made on the report and customers can maintain it.) To create a standard text we begin by opening the standard text request screen. The path is **Tools → Word processing → Standard text** (transaction SO10).

Creating Standard Text

In Figure 2.10 we have typed in a unique standard text name, z_contact_info. Selecting the create/change button, we get the standard text editor screen in Figure 2.11.

NOTE

To create more than three standard texts, it may be desirable to group them in a custom TEXT ID. This will make them easier to manage later. Refer to the instructions at the end of this section.

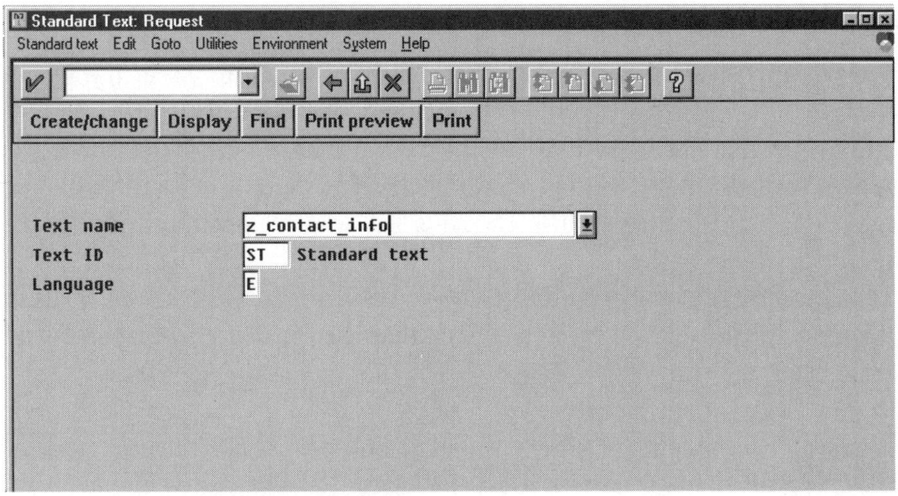

FIGURE 2.10   Standard text request
Copyright by SAP AG

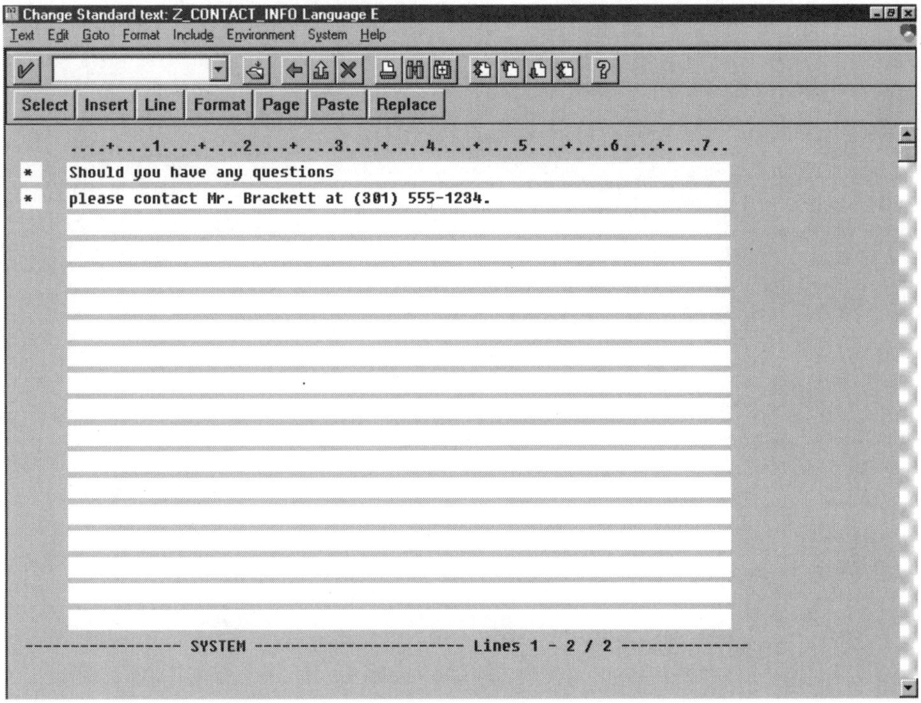

FIGURE 2.11   Standard text editor
Copyright by SAP AG

The Standard Text Editor

In Figure 2.11, I have typed in the text as shown. The asterisk at the left of both lines tells SAPscript that the following line should use the default paragraph for the format settings of the text. When a new standard text is created the default layout set is called system. The default paragraph for the system layout set is called L. The L paragraph uses left-justified Courier 12 for the settings. As it stands now, our text will print as left-justified Courier 12. Change the tag column setting (where the asterisk is) by selecting from the possible entries. Notice in Figure 2.12 that there other paragraphs B and C can be used if desired.

WARNING

If a line is set up incorrectly in the Editor there will be no error message. The text will just not appear.

FIGURE 2.12   Tag column
Copyright by SAP AG

Standard texts work almost exactly as text elements do. Text elements are just standard texts within a layout set. As with text elements, commands and symbols can be used in the standard text. The other options, shown as tag columns, can control how the line is handled. Each of these options is explored in the section on text elements in Chapter 4.

The layout set and style used by the standard text can be changed in the format menu. Those currently in use are shown at the bottom of the screen. In our example we use layout set SYSTEM and no style is selected. If a style were selected, the name would appear to the left of the layout set name. The tag columns available are always those of the layout set or style selected. If a layout set and style are selected, then only the tag columns of the style will be given.

Moving Around in the Editor

Here are a few helpful hints for moving around the editor:

▲ **Moving up and down**—Use arrow keys or go to **Edit ➔ Position** and enter the line number desired.

▲ **Moving horizontally**—The arrow, space bar, backspace and delete keys all work as expected. If text pasted into a line (**CTRL + V**) runs beyond the 72-character line length shown, use shift **F8** to jump to the right and view the text. Use shift **F8** to go back to the left again when finished.

▲ **Windows select, copy and paste**—Perform a typical windows select on characters in a single line by holding the left mouse button down and dragging the cursor. To select more than a single line use **CTRL + Y** to get a cursor that looks like a "+," then hold the left mouse button down and drag the cursor to select the lines required. Use **CTRL + C** to copy and **CTRL + V** to paste.

▲ **SAPscript select, copy and paste**—Double clicking, choosing the select button, **F2** and **Edit ➔ Select** will all begin the select at the current position. If another position is selected just after that, all the characters between the two will be selected. When text is properly selected, a sample of the beginning and ending text will appear at the bottom of the editor. To select a whole line at a time, make selections from the tag column. To select the entire document, put the cursor in the tag column and hit the select button three times. Once lines are selected, make a copy using the copy button or **F6**. To paste, use **F9**, the paste key or **Edit → Paste**.

Save the standard text by selecting the **Save** icon, **Text → Save** or **F11**. It is not necessary to activate a standard text. Once text is saved, it can be accessed by the layout set.

Creating a Layout Set for the Standard Text

To build a simple layout set we begin with **Tools → Word Processing → Layout set** (transaction SE71). In Figure 2.13, the new layout set is called Z_LS_CONTACT_411. The language is English.

Selecting the create button opens an information screen that says "Z_LS_CONTACT_411 language E is not available in this client." Press the green check mark to acknowledge and pass through to the header screen (Figure 2.14).

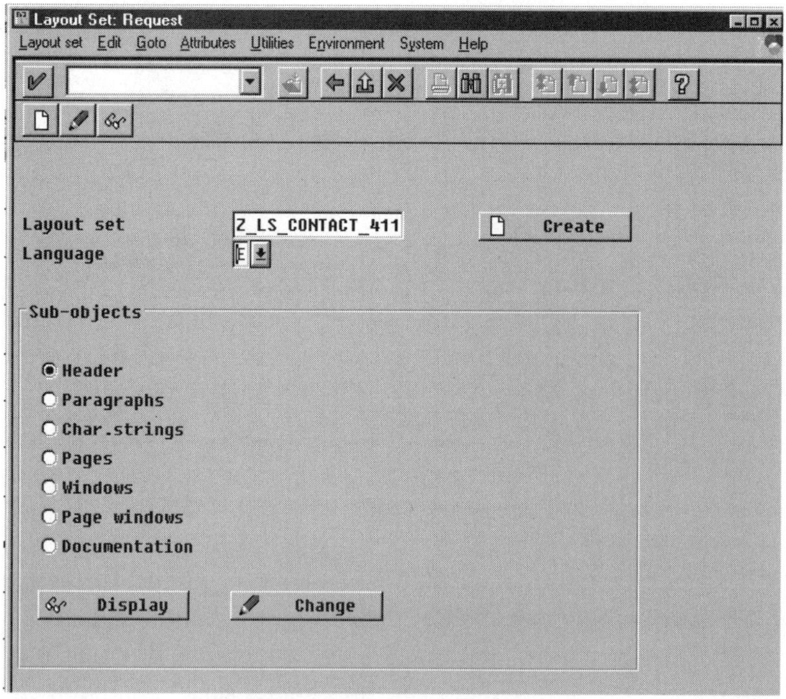

FIGURE 2.13   Creating a new layout set
Copyright by SAP AG

Z_LS_CONTACT_411 fe002

CD-ROM

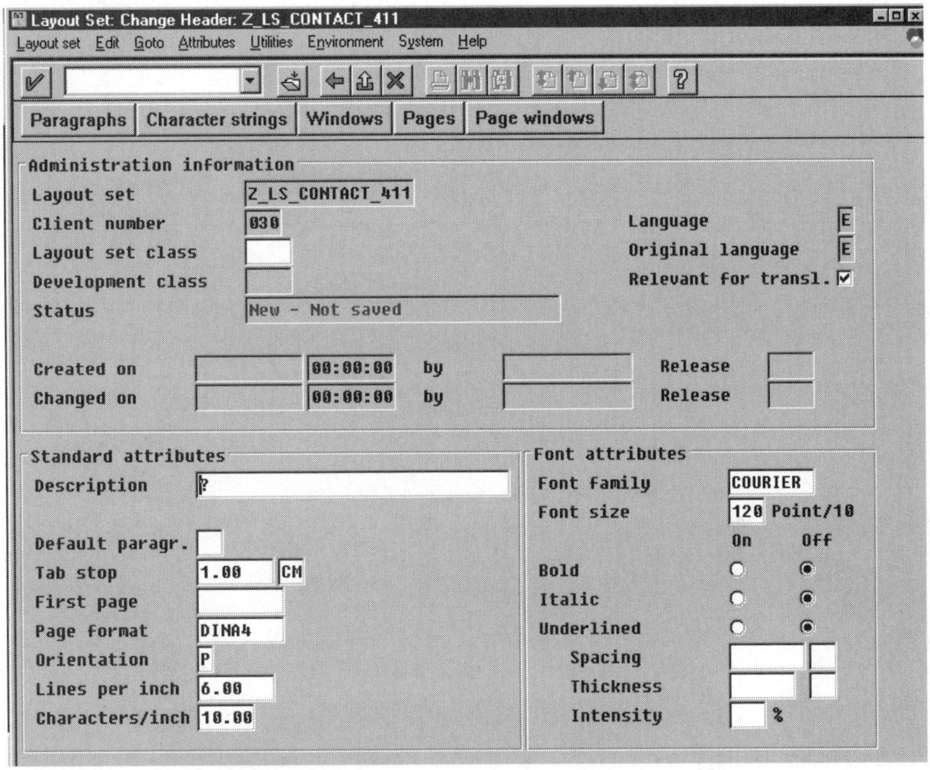

FIGURE 2.14   Layout set header
Copyright by SAP AG

A description must be entered before the layout set can be saved. Once the description is entered, saving will prompt for the correction number information. This example is a local private object.

Creating the Layout Set Paragraph

Although the layout set can be saved, it still needs several essential elements before it can be useful. The default paragraph and first-page entries are mandatory. Place the cursor on the field and select the dropdown arrow; the message indicates that there are no paragraphs from which to choose. The first step is to create a paragraph, which will be the one most typical of the text used in the layout set. Our "contact information phrase" will be in Courier New, 14 CPI, bold. Since this is all we intend to use this layout set for, we will create a paragraph with this font and use it as our default paragraph for the entire layout set. This is accomplished by moving to the paragraph either by clicking the **Paragraphs** button or by choosing **Goto → Paragraphs**. The new paragraph is added by selecting the **Edit → Create** element. In this example the new paragraph name is "P1."

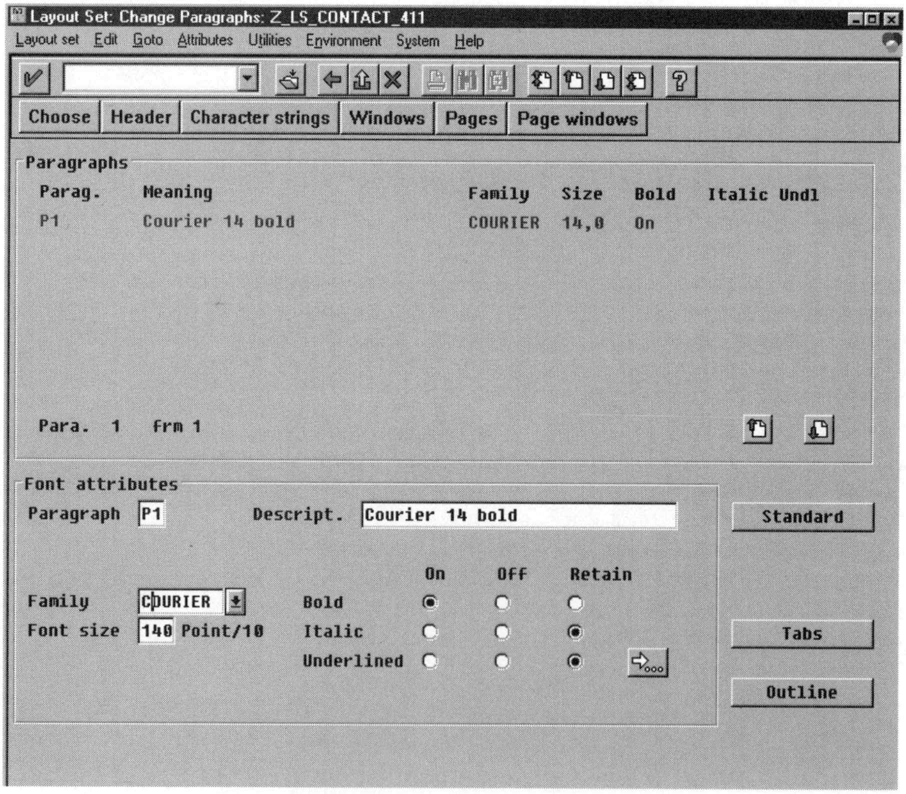

FIGURE 2.15 Creating a new paragraph
Copyright by SAP AG

The description is Courier 14 bold. The font for the new paragraph is chosen by clicking on the font tab, in the lower right corner of the screen (the selected tab is never shown, so we cannot see it now). Once the tab has been selected the font attributes screen appears and the font choice can be entered (Figure 2.15). Use the pick list to select the font family and size. Once the paragraph is created, "P1" can be entered in the header screen as the default paragraph.

Creating the Layout Set Page

Moving to the Page screen is accomplished by selecting the **Pages** button from the top of the screen or using the **Goto** menu. (All necessary views in the layout set can be accessed in this same way.) We must define a page on which to put our text. To do that, select **Edit → Create element**. In this example the page is named, "Page1" and the description is "Page for text" (see Figure 2.16). Once this page is defined it can be entered on the header page as the first page.

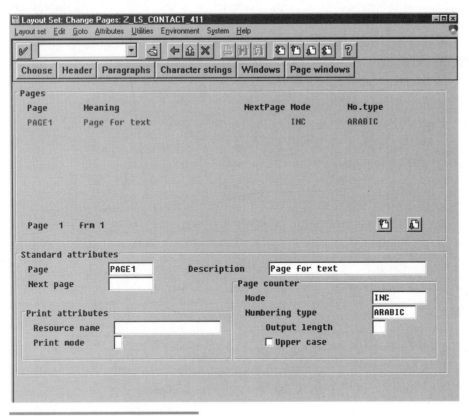

FIGURE 2.16   Creating a page
Copyright by SAP AG

Creating the Layout Set Window

Thus far we have defined a page and a paragraph. Now we need to tell the layout set where to put the window on the page and what to put in the window. To do this we need to create a window and a Page window. In the Page window we tell the layout set what text to use. The window must be created before the Page window. Navigating to the window view, we select the **Edit → Create** element and enter the name and description for the window, "win1" and "window for contact info" respectively. The window type is CONST because the window is not subject to change. If symbols were included in the window they could change from page to page; we would then want to use window type VAR, for variable. In the example given in Figure 2.17, the default paragraph is P1. Although we do intend to use this paragraph in the window, we could have left it blank and used the layout set default, which is also P1.

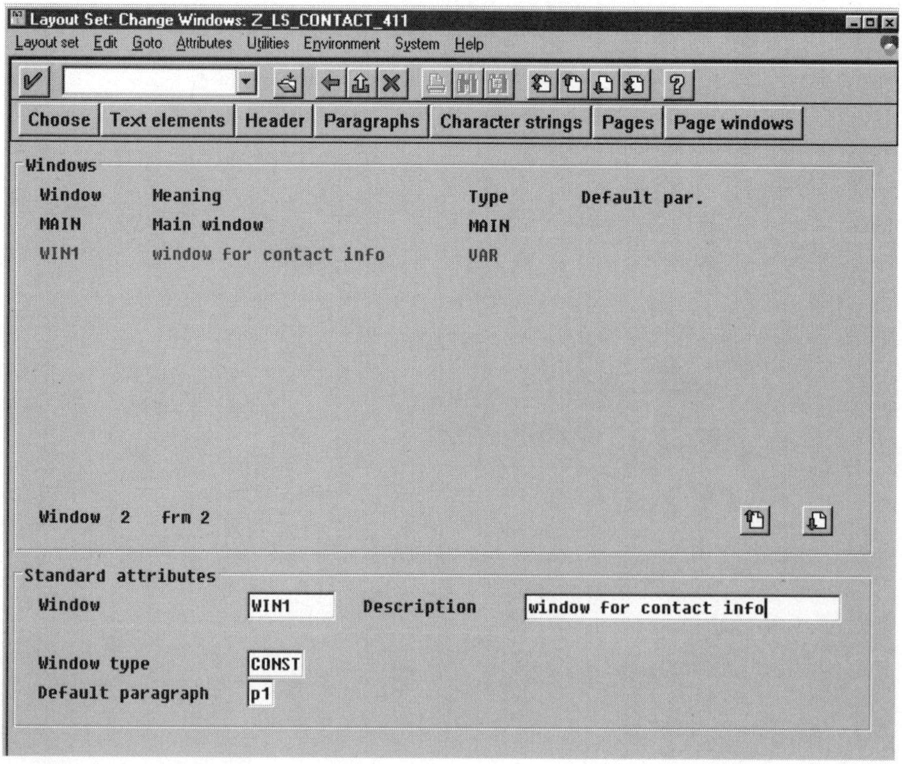

FIGURE 2.17   Create a window

Creating the Page Window

Before creating the Page window, thought should be given to where the window will reside on the page. Refer to the header view in Figure 2.14 to see that the default page format is DINA4. For our purposes, this is changed to LETTER, because this is the size paper to be printed. Check the Paper format sizes by following **Tools → Administration → Spool → Spool administration**, then click the **Page formats** button and press the **Display** key. This will produce a screen similar to the one shown in Figure 2.18.

The page format Letter is 215 mm across and 279 mm deep. Let us say we want to create our Page window in the middle of the upper third of the page, and make it large enough to fit our text. The Page window could be laid out something like Figure 2.19.

Format	P	L	Width		Height	
DINA3	X		297	MM	420	MM
DINA4		X	297	MM	210	MM
DINA4	X		210	MM	297	MM
DINA5		X	210	MM	148	MM
DINA5	X		148	MM	210	MM
ESR	X		86	CH	25	LN
EXECUTIV		X	266	MM	184	MM
EXECUTIV	X		184	MM	266	MM
FORMDISP	X		175	CM	175	CM
INCH11	X		864	PT	792	PT
INCH12	X		864	PT	864	PT
INCH4	X		864	PT	300	PT
INCH4C	X		864	PT	288	PT
INCH6	X		864	PT	432	PT
INCH7	X		864	PT	504	PT
INCH8	X		864	PT	576	PT
LEGAL		X	355	MM	215	MM
LEGAL	X		215	MM	355	MM
LETRA	X		210	MM	102	MM
LETTER		X	279	MM	215	MM
LETTER	X		215	MM	279	MM
LINE_21	X		864	PT	252	PT

FIGURE 2.18   Page formats
Copyright by SAP AG

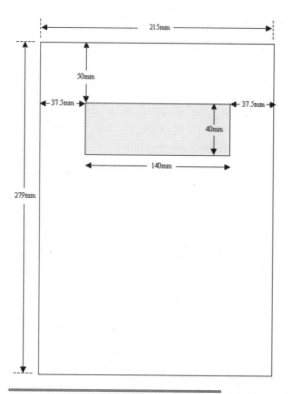

FIGURE 2.19   Laying out the page

Using these dimensions we are now ready to create the Page window. The Page window screen is accessed like the others by selecting the **Page window** button or choosing **Goto → Page windows**. Once in the Page window screen, select **Edit → Create element**. Select "WIN1" and make the following entries:

▲ **Left margin–37.5 mm**—This is the distance between the left side of the window and the left side of the page.

▲ **Upper margin–50 mm**—The distance between the top of the window and the top of the page.

▲ **Window width–140 mm**—Width of the window

▲ **Window height–40 mm**—Height of the window

Create another page window, this time selecting the Main window and enter the following dimensions: left margin 37.5 mm; upper margin 100 mm; width 140 mm; height 150 mm. This will place the Main window just below our text box.

Press the **Save** button and the Page Window definition should look like Figure 2.20.

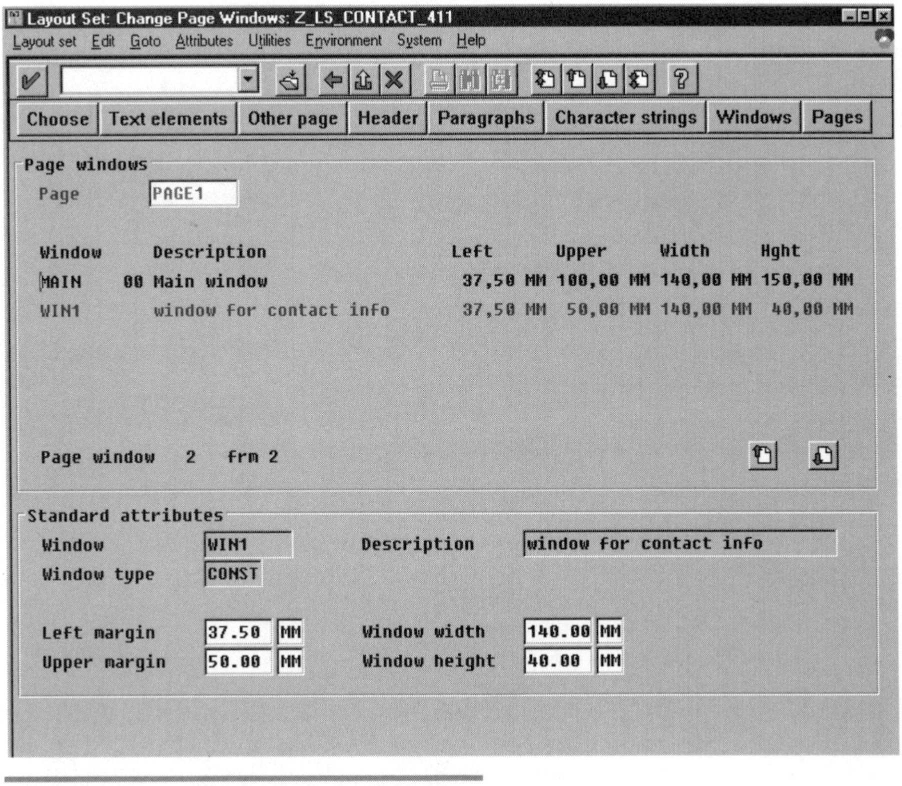

FIGURE 2.20 Page window definition
Copyright by SAP AG

Creating the Text Element

At this point the Page window is defined but SAPscript still does not know what to put in the window. From the Page Window screen, press the **Text Elements** button or choose **Edit → Text elements** from the pulldown menu. This will produce the Text Elements screen where text can be entered directly. In this case we are going to include text we have already defined in the standard text editor. This is done with the Include command as follows.

```
INCLUDE Z_CONTACT_INFO OBJECT TEXT ID ST
```

INCLUDE is the command; Z_CONTACT_INFO is the name of the standard text we want to include; TEXT is the type of object; and ST is the name of the text ID (the default text ID). The parameters come from the standard text header. To view them, go back to the Standard Text Entry screen and choose **Goto → Header** from the pulldown menu. Since a command is being entered in the line, "/:" should be used in the tag column. The Text Element screen should look like Figure 2.21.

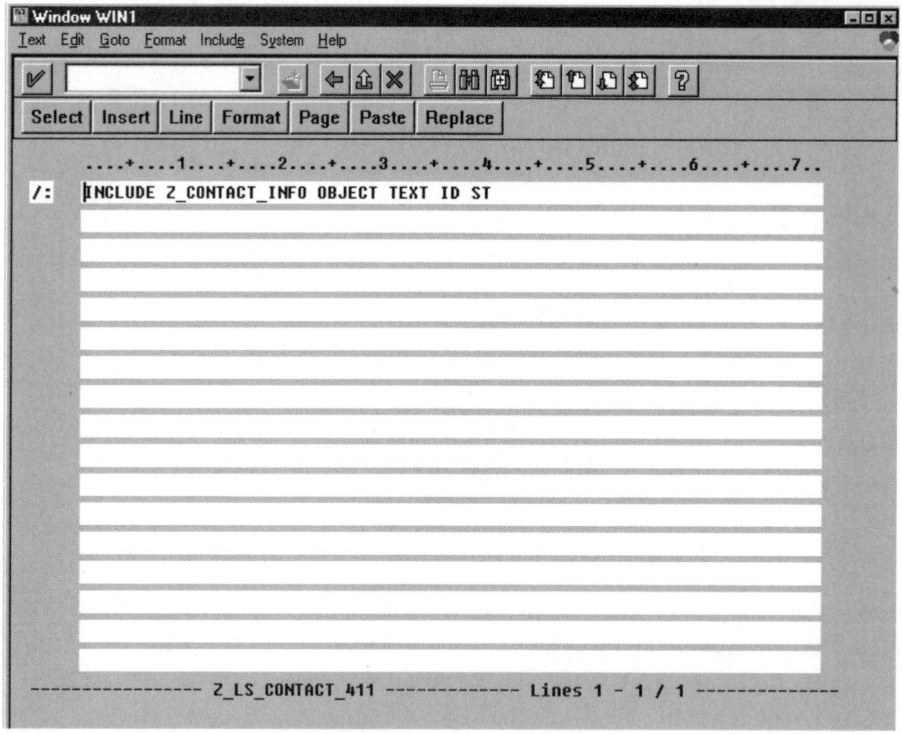

FIGURE 2.21   Include statement
Copyright by SAP AG

Testing the Output

To test the output, backup to the Page Window screen and select **Utilities →**
Test print. Provide the name of a valid printer and select **Print Preview** to
look at the output on the screen. Figure 2.22 shows what the Print Preview
should look like.

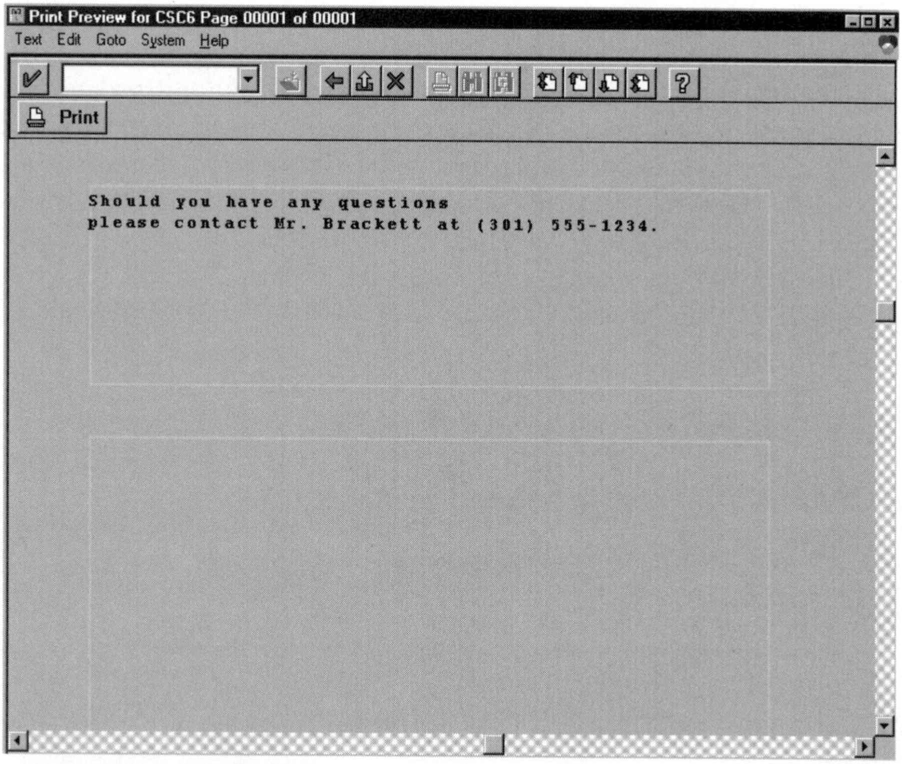

FIGURE 2.22   Print preview
Copyright by SAP AG

Standard text is routinely included in layout sets to get "user notes" that are added to the correspondence, sales text, company names, point of contact names and long legal paragraphs. Companies like the idea of having a "window" where they can add comments to their correspondence when necessary.

Creating a New Text ID

Create a new text ID to group your standard texts. With more than a few standard texts it may be advisable to group them for easier identification. Often a text ID is created for standard texts created in support of a particular development effort, much in the way that development classes are used. To create a new text ID, we begin in the SAPscript Settings screen (Figure 2.23). The path is **Tools → Word Processing → Settings** (SE75). Select **Text**

Objects and IDs and press the **Change** button. Note that text IDs are client independent.

Highlight the object called Text and press the **Text ID** button. Text IDs are subsets of text objects. The object Text is defaulted in the Standard Text editor. When creating a text ID to be used in the Standard Text editor, create the text ID for the object Text only. After selecting the Text ID button, press the **Create** button. The screen in Figure 2.24 will appear. Use the accepted naming standards when creating the new text ID. Since our text ID is for standard texts that will be used in layout sets, use the default options shown in the figure.

Object	Description	Format	Save mode	Interface	Line width
STYLEVERS	Old (German) text		Dialog	TN	
SUPM	Serv. master plant data text		Update	TN	
T090			Dialog	TN	
T093			Dialog	TN	
T096			Dialog	TN	
T357G	Permits		Update	TN	
TASKTEXT	Texts for tasks		Not in text file	TY	
TERM			Dialog	TN	
TEXT	SAPscript standard texts		Dialog	TX	
TNABG	Texts, bus.partner, employer		Update	TX	
TNDEB	Texts, bus.partner, customer		Update	TX	
TNGPA	Texts, gen. business partner		Update	TX	
TNKRH	Texts, bus.partner, hospital		Update	TX	
TNKTR	Texts, bus. partner, cost obj.		Update	TX	
TNPER	Texts, bus. partner, person		Update	TX	
TNTPT	Tariff item texts		Update	TX	
VARI	Relationship maintenance texts		Update	TN	
VBBK	Sales Header texts		Update	TN	
VBBP	Sales Item texts		Update	TN	
VBKA	Sales CAS texts		Update	TN	
VK02			Dialog	DS	
VTTK	Transport header texts		Update	TN	
WF_NOTE	Notes within workflows		Dialog	TN	
WLBM	Texts for layout area item		Update	TX	

FIGURE 2.23   Text objects
Copyright by SAP AG

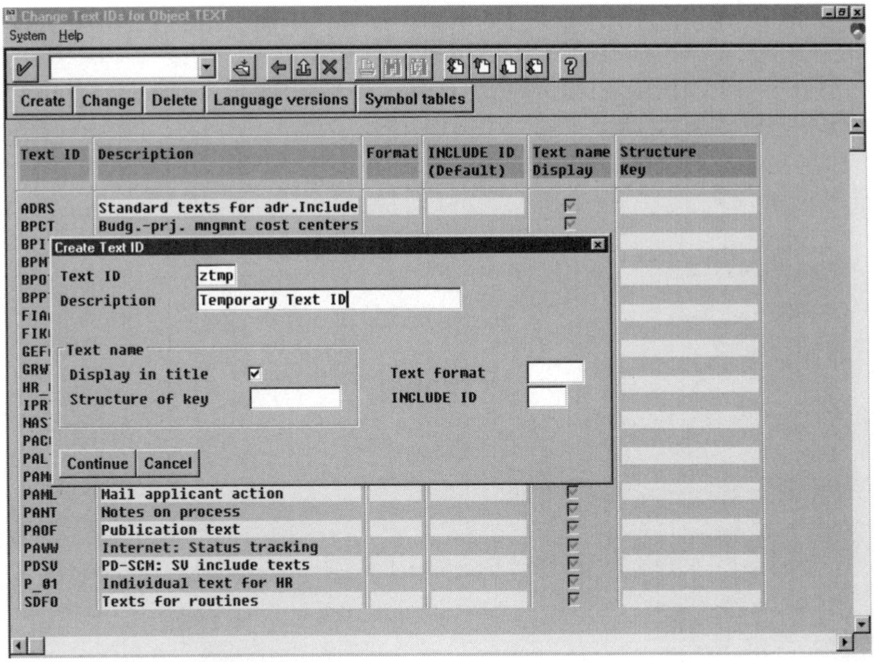

Figure 2.24   Creating a text ID
Copyright by SAP AG

Using Layout Sets with Different Languages

Layout Set Languages

Some users may see the screens in French, others in English, but all may need to print correspondence in Spanish because the customer is Spanish. Layout sets are language dependent. When a layout set is created for the first time it is created in a particular language referred to in the layout set header as the *original language.* LAYOUT SETS CAN ONLY BE MAINTAINED IN THEIR ORIGINAL LANGUAGE. Only the text elements of the other languages can be changed. This makes sense, because the text is all that needs to be changed. For instance, if a Swedish manufacturer of fire extinguishers wanted to sell a top model in Japan, the instruction label on the canister would be changed to Japanese; the entire fire extinguisher would not be reengineered. It is the same with the layout set. The windows are still in the same place, the pages still have the same orientation, the document has the same look and feel, it is only the language of the text that has changed.

Using our layout set from the previous section as an example (Figure 2.22), we will create a derivative of this layout set in Spanish. Initially, the layout set was called Z_LS_CONTACT_411 and the original language was English.

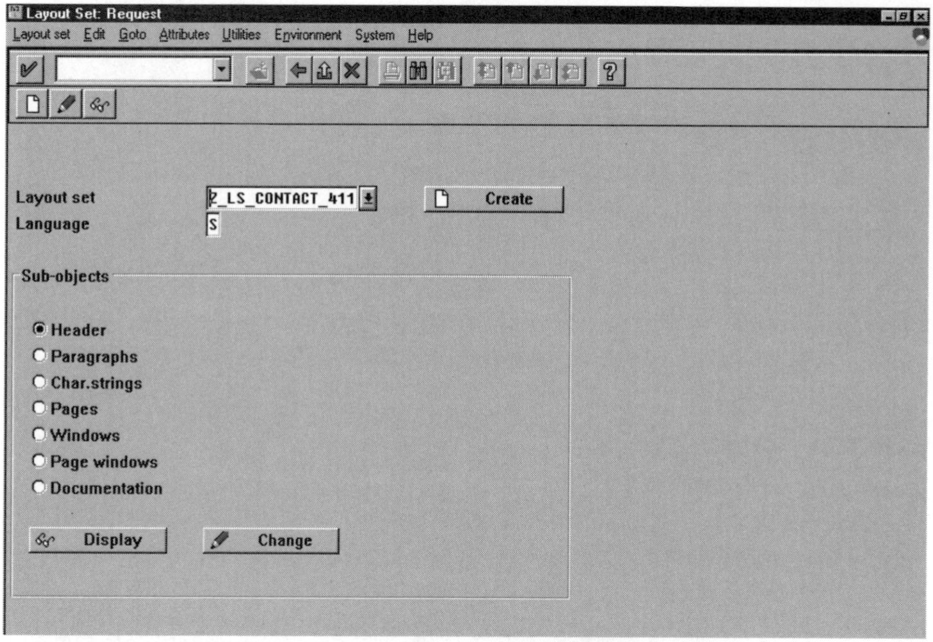

FIGURE 2.25   Creating a layout set in a different language
Copyright by SAP AG

Beginning at the Layout Set: Request screen (see Figure 2.25), we enter the layout set name Z_LS_CONTACT_411. Enter **S** for the language and press the **Create** key.

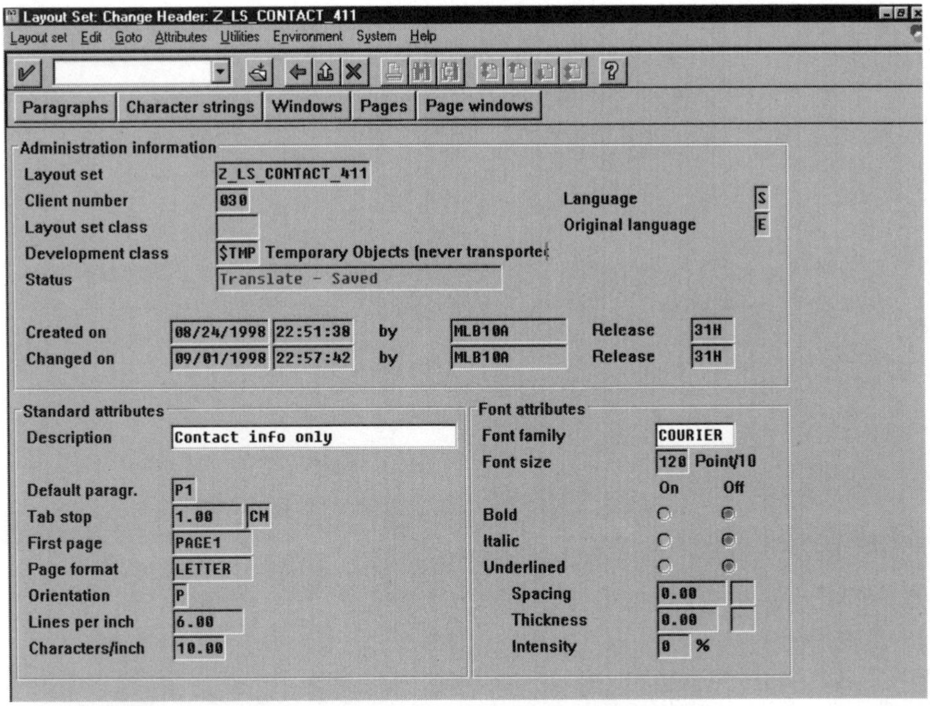

FIGURE 2.26 Layout set: Header for alternate language
Copyright by SAP AG

Layout Set Header for the New Language

Everything on the layout set Header screen looks the same as the header screen for the original language, except that the Language field has an S (Figure 2.26). Notice that only the Description and Font Family fields are highlighted and available for change. As we move to each of the other screens in the layout set definition, notice that almost nothing is available for change. The only thing than can be changed is the text (in the Text Element screen). Borrowing from our analogy, SAP only allows us to change the text on the label, not anything else—not even the placement of the label. As we can see from the Page Window screen in Figure 2.27, the placement of the Page window is locked. If we select WIN1 and go to the Text Element screen, we will find that text is available for change.

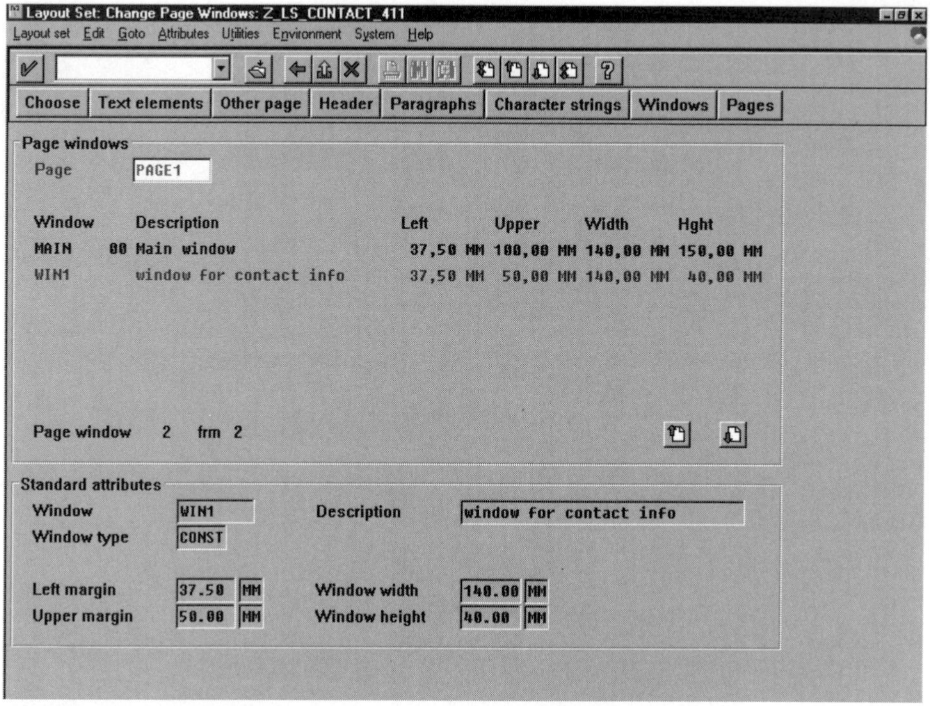

FIGURE 2.27   Page window screen for alternate language
Copyright by SAP AG

Text Element for the New Language

The text from the original text element was copied over to the Spanish version of the layout set. This is a problem because that text is in English; we need to change it to Spanish. At this time we open the text element in each Page window and change the text to Spanish. Instead of using an INCLUDE like we did in the English version, we are typing the text directly into the Text Element window. We could do it either way. The translated window should look like the one in Figure 2.28.

Before we save this work notice that the status field in the Header screen says "Translate–Not saved;" this is because we have translated the text but not saved or activated it. If we save the work it will say, "Translate–Saved." If we then activate it will say, "Active–Saved." Original-language layout sets are "Revised," alternate-language layout sets are "Translated."

```
Window WIN1                                                      _ □ ✕
Text  Edit  Goto  Format  Include  System  Help

 ✔  [            ▼]  ◄  ⇧ ✕   ▦▦  ▦▦  ▦▦▦▦  ▦
 Select | Insert | Line | Format | Page | Paste | Replace

 ....+....1....+....2....+....3....+....4....+....5....+....6....+....7..
 *    Si usted tiene preguntas
 *    por favor llame al Sr. Brackett al (301) 555-1234│




---------------- Z_LS_CONTACT_411 ------------ Lines 1 - 2 / 2 --------------
```

FIGURE 2.28   Text element for Z_LS_CONTACT_411 converted to Spanish
Copyright by SAP AG

Standard Texts in Different Languages

Like layout sets, standard text is language dependent. When creating our standard text (Figure 2.10) we used "E" for English. We could have used any language, but our layout set (as written) would only have picked up the English version. This is because our layout set is in English. If we use an INCLUDE in our text element the layout set will always look for the standard text with the same language as layout set language—not necessarily the original language. For instance if we use an INCLUDE here in our Spanish layout set, we will also need to create a Spanish standard text called Z_CONTACT_INFO. We can override this by specifically identifying the language in the INCLUDE statement. If we wanted to include the English standard text in the Spanish Layout Set text element, the command line would be changed to look like this:

```
INCLUDE Z_CONTACT_INFO OBJECT TEXT ID ST LANGUAGE E
```

In our case this would defeat the purpose. In some cases, however, there might be a requirement to print a standard text in a certain language based on user inputs or settings.

This could be done by defining the language as a symbol which can be passed in the calling ABAP program.

Suppose you are printing a Spanish layout set but one line should print in a secondary language that says, "If you need this printed in English, please see Mrs. Barnes at the administration desk." The secondary language is defined by user input. A standard text in English called ZENGHELKP holds the phrase as stated. If the user input were captured in a field called ZLANGU in a structure called ZSTRUCT, the resulting include command would look like this:

```
INCLUDE ZENGHELP OBJECT TEXT ID ST LANGUAGE Z STRUCT-ZLANGU
```

This means that Mrs. Barnes can access the standard text and change the English message as needed. This message would show up on Spanish printouts as well as those of any other layout-set language combination as long as the include statement is used this way.

Determining the Language of the Layout Set

We have created layout sets in multiple languages. Which language is used? The short answer is—the language that is used in the Function module that initiates the layout set. The Function module is examined in more detail in Chapter 3. If a language is not provided, then SY-LANGU (SAP logon language key) is used. If a language is provided but the layout does not exist in that language, then the original language of the layout set is used.

The print program initiates the layout set. So the print program is going to get the language parameter from user settings, normally in output determination. In standard print programs, the Language parameter is passed in different ways depending on the application area. For example, if you are printing customer invoices in the SD module, and you want Spanish customers to get Spanish invoices. Set the output determination criteria so that these customers are linked with the appropriate output type and language "S." This Language parameter would then be passed to the print program in NAST-SPRAS. The print program would in turn call its layout set using LANGUAGE = NAST-SPRAS.

Architecture in Review

1. Layout sets used for external correspondence are called by ABAP processing programs.
2. Processing programs and layout sets are attached to outputs in the respective application areas. Custom processing programs can call layout sets without being triggered by output determination if SAPscript capabilities are needed in a report.
3. If there is text defined, there is a language. SAPscript objects that contain text have a language key.

3

Calling Layout Sets Directly from an ABAP Program

Example Programs

First Example Program

To illustrate how an ABAP program calls a layout set we need to look at a sample program. The following print program produces a simple list. When working on layout sets, I usually make a list of the paragraphs and character strings I have created in the layout set. On the list I include the font and other characteristics associated with each so I know which one to choose from the tag list as I am writing the text element. To illustrate layout set concepts, I used a layout set (Z_LS_INFO), to output the lists. The program is called ZLSINFO.

```
1    REPORT ZLSINFO MESSAGE-ID 00.
2
3    * DESCRIPTION: Print Layout Set Paragraph and Character
                    Examples
4    */ Database Tables Used in Report
5    TABLES: ITCDP,
6    ITCDS,
7    ITCTA.
8
9    */ Database Tables Used by Layout Set
10
11   TABLES: ITCPP,      "Script output parameters
12   ITCPO.              "Script com parameters
13
14   */ Program Selections
15   PARAMETERS:  S_TDFORM      LIKE ITCTA-TDFORM,
16                P_LANG        LIKE RSSCF-TDSPRAS.
17
18   */ Data Definitions
19   DATA: LFOUND,
20      ELEMENT_NAME(30).
21
22   */ Internal Tables
23   DATA: BEGIN OF I_ITCDP OCCURS 10. "paragraphs
24      INCLUDE STRUCTURE ITCDP.
25   DATA: END OF I_ITCDP.
26
27   DATA: BEGIN OF I_ITCDS OCCURS 10. "strings
28      INCLUDE STRUCTURE ITCDS.
29   DATA: END OF I_ITCDS.
```

```
30
31 DATA: BEGIN OF I_ITCTA OCCURS 10.
32     INCLUDE STRUCTURE ITCTA.
33 DATA: END OF I_ITCTA.
34
35 DATA: BEGIN OF I_THEAD OCCURS 10.
36     INCLUDE STRUCTURE THEAD.
37 DATA: END OF I_THEAD.
38
39 */ Programmatic Checks of User Selections
40 AT SELECTION-SCREEN.
41 IF S_TDFORM = ' '.
42     MESSAGE E398 WITH 'Enter valid layout set name'.
43 ENDIF.
44
45 */ Begin Main Processing
46 START-OF-SELECTION.
47 PERFORM GET_FORM_INFO.
48 PERFORM OPEN_LAYOUT_SET.
49 PERFORM PROCESS_INFO.
50 PERFORM CLOSE_LAYOUT_SET.
51 */ Program Subroutines
52 */ Form: Get_form_info
53 */ Description: Retrieve information about the layout set
54 */
55 FORM GET_FORM_INFO.
56 CALL FUNCTION 'READ_FORM'
57     EXPORTING
58         LANGUAGE          = P_LANG
59         FORM              = S_TDFORM
60     IMPORTING
61         FOUND             = LFOUND
62         FORM_HEADER       = I_ITCTA
63     TABLES
64         PARAGRAPHS        = I_ITCDP
65         STRINGS           = I_ITCDS.
66     MOVE S_TDFORM TO ITCTA-TDFORM.
67 ENDFORM.
68
69 */ Form: open_layout_set
70 */ Description: Open the layout set
71 */
72 FORM OPEN_LAYOUT_SET.
73 CALL FUNCTION 'OPEN_FORM'
74     EXPORTING FORM          = 'Z_LS_INFO'
```

```
75        LANGUAGE           = 'E'
76        DEVICE             = 'PRINTER'
77        APPLICTION         = 'TX'
78        DIALOG             = 'X'.
79  ENDFORM.
80
81  */ Form: process_info
82  */ Description: Loop through information about the
83  */ paragraph and strings and call layout set
84  FORM PROCESS_INFO.
85     PERFORM WRITE_TO_MAIN USING 'PARA_HEADER'.
86     LOOP AT I_ITCDP.
87        MOVE-CORRESPONDING I_ITCDP TO ITCDP.
88        PERFORM WRITE_TO_MAIN USING 'PARA_LINE'.
89     ENDLOOP.
90     PERFORM WRITE_TO_MAIN USING 'STRING_HEADER'.
91     LOOP AT I_ITCDS.
92        MOVE-CORRESPONDING I_ITCDS TO ITCDS.
93        PERFORM WRITE_TO_MAIN USING 'STRING_LINE'.
94     ENDLOOP.
95  ENDFORM.
96
97  */ Form: close_layout_set
98  */ Description: Close the layout set
99  */
100 FORM CLOSE_LAYOUT_SET.
101    CALL FUNCTION 'CLOSE_FORM'.
102 ENDFORM.
103
104 */ Form: write_to_main
105 */ Description: Do write
106 */
107 FORM WRITE_TO_MAIN USING ELEMENT_NAME.
108    CALL FUNCTION 'WRITE_FORM'
109       EXPORTING WINDOW    = 'MAIN'
110       ELEMENT             = ELEMENT_NAME.
111 ENDFORM.
```

ZLSINFO CE003

CD-ROM

CD-ROM

Layout set Z_LS_INFO FE001

The basic processing steps in this program are as follows:

1. Retrieve layout set name and language from parameters
2. Get layout set information using function module
3. Open the layout set
4. Process the data/print loop
5. Close the layout set.

Each of these tasks is partitioned as a perform statement in lines 47–50. The function module READ_FORM on line 56 is a standard SAP function module that retrieves information about layout sets. In our case, the information about the paragraphs is exported to an internal table called I_ITCDP and the character string information is exported to an internal table called I_ITCDS.

In step three the layout set is opened with the function module OPEN_FORM. Form equals Z_LS_INFO because that is the name of the layout set we want to open. Language is E for English. Device is printer because, we are outputting the layout set to a printer. The Application is TX because that is the type of transaction we want to use for print previews. Dialog is X because we need the user dialog screen that allows us to enter the output information (printer name etc.). If Dialog is blank then we have to pass the output information to Options in a structure that is like ITCPO.

Step four is the print loop. In Figure 3.1 we see that the paragraph information is printed first. To print the section header **Paragraphs**, we need to print a text element in the Main window called PARA_HEADER. The text elements for the Main window of Z_LS_INFO look like this:

```
/E PARA_HEADER
*
P2 Paragraphs
*
P4 Name,,Description,,Just,,Spacing,,Font,,Bold
/E PARA_LINE
*   &ITCDP-TDPARGRAPH(2)& &ITCDP-TDTEXT(30)&
          &ITCDP-TDPJUSTIFY(10)&
    &ITCDP-TDPLDIST(5)&&ITCDP-TDPDISTU(2)& &ITCDP-TDFAMILY(8)&
    &ITCDP-TDHEIGHT(3)& &ITCDP-TDBOLD(1)&
```

```
/E  STRING_HEADER
*

*

P2  Character Strings
*

P4  Name,,Description,,Font,,Bold
/E  STRING_LINE
*    &ITCDS-TDSTRING(2)& &ITCDS-TDTEXT(30)& &ITCDS-TDFAMILY(8)&
     &ITCDS-TDHEIGHT(3)& &ITCDS-TDBOLD(1)&
```

```
Print Preview for CSC6 Page 00001 of 00001                              _ 8 X
Text  Edit  Goto  System  Help

                              Layout set Z_TEMP
                       Paragraphs and Character Strings


    Paragraphs

    Name         Description                 Just      Spacing Font      Bold
    P1 courier 10                            LEFT        1.00  HELVE     080 *
    P2 helvetica 16 bold                     LEFT        1.00  HELVE     160 X
    P3 helvetica 14                          LEFT        1.00  HELVE     140 X
    P4 helvetica 10                          LEFT        1.00  HELVE     100 X
    P5 helvetica 6                           LEFT        1.00  HELVE     060 *
    P6 Times 16 bold                         CENTER      0.25  TIMES     160 X
    P7 HELVETICA 8 BOLD CENTER HEADER        CENTER      1.00  HELVE     080 X
    P8 HEL 8 BOLD CENT CLOSE                 CENTER      2.70  HELVE     080 X
    P9 HEL 8 BOLD CENT (NUMBERS)             CENTER      5.00  TIMES     080
    Q1 HELVETICA 8 LEFT BOLD                 LEFT        3.50  HELVE     080 X
    Q2 hel 10 bold left-right tab            LEFT        1.00  HELVE     100 X
    Q3 TIMES 10 BOLD LEFT                    LEFT        3.50  TIMES     100 X


    Character Strings

    Name         Description                 Font      Bold
    C1 HEL 8 BOLD                            HELVE     080 X
    C2 TIMES 6                               TIMES     060 *
```

FIGURE 3.1   ZLSINFO output
Copyright by SAP AG

CD-ROM

Layout set Z_LS_INFO FE001

PARA_HEADER just prints a blank line, then the word "Paragraphs" in bold, then another blank line and finally the field headers for Paragraphs. It prints in bold because paragraph P2 is bold. For the blank lines it does not matter if bold is turned on because nothing is printed on those lines, so we use "*" for the default paragraph. For a blank line the only thing that is relevant is the line spacing. The headers use P4, which is not bold but has tab stops set up that line up the field headers appropriately.

At line 86, we start looping at I_ITCDP which holds the paragraph information that we collected with step two. I_ITCDP has one record for each paragraph contained in the layout set. Each record has 55 fields, which contain all the information about each paragraph. (The function module returns more information than we use in our report). As we loop through each record in the internal table I_ITCDP, we need to move the record information to a structure so that the fields can be used by the layout set (line 87). At line 88 we tell the layout set to print the text element PARA_LINE in the Main window. The text element PARA_LINE does not contain any literals, only symbols. The eight symbols printed contain the paragraph information as shown in the header. We do not want the record to get thrown out of alignment if one of the fields is blank, so we use explicit lengths for each, thus the number in parenthesis after each symbol.

At lines 91 through 94, we print the character string information in the same way. There are 13 paragraphs and two character strings in the example output shown in Figure 3.1. The header at the top of the page is printed in a separate page called Title. The contents of Title will print each time the page is generated. The text element for Title is as follows:

```
P3  Layout set &itcta-tdform&
P3  Paragraphs and Character Strings
```

The paragraph P3 is 14 CPI, bold and centered. The field TDFORM from the structure ITCTA contains the name of the layout set for which the utility is being run.

Second Example Program

There are other ways of calling layout sets. The example above illustrates the common method used for most correspondence. The function modules OPEN_FORM, WRITE_FORM and CLOSE_FORM were used. In the sections that follow, we look at other function modules used to control layout sets.

START_FORM and END_FORM are used to start and stop layout sets. Suppose we are generating a report for each customer in a list. All the information about the customer is included on the customer's report. We want to print one copy of the report for each customer. In this case we will need to use START_FORM and END_FORM. Since we want to print one "copy" of the layout set for each customer in the list, we need to stop the layout set after customer "1" is finished and then start again at the first page of the layout set with customer "2". It is not necessary to open and close the layout set each time. The answer is to structure processing steps in the following manner:

1. Open the layout set
2. Start the layout set
3. Print customer "1" info
4. End the layout set
5. Start the layout set
6. Print customer "2" info....

WRITE_FORM_LINES is another function module that passes text to a layout set for printing. What follows is a simple example of all three of these function modules. This program called ZLSEXP follows the steps above, but instead of using the WRITE_FORM function module, it uses WRITE_FORM_LINES.

```
 1   REPORT ZLSEXP.
 2
 3   DATA: BEGIN OF PHEAD.
 4       INCLUDE STRUCTURE THEAD.
 5   DATA: END OF PHEAD.
 6
 7   DATA: BEGIN OF MYLINES OCCURS 50.
 8       INCLUDE STRUCTURE TLINE.
 9   DATA: END OF MYLINES.
10
11   APPEND '* This is the first line' TO MYLINES.
12   APPEND '* This is the second line' TO MYLINES.
13   APPEND '* This is the third line' TO MYLINES.
14   PERFORM OPEN_LAYOUT.
15   PERFORM START_LAYOUT.
16   PERFORM WRITE_LINES.
17   PERFORM END_LAYOUT.
18   APPEND '* This is the fourth line on the second form'
             TO MYLINES.
19   PERFORM START_LAYOUT.
```

```
20 PERFORM WRITE_LINES.
21 PERFORM END_LAYOUT.
22 PERFORM CLOSE_LAYOUT.
23
24 FORM OPEN_LAYOUT.
25     CALL FUNCTION 'OPEN_FORM'
26         EXPORTING
27             LANGUAGE       = 'E'
28             DEVICE         = 'PRINTER'
29             APPLICTION     = 'TX'
30             DIALOG         = 'X'.
31 ENDFORM.
32
33 FORM START_LAYOUT.
34     CALL FUNCTION 'START_FORM'
35         EXPORTING
36             FORM               = 'S_DOCU_SHOW'.
37 ENDFORM.
38
39 FORM WRITE_LINES.
40     CALL FUNCTION 'WRITE_FORM_LINES'
41         EXPORTING HEADER  = PHEAD
42         TABLES LINES      = MYLINES.
43 ENDFORM.
44
45 FORM END_LAYOUT.
46     CALL FUNCTION 'END_FORM'.
47 ENDFORM.
48
49 FORM CLOSE_LAYOUT.
50     CALL FUNCTION 'CLOSE_FORM'.
51 ENDFORM.
```

CD-ROM

Program ZLSEXP CE004

This will print the following lines on the first printing of the form:
  This is the first line
  This is the second line
  This is the third line

These lines follow on the next occurrence of the form:
This is the first line
This is the second line
This is the third line
This is the fourth line on the second form

MYLINES is an internal table that matches the structure of TLINE. TLINE has two fields, one for the tag column (2 characters) and one for the text (132 characters). The text for the first report is appended to MYLINES at lines 11-14. OPEN_FORM is then called without identifying a layout set. START_FORM is called to name the layout set. WRITE_FORM_LINES is called to pass the internal table MYLINES to the Main window of the layout set.

When using WRITE_FORM_LINES provide the export Header and the Table Lines. I have declared the internal table PHEAD and passed it to the function module but it has no entries. This gets confusing, but if I wanted to use any formatting options with my text in MYLINES, the entries would be made accordingly in PHEAD. In PHEAD I could identify a style or layout set as formatting options for my text.

After the first "report" is printed, the form is terminated with ENDFORM and the fourth line is appended to MYLINES. The form is then re-engaged with START_FORM and printed again with WRITE_FORM LINES. When OPEN FORM is called the user inputs are gathered and used for both occurrences of the report.

An Alternative to START_FORM and END_FORM

Sometimes it is necessary to open and close the layout set each time a report is generated. In this case we need to capture the output parameters after the first loop, and set the dialog parameters to " " for subsequent loops so users do not get prompted for the output parameters every time the loop passes. After the first loop, set the output parameters with Options in the OPEN_FORM function. Capture these Options in the first pass with Result. Here is an example of how to open a form in this manner.

```
1    FORM OPEN_LS_FORM.
2    IF LSVAR-OPEN_FLAG  = 'X'.
3        LSVAR-DIALOG     = ' '.
4        MOVE-CORRESPONDING I_ITCPP TO ITCPO.
5    ELSE.
6        LSVAR-DIALOG     = 'X'.
```

```
 7        ITCPO-TDNEWID    = P_NEWID.
 8        ITCPO-TDDEST     = P_DEST.
 9        ITCPO-TDIMMED    = P_IMMED.
10        ITCPO-TDDELETE   = P_DELETE.
11 ENDIF.
12
13 CALL FUNCTION 'OPEN_FORM'
14      EXPORTING FORM    = 'Z_AR_UNDIS_INV'
15         LANGUAGE       = 'E'
16         OPTIONS        = ITCPO
17         DEVICE         = 'PRINTER'
18         APPLICTION     = 'TX'
19         DIALOG         = LSVAR-DIALOG
20      IMPORTING
21         RESULT         = I_ITCPP.
22 ENDFORM.
```

CD-ROM

Capture options CE005

The examples above provide "real-life" uses can be of the function modules typically used as well to control layout sets. Other function modules are used to control SAPscript objects: all possible function modules can be found by searching for those that have a function group that begins with STX (search with STX*). The sections that follow provide the syntax and Import/Export parameters for the commonly used function modules.

Layout Set Function Modules

OPEN_FORM

OPEN_FORM must be used when information will be passed to a layout set. OPEN_FORM can be used in combination with START_FORM but must always be used first. If the layout set name is not identified in OPEN_FORM, it must be identified in START_FORM. Once OPEN_FORM is used, CLOSE_FORM must be used before using OPEN_FORM again or there will be an error.

```
Call Function 'OPEN_FORM'
EXPORTING FORM         = SPACE
    LANGUAGE           = SY-LANGU
    DEVICE             = 'PRINTER'
```

```
        DIALOG              = 'X'
        OPTIONS             = SPACE
        APPLICATION         = 'TX'
        ARCHIVE_INDEX       = SPACE
        ARCHIVE_PARAMS      = SPACE
    IMPORTING
        LANGUAGE            =
        RESULT              =
        NEW_ARCHIVE_PARAMS  =
    EXCEPTIONS
        CANCELED            =
        DEVICE              =
        FORM                =
        OPTIONS             =
        UNCLOSED            =
```

Exports

FORM—Provide the name of the layout set here or in START_FORM. The default value is space.

LANGUAGE—When a layout set is opened, a language must be provided. If it is not, the logon language SY-LANGU is used. Examples are "E" for English, "D" for German, "S" for Spanish.

DEVICE—When creating output correspondence, Printer or Telefax will probably be used. Other options available are: Telex for telex output; ABAP to output as a list; and Screen which is also a list, except that the application that displays the list can be chosen with the Application Export parameter. The default value is Printer.

DIALOG—This tells the Function module whether or not to display the user interface to get the Output parameters. X means do show the Dialog screen. " " means do not show the Dialog screen. The default value is X.

OPTIONS—Use this instead of the Dialog screen. The structure should be like ITCPO. Standard SAP outputs collect these settings from the output determination area of the application document and pass the settings to the layout set with the Options parameter. The default is space.

APPLICATION—When text is output to the screen, an application must be used to display the information. This option makes it possible to pick the type of application. The default is TX. The acceptable values are given in table TTXOB. When calling layout sets, the text object is always Text. The text editor application interface for Text is TX according to table TTXOB. I have never had an occasion to use anything other than TX when creating correspondence.

ARCHIVE INDEX—To archive printed output, add information about the output to help retrieve it later. A structure like TOA_DARA must be used. The default is space.

ARCHIVE PARAMS—Archiving parameters can be set dynamically by passing values in a structure like ARCPARAMS. The default value is space.

Imports

LANGUAGE—Why are we getting the language back if we already provided it in the export? Answer: Because it may not be the same. If a language is provided that does not exist, (or is not active) the original language of the layout set is used. The format will be like SY_LANGU or THEAD-TDSPRAS.

RESULT—This returns the output settings the user gave in the Output Dialog screen. The structure is like ITCPP.

NEW_ARCHIVE_PARAMS—This contains the parameters provided as a result of the archiving process. Structure is like ARC_PARAMS.

Exceptions

CANCELED—The user hit cancel on the Output Options screen.

DEVICE—Invalid device type provided in the Device Export parameter.

FORM—An invalid form was provided in the Form Export parameter.

OPTIONS—The Options Export parameter contains invalid entries.

UNCLOSED—The previous layout set has not been closed.

EXAMPLE

```
1   call function 'OPEN_FORM'
2   exporting
3      language        = 'E'
4      device          = 'PRINTER'
5      application     = 'TX'
6      dialog          = 'X'
7   importing
8      new_archive_params      = prc_params
9   exceptions
10     options                 = 01.
```

CD-ROM

Open form CE006.

CLOSE_FORM

As the name implies, CLOSE_FORM is used to close the layout set. This tells SAPscript that it has all the information needed to print. The layout set will not print until CLOSE_FORM is called.

```
CALL FUNCTION 'CLOSE_FORM'
IMPORTING    RESULT    =
TABLES       OTFDATA   =
EXCEPTIONS   UNOPENED  =
```

Imports

RESULT—This returns the output settings the user gave in the output dialog screen. The structure is like ITCPP. Structure is the same as import parameter Result in OPEN_FORM.

Tables

OTFDATA—It is possible to have all the output sent back in an internal table in the OTF format (tag columns and text strings). To do this, TDGETOTF in the Options export parameter of OPEN_FORM should be set to X. OTFDATA should be piped to an internal table with a structure like ITCOO.

Exceptions

UNOPENED—Layout set is not open.

EXAMPLE

```
1   FORM CLOSE_LS_FORM.
2   CALL FUNCTION 'CLOSE_FORM'.
3   ENDFORM.
```

WRITE_FORM

WRITE_FORM is how the layout set knows to write out the contents of a particular text element. The text element can be the entire contents of a Page

Windows text element or it can be a portion of the Page Windows text element identified with the Text Element tag column. A particular window can be identified so only that window prints. Usually WRITE FORM is used to trigger the printing of a particular text element in the Main window; when the Main window is filled on the page being written to, all the other windows on that page that have default text elements are then printed. That is why we do not see the other non-Main windows being called from the print program.

```
CALL FUNCTION 'WRITE_FORM'
EXPORTING        ELEMENT        = SPACE
                 WINDOW         = 'MAIN'
                 FUNCTION       = 'SET'
                 TYPE           = 'BODY'
IMPORTING        PENDING_LINES  =
EXCEPTIONS       ELEMENT        =
                 FUNCTION       =
                 TYPE           =
                 UNOPENED       =
                 UNSTARTED      =
                 WINDOW         =
```

Exports

ELEMENT—The name of the text element (as assigned by a Text Element tag column) in a Page window. If an element is not provided then SAPscript will print anything in the Page Windows text element not identified with a Text Element Tag column. The default value is space.

In Figure 3.2, if ELEMENT is OTHER_TEXT and the Window is V3, then only the text "Please mail your invoice to the address above" will print. If no Element is identified and Window is V3, then only the standard text called Invoice will print.

WINDOW—This is where to enter the window to be printed. If a window is not entered then the Main window is used.

FUNCTION—There are two types of windows, Main windows and all others. Main windows are special because they control when a new page is issued. Main windows are to output the list part of the printout. We normally do not know in advance how much of the Main window is going to be used. Main windows can be continued on subsequent pages. The TOP and BOTTOM commands (or Type export parameter) can be used so that identified texts appear only at the top or bottom of the Main window.

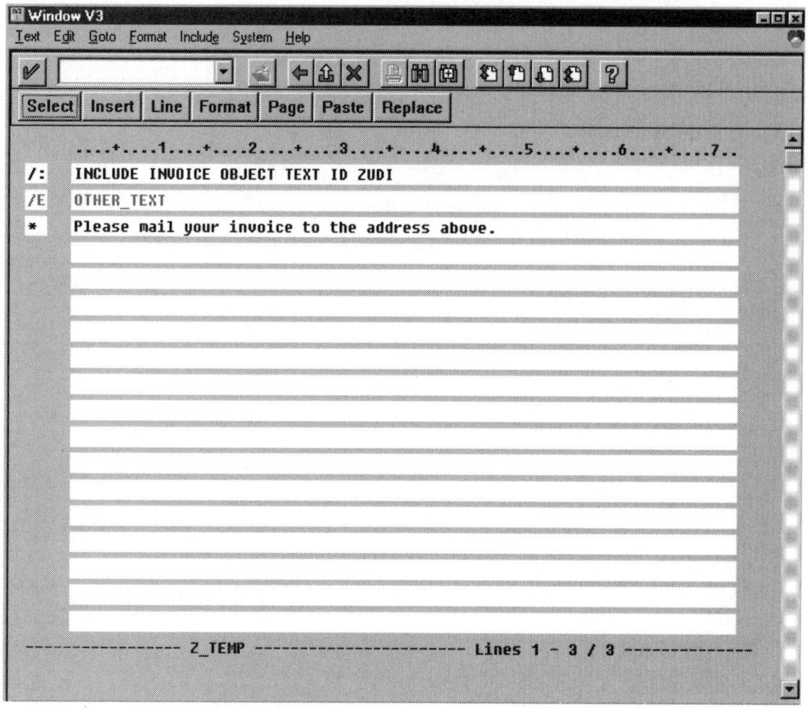

FIGURE 3.2   Text element in a text element
Copyright by SAP AG

Rules for FUNCTION:

- ▲ In the Top or Bottom sections of MAIN as described or any window other than MAIN with the Function set to SET, then: the text there is overwritten with the new text.
- ▲ In the Top or Bottom sections of MAIN as described or any window other than MAIN with the Function set to APPEND, then: the text is appended to the previous outputs to this window.
- ▲ In the Top or Bottom sections of MAIN as described or any window other than MAIN with the Function set to DELETE, then: the element being identified will be cleared of any contents.
- ▲ In MAIN with the Function set to SET or APPEND, then: the text is appended to the previous outputs to this window.
- ▲ In MAIN with the Function is set to DELETE, then: The Function statement will have no effect on the window.

The default value is SET.

TYPE—Use this to tell SAPscript to output text only at the top of the Main window with TOP. To output only at the bottom of MAIN use BOTTOM. BODY will put text in the "body" (not the top or bottom) of MAIN. The default is BODY.

Imports

PENDING_LINES—If something is triggered to print at the Bottom of MAIN, as described above, and it won't fit, then it is printed at the bottom of the MAIN on the next page. In this case PENDING_LINES will have an X to indicate (programmatically) not to re-output the same thing.

Exceptions

ELEMENT—Value given with Export parameter ELEMENT could not be found.

FUNCTION—FUNCTION provided in the Export parameters was not found.

TYPE—TYPE provided in the Export parameters was not valid.

UNOPENED—OPEN_FORM has not been called. OPEN_FORM must always precede WRITE_FORM.

UNSTARTED—OPEN_FORM was called but not START_FORM. START_FORM is needed because no layout set name was given in OPEN_FORM.

WINDOW—Invalid window provided in the Window export parameter.

This is a frequently used Function module, so there are three examples:

EXAMPLE 1

```
1   CALL FUNCTION 'WRITE_FORM'
2        EXPORTING WINDOW = 'V8'
3            ELEMENT     = 'REMIT_TO'.
```

EXAMPLE 2

```
1   CALL FUNCTION 'WRITE_FORM'
2        EXPORTING
3            PAGE        = 'NEXT'
4            ELEMENT     = 'FOOTER_TEXT'
5            WINDOW      = 'FOOTER'.
6   IF SY-SUBRC NE 0.
7       PERFORM ERROR_PROTOCOL.
8   ENDIF.
```

EXAMPLE 3

```
1   FORM WRITE_LS_FORM.
2      IF ZUDI-N_INV_NUM <> LSVAR-LAST_INV.
3         MOVE 'NEW_INVOICE' TO LSVAR-ELEMENT.
4      ELSE.
5         MOVE 'SAME_INVOICE' TO LSVAR-ELEMENT.
6      ENDIF.
7      IF LSVAR-LAST_INV = 'FIRST'.
8         MOVE 'SAME_INVOICE' TO LSVAR-ELEMENT.
9      ENDIF.
10        MOVE ZUDI-N_INV_NUM TO LSVAR-LAST_INV.
11     CALL FUNCTION 'WRITE_FORM'
12        EXPORTING WINDOW    = 'MAIN'
13             ELEMENT   = lsvar-element.
14  ENDFORM.
```

CD-ROM

Write_form CE007

WRITE_FORM_LINES

WRITE_FORM_LINES is used to output text lines to a Window. The text lines are moved to an internal table that is like TLINE, and then passed to the Function module. TLINE is structured in the ITF format, just like what we see in text elements (tag columns and text lines).

```
CALL FUNCTION 'WRITE_FORM_LINES'
EXPORTING      HEADER          = (mandatory)
               WINDOW          = 'MAIN'
               FUNCTION        = 'SET'
               TYPE            = 'BODY'
IMPORTING      PENDING_LINES   =
               FROMPAGE        =
TABLES         LINES           = (mandatory)
EXCEPTIONS     FUNCTION        =
               TYPE            =
               UNOPENED        =
               UNSTARTED       =
               WINDOW          =
```

HEADER—When we create a standard text it is possible to associate a style or a layout set that goes with the standard text (the layout set *may* not be the same as the layout set to which the text is sent). With the Header export parameter it is possible to identify a layout set or style to accompany the text by providing values in TDSTYLE (for the style) and TDFORM (for the layout set) of a structure like THEAD. A header must be passed even if it is not populated.

WINDOW—This is where to enter the window to be printed. If one is not entered then the Main window is used.

FUNCTION—There are two types of windows, Main windows and all others. Main windows are special because they control when a new page is issued. Main windows are where to output the list part of the printout. We normally do not know in advance how much of the Main window is going to be used. Main windows can be continued on subsequent pages. The Top and Bottom commands (or Type Export parameter) can be used so that identified texts appear only at the top or bottom of the Main window.

Rules for FUNCTION:

▲ In the Top or Bottom sections of MAIN as described or any window other than MAIN with the Function set to SET, then: the text there is overwritten with the new text.

▲ In the Top or Bottom sections of MAIN as described or any window other than MAIN with the Function set to APPEND, then: the text is appended to the previous outputs to this window.

▲ In the Top or Bottom sections of MAIN as described or any window other than MAIN with the Function set to DELETE, then: the element being identified will be cleared of any contents.

▲ In MAIN with the Function set to SET or APPEND, then: the text is appended to the previous outputs to this window.

▲ In MAIN with the Function is set to DELETE, then: The Function statement will have no effect on the window.

The default value is SET.

TYPE—Use this to tell SAPscript to output text only at the top of the Main window with TOP. To output only at the bottom of MAIN use BOTTOM. BODY will put text in the "body" (not the top or bottom) of MAIN. The default is BODY.

Imports

PENDING_LINES—If something is triggered to print at the Bottom of MAIN, as described above, and it won't fit, then it is printed at the bottom of the MAIN on the next page. In this case PENDING_LINES will have an X to indicate (programmatically) not to re-output the same thing.

FROMPAGE—When the text is output, we do not know how much of MAIN is already full and which page the text actually printed on. The page number is returned, not the page name. The page name would not help much if we always continue with NEXTPAGE for example.

Tables

LINES—This internal table is mandatory and is the whole reason to use this function module. We must use an internal table like TLINE, which is in the ITF format, tag column (2 characters) and a text line (132 characters).

Exceptions

FUNCTION—FUNCTION provided in the export parameters was not found.

TYPE—TYPE provided in the export parameters was not valid.

UNOPENED—OPEN_FORM has not been called. OPEN_FORM must always precede WRITE_FORM.

UNSTARTED—OPEN_FORM was called but START_FORM was not called. START_FORM is needed because no layout set name was given in OPEN_FORM.

WINDOW—Invalid window provided in the Window export parameter.

EXAMPLE
```
1   call function 'WRITE_FORM_LINES'
2       EXPORTING  HEADER     = phead
3       IMPORTING  FROMPAGE   = pfrompage
4       TABLES     LINES      = mylines.
```

START_FORM

START_FORM is used to start a layout set. If the layout set name was not identified in OPEN_FORM, then use START_FORM and identify the layout set name. START_FORM is primarily used when you need to start back at the beginning of a layout set multiple times. To print one report per customer (with all the associated customer information) for each customer in a list, start back at the top of the layout set but do not close and open the layout set (and reacquire the output parameters) each time.

```
Call Function 'START_FORM'
EXPORTING ARCHIVE_INDEX       = SPACE
          FORM                = SPACE
          LANGUAGE            = SPACE
          STARTPAGE           = SPACE
          PROGRAM             = SPACE
IMPORTING
          LANGUAGE            =
EXCEPTIONS
          FORM                =
          FORMAT              =
          UNENDED             =
          UNOPENED            =
          UNUSED              =
```

Exports

ARCHIVE INDEX—To archive printed output, add information about the output to help retrieve it later. A structure like TOA_DARA must be used. The default is space.

FORM—Provide the name of the layout set here or in OPEN_FORM. The default value is space.

LANGUAGE—If the layout set name is provided in START_FORM the language must be provided as well. Default is space.

STARTPAGE—This is where to provide the *name* of a page to start with as opposed to the default start page assigned in the layout set header. Default is space.

PROGRAM—The layout set will look at the tables statement in this program to define the symbols (this is not used much). Default is space.

Imports

LANGUAGE—If an exported language does not exist, (or is not active) the original language of the layout set is used. The language used to render the layout set will be given with LANGUAGE. The format will be like SY_LANGU or THEAD-TDSPRAS.

Exceptions

FORM—An invalid form was provided in the Form export parameter.

FORMAT—Page format attempted is invalid.

UNENDED—Layout set has been started already, end it first.

UNOPENED—Layout set not opened, output parameters not set.

UNUSED—Layout set not opened.

EXAMPLE
```
1   call function 'START_FORM'
2       exporting
3       form = 'S_DOCU_SHOW'.
```

END_FORM

Use this to end a layout set that has been started with START_FORM. After using END_FORM, issue either CLOSE _FORM to finish processing or START_FORM to start another layout set.

```
CALL FUNCTION 'END_FORM'
    IMPORTING   RESULT      =
    EXCEPTIONS  UNOPENED    =
```

Imports

RESULT—This returns the output settings the user gave in the output dialog screen when OPEN_FORM was issued. The structure is like ITCPP.

Exceptions

UNOPENED—Layout set is not open, therefore it cannot be ended.

EXAMPLE
```
1   form end_layout.
2       call function 'END_FORM'.
3   endform.
```

CONTROL_FORM

This function module is used to send control commands to the Layout set. Usually PROTECT, ENDPROTECT and NEW-PAGE are used. Consult the command reference section for a complete list of commands.

```
1   CALL FUNCTION 'CONTROL_FORM'
2   EXPORTING    COMMAND      = (mandatory)
3   EXCEPTIONS   UNOPENED     =
4                UNSTARTED    =
```

Exports

COMMAND—Enter the command to be executed.

Exceptions

UNOPENED—OPEN_FORM has not been issued, open the form first.

UNSTARTED—OPEN_FORM was called but START_FORM was not. START_FORM is needed because no layout set name was given in OPEN_FORM.

EXAMPLE

```
1   CALL FUNCTION 'CONTROL_FORM'
2        EXPORTING
4            COMMAND = 'NEW-PAGE'.
```

Calling Layout Sets Directly from an ABAP Program in Review

1. Function modules are used to control the layout set.
2. OPEN_FORM and CLOSE_FORM must always be present.
3. The Main window is different from the other windows and is where to post the recurring data (item levels loops).
4. All layout sets are driven by print programs. Print programs can be standard SAP objects or custom developed.

CHAPTER

4

Building Blocks

Header

Description

Headers are to layout sets what attributes are to ABAP programs. The header is the place to provide all the administrative information about the layout set and a few default parameters. We will use Z_LS_INFO for an example (see Figure 4.1). To get to this screen choose **Tools → Word processing → Layout set** then enter a layout set name and press **Change** or **Display** (with display, the fields that are changeable will not show up in white.) Z_LS_INFO is the Layout set we used in the first ABAP example in Chapter 3.

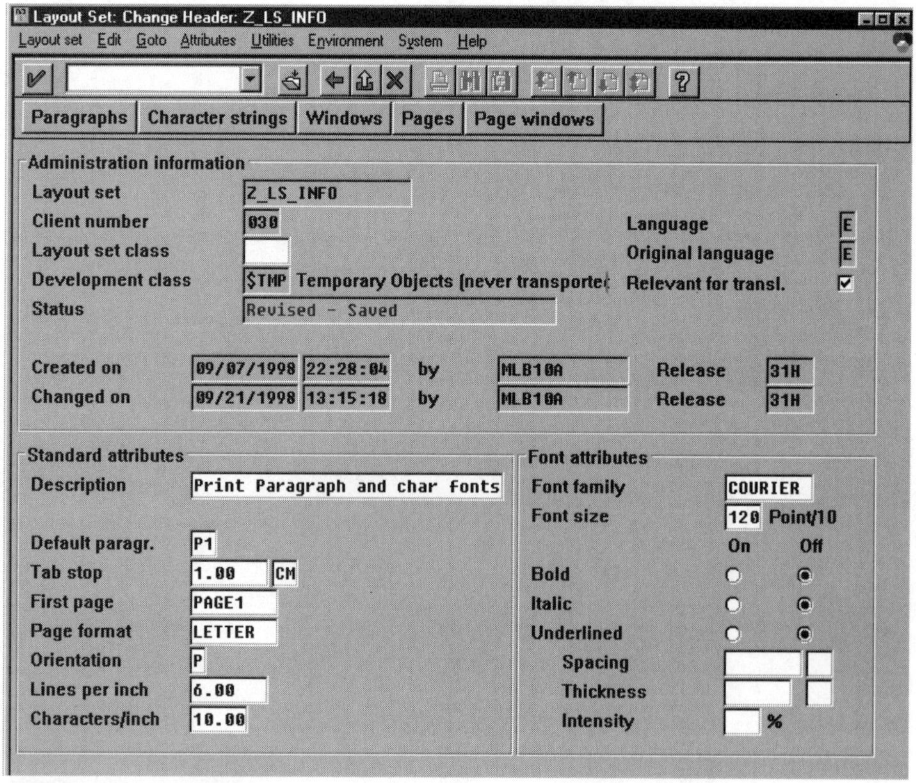

FIGURE 4.1 Header

Copyright by SAP AG

Header Fields

Layout set—This is the name of the layout set.

Client number—This is the currently occupied client number. The client cannot be changed. The client currently occupied always shows.

Layout set class—This is a way of grouping layout sets. Layout set classes can be viewed/ maintained in **Tools → Word processing → Settings**.

Development class—Objects are grouped by development class. Development classes are the same here as they are for other development objects.

Status—**Revised-Saved** means the layout set has been changed and saved, but not activated.

> **Active-Saved** means the layout set was saved and activated.

> **Translate-Not saved** means a new version of the layout set was created in a language other than the original language but not saved.

> **Translate-Saved** means that the translated layout set has been saved but not yet activated.

> **New**—New layout set.

Language—The language of the layout set; this may not be the same as the original language.

Original language—The original language in which the layout set was created.

Relevant for transl.—If this box is checked, then other languages of the layout set can be created (same layout set name, different language). If the box is not checked then they cannot.

Created on—The date and time the layout set was created; the user ID of the person who created the layout set and the release number at time of creation.

Changed on—The last date and time the layout set was changed; the user ID of the person who last changed the layout set and the release number when it was changed.

Description—A description of the layout set.

Default Paragr.—The default paragraph for the whole layout set. Unless specified otherwise, this paragraph format will be used.

Tab stop—Unless otherwise provided in the Paragraph tab settings, this is the default tab spacing that will be used when (two commas) are used in the text element to identify a tab stop.

First page—This is the page with which the layout set will start.

Page format—The page format for the printed output.

Orientation—The orientation of the page, (portrait or landscape).

Lines per inch—The number of text lines that appear per vertical inch.

Characters/inch—The number of characters that appear for each horizontal inch.

Font family—The default font for the layout set (example: Courier, Helvetica).

Font Size—The default font size for the layout set.

Bold—The default font can be bold (or not).

Italic—The default font can be italicized (or not).

Underlined—The default font can be underlined (or not).

Spacing—When an underline is used this is the spacing between the line and the bottom of the letters for characters that are underlined.

Thickness—The thickness of the underline, when it is used.

Intensity—The brightness of the underline when it is used (0–100, darkest to lightest respectively).

Paragraph

Description

As the name implies, *paragraphs* are default paragraph settings that can be applied to text elements. When a new paragraph is created, its name shows up as a tag column option. Get to the screen in Figure 4.2 by clicking the **Paragraphs** button from the layout set Header screen (**Tools → Word** processing → **Layout set** then enter a layout set name and press **Change** or **Display**).

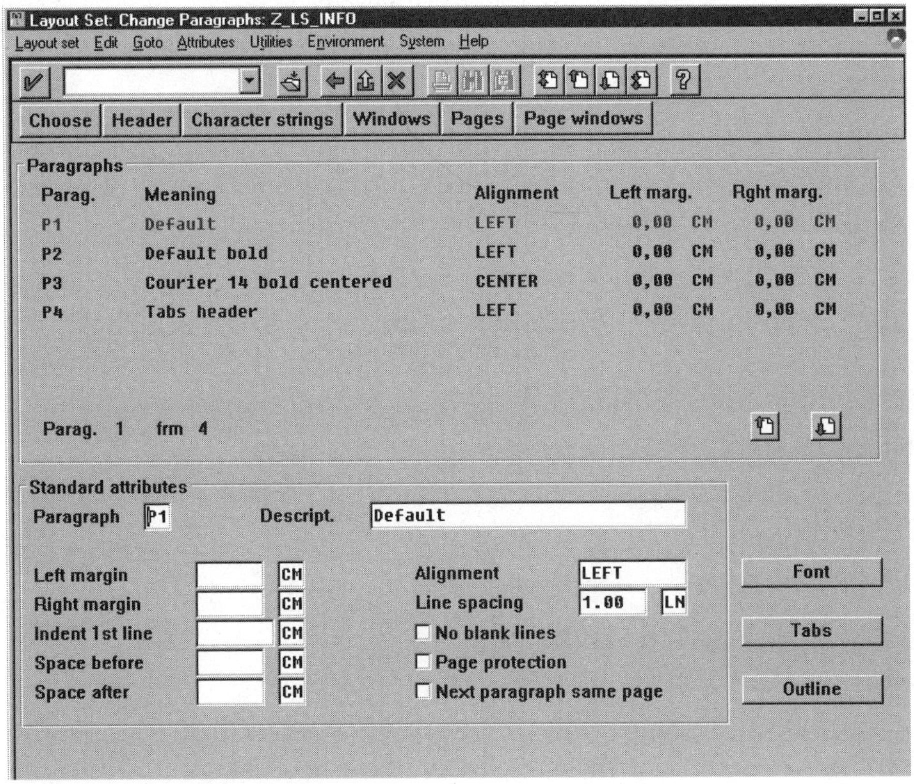

FIGURE 4.2   Paragraphs
Copyright by SAP AG

Paragraph Standard Attributes

In Figure 4.2, the paragraphs section shows all the paragraphs for the layout set. The Standard attributes section shows the standard attributes for the paragraph selected in the paragraphs section.

In the paragraphs section of the screen in Figure 4.2:

Paragraph—The name of the paragraph.

Description—The description of the paragraph.

Left margin—The left margin of the paragraph.

Right Margin—The right margin of the paragraph.

Indent 1st line—The amount to indent the first line of text; if the value is negative, the line will begin to the left of the margin.

Space before—It is possible to assign a "buffer" space before the paragraph.

Space after—Or assign a buffer space after the paragraph.

Alignment—The way the lines in the paragraph are aligned; acceptable values are: left, right, centered and block. Block means the text is spread across the line so that the characters are evenly spaced.

Line spacing—The amount of vertical space between lines.

No blank lines—If this is checked, then blank lines in the paragraph will not print.

Page protection—If this switch is set, the paragraph will not be split on multiple pages. The paragraph will print on the next page if necessary.

Next paragraph same page—If this switch is set, this and the next paragraph will not be separated by a page break.

Paragraph Font Attributes

If the Font button on the Paragraphs screen is selected, the lower half of the screen will display the font attributes as shown in Figure 4.3.

The following additional fields are shown when paragraph fonts are selected:

Family—The type of font (example: Courier, Helvetica).

Font size—The size of the font.

Bold—If this is turned on, everything in the paragraph will be in bold. If Retain is chosen, then the setting from the header is retained. If Off is chosen, then the paragraph will not be in bold regardless of what is in the header.

Italic—If this is turned on, everything in the paragraph will be italicized. If Retain is chosen, then the setting from the header is retained. If Off is chosen, then the paragraph will not be italicized regardless of what is in the header.

Underlined—If this is turned on, everything in the paragraph will be underlined. If Retain is chosen, then the setting from the header is retained. If Off is chosen, then the paragraph will not be underlined regardless of what is in the header. When On is selected it is possible to click the "→..." button in the lower right corner of the Font Attributes screen and set the spacing thickness and intensity of the paragraph underline.

> **Spacing**—The spacing between the line and the bottom of the letters being underlined.

> **Thickness**—The thickness of the underline.

> **Intensity**—The brightness of the underline (0–100, darkest to lightest respectively).

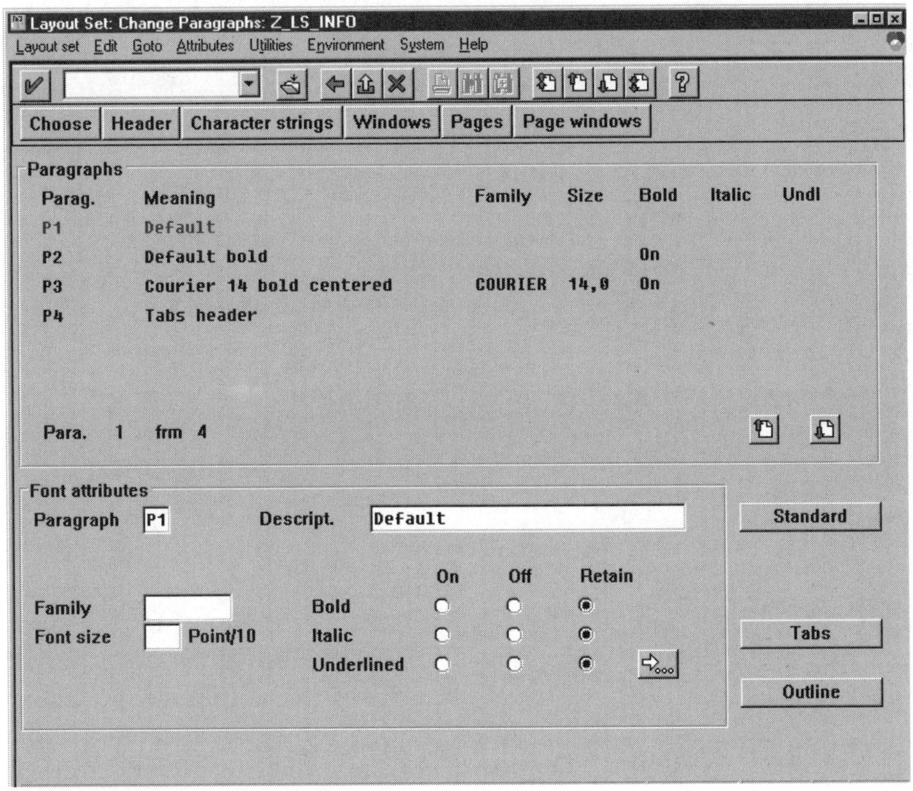

FIGURE 4.3   Paragraph font
Copyright by SAP AG

Paragraph Tab Attributes

When the Tabs button is selected (Figure 4.4), the following additional fields are shown:

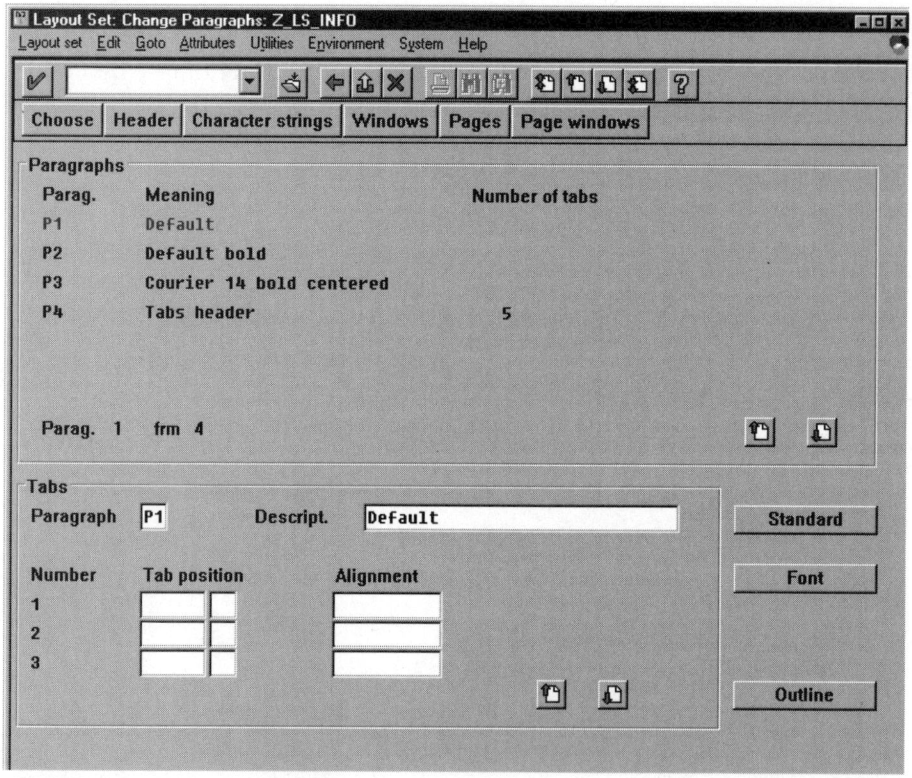

FIGURE 4.4   Paragraph tabs
Copyright by SAP AG

Tab position—This is where to put tab positions. For example, for tab stops at 3, 4 and 6 cm across the page, make three entries. When entering tab positions, use decimals. (Use F4 to get a list of possible entries for the unit of measure.) Normally tabs are left justified but they can be set as desired in the alignment field. Acceptable alignments are: left, right, centered, decimal (lined up on the decimal point) or sign (right aligned with a sign). In our example our entries would look like this:

Number	Tab position	Alignment
1	3 CM	Left
2	4 CM	Left
3	6 CM	Left

To enter more tab positions, page down to get entry locations for more.

Paragraph Outline Attributes

If the Outline button in the paragraphs screen is selected, the outline attributes will show on the lower half of the screen (Figure 4.5).

The following fields are shown when the Outline button is selected (refer to Figure 4.5).

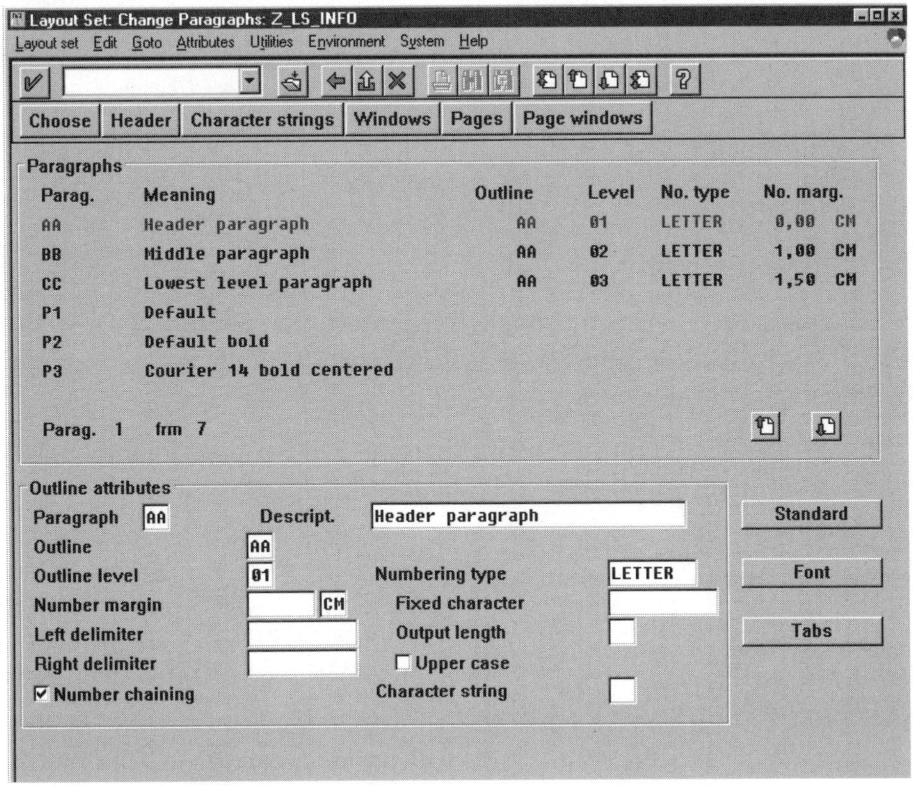

FIGURE 4.5   Paragraph outlines
Copyright by SAP AG

Outline—The name of the chief paragraph; in our example the highest paragraph in the outline is AA.

Outline level—Where does the outline fit in the hierarchy? 1 is the highest. In our example 1 is the Title, 2 is the chapter, and 3 is the section.

Number margin—How far the outline number/character should be bumped to the right.

Left delimiter—This is the character to use at the left of this level outline number.

Right delimiter—This is the character to use at the right of this level outline number. Had I used ". " for each of my paragraphs the outline letters would have been arranged like this:

```
a.
        a.a.
                a.a.a.
                a.a.b.
                a.a.c.
        a.b.
                a.b.a.
                a.b.b.
                a.b.c.
```

Number chaining—If this is checked, then all the paragraphs will be numbered relative to one another. If it is not checked, then each paragraph will be numbered independently.

Numbering type—Different numbering schemes can be used in the outline (example: Roman numerals, letters and numbers).

Fixed Character—In numbering type Char, this indicated a fixed character for this level. Enter the fixed character here.

Output length—The output length of outline numbers, if they exist, the numbers will be filled with leading zeros, if necessary, to pad the number to the desired length.

Upper case—Numbers and characters will be in upper case if the box is checked; if it is not, they will be in lower case.

Character string—Assign a character string to an outline number/character. The attributes of the character string will be used to render the outline number/character but the text line that follows will retain the attributes of the paragraph to which it is assigned.

In Figure 4.5 in the paragraphs section of the screen, I have added three paragraphs, AA, BB and CC, one for each hierarchy of the outline that I want to create. Paragraph AA is the highest of the three paragraphs (like a title). Paragraph BB, in Figure 4.6, is in the middle (like a chapter). Paragraph CC, shown in Figure 4.7, is at the lowest level of the outline (like a section).

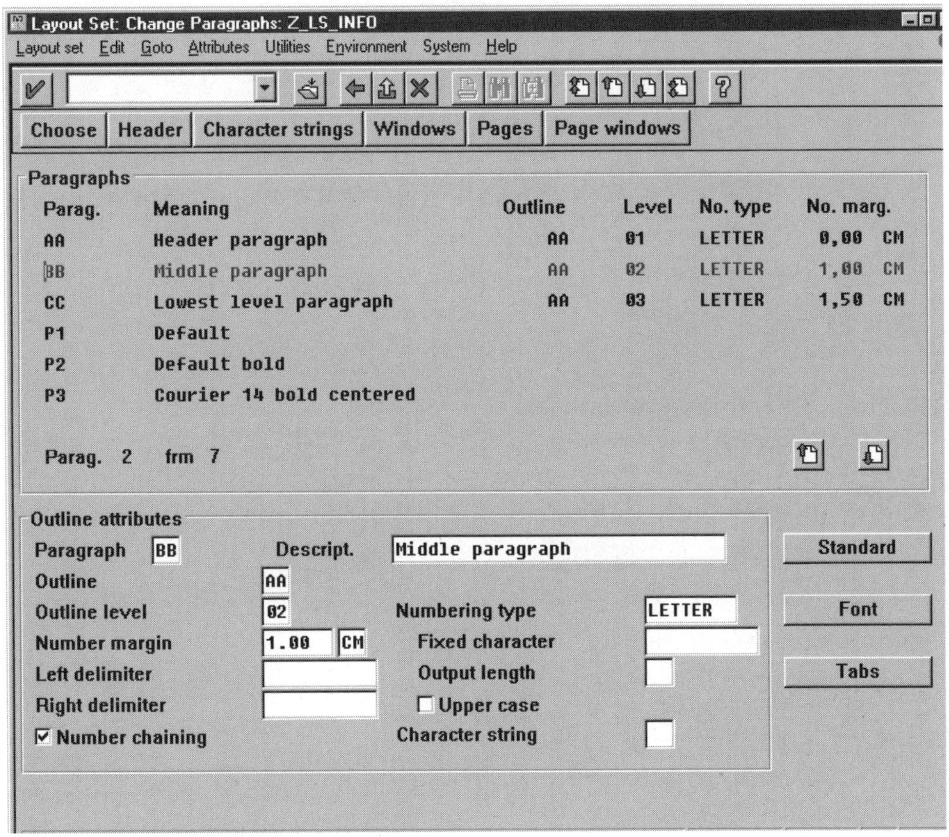

FIGURE 4.6   Paragraph outline BB
Copyright by SAP AG

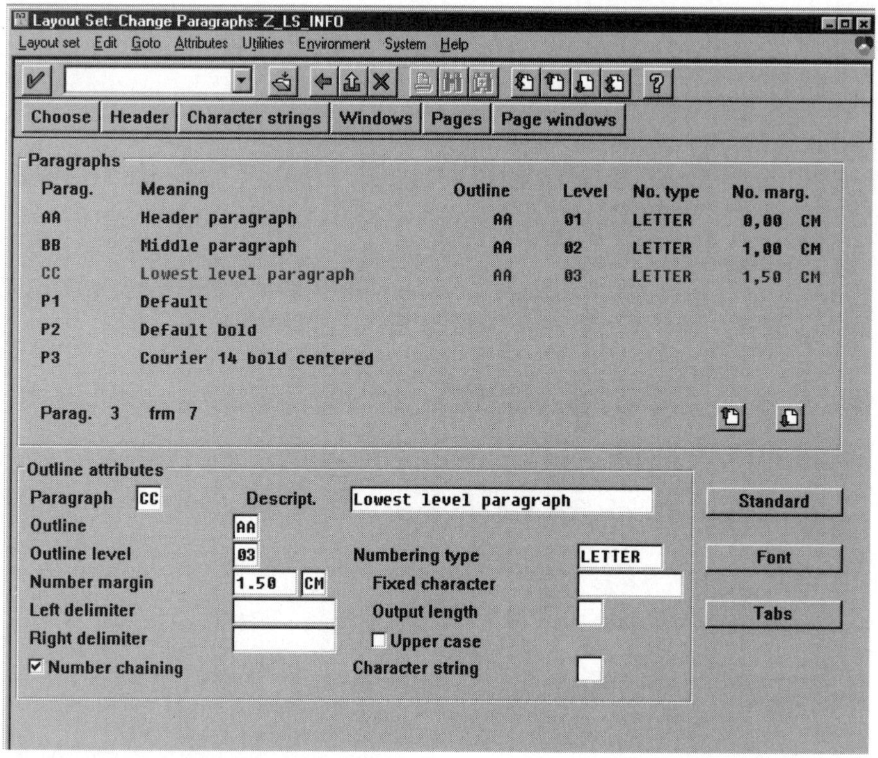

FIGURE 4.7 Paragraph outline CC
Copyright by SAP AG

In this example I want to show an outline that has the following format:

Title
- Chapter 1
  - Section 1
  - Section 2
  - Section 3
- Chapter 2
  - Section 1
  - Section 2
  - Section 3

To do this, I have interjected a New Page window into layout set `Z_LS_INFO` called W3, a plain window placed just above the Main window. The Main window had to be moved down so that W3 could fit. The text element for W3 looks like this:

```
AA  Title
BB  chapter 1
CC  section 1
CC  section 2
CC  section 3
BB  chapter 2
CC  section 1
CC  section 2
CC  section 3
```

This window will produce the output shown in Figure 4.8 when the layout set is called by the ABAP program ZLSINFO.

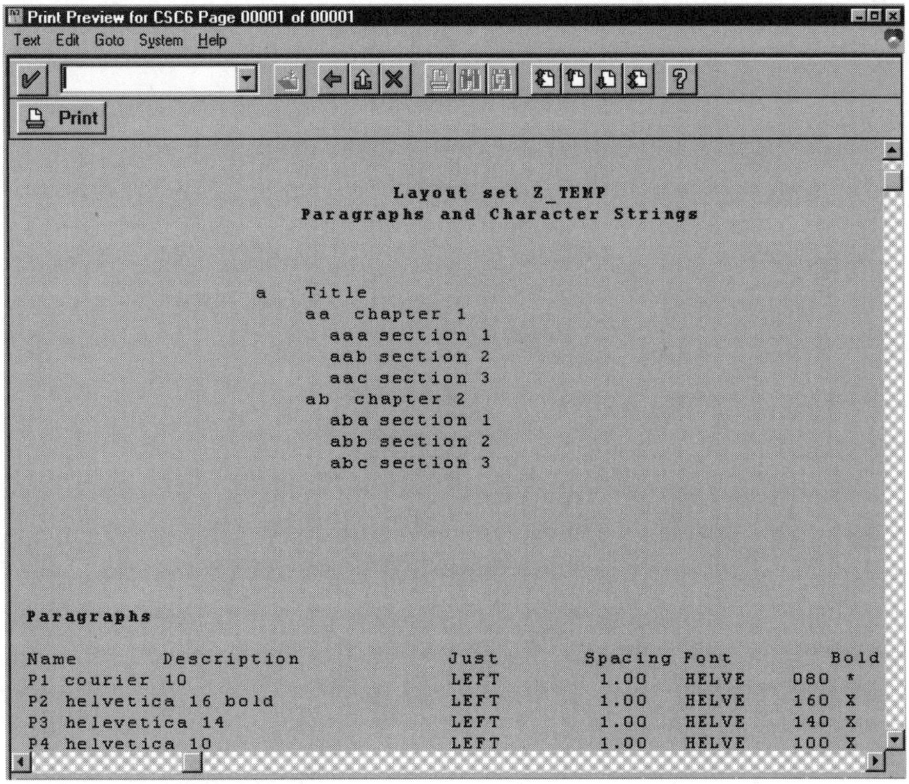

FIGURE 4.8   Outline output
Copyright by SAP AG

It is important to note that the outline numbers are indented according to the number margin provided in the paragraph outline parameters, but the text is indented according to the left margin of the paragraph. In paragraph CC, the outline letter is indented 1.5 cm; for this reason the left margin of paragraph CC is set to 2.5 cm. *The outline function does not indent text,* the left margin for the paragraph must be set to take into account the space needed by the outline number/character and its possible growth.

WARNING

The outline function does not indent the text.

Character Strings

Description

Character strings are predefined settings for text. As with paragraph definitions, assign a unique name to the character string and then set the attributes associated with it (bold, underlined, font etc.). To use the character string, surround the characters to be changed with <C1> and </> (where C1 is the name of the character string). Get to the character strings menu by selecting the **Character String** button from the Header screen (see Figure 4.9).

Character String Standard Attributes

String—The name assigned to the character string.

Description—A description of the character string. Whatever is put here will show up on the Possible Entries dropdown list. I usually include some unique characteristics of the string so I can recognize it in the Possible Entries list.

Marker—To mark the use of the character string, do so by adding characters next to the name of the character string when it is called. If I wanted to mark the character string H1 with 1234, I would make sure this box is checked and then create my text element like this:

```
*    Please send all inquiries to <H1:1234>John Doe</>
```

Bar code—Check with the basis team to see if the printer is set up to handle bar codes. If so, a bar code can be entered from the possible entries list. The bar code selected depends on the style of bar code required. With a bar code selected, it is possible to use digits within the character string to render the equivalent bar code. Bar codes are larger than digits, so allow enough room in the window. Usually the bar code value is a symbol. If my field for UPC code were Z_ITEMS-ZUPC and my character string for bar codes were B1, the text element line to render the bar code would look like this:

```
*    <B1>&Z_ITEMS-ZUPC&</>
```

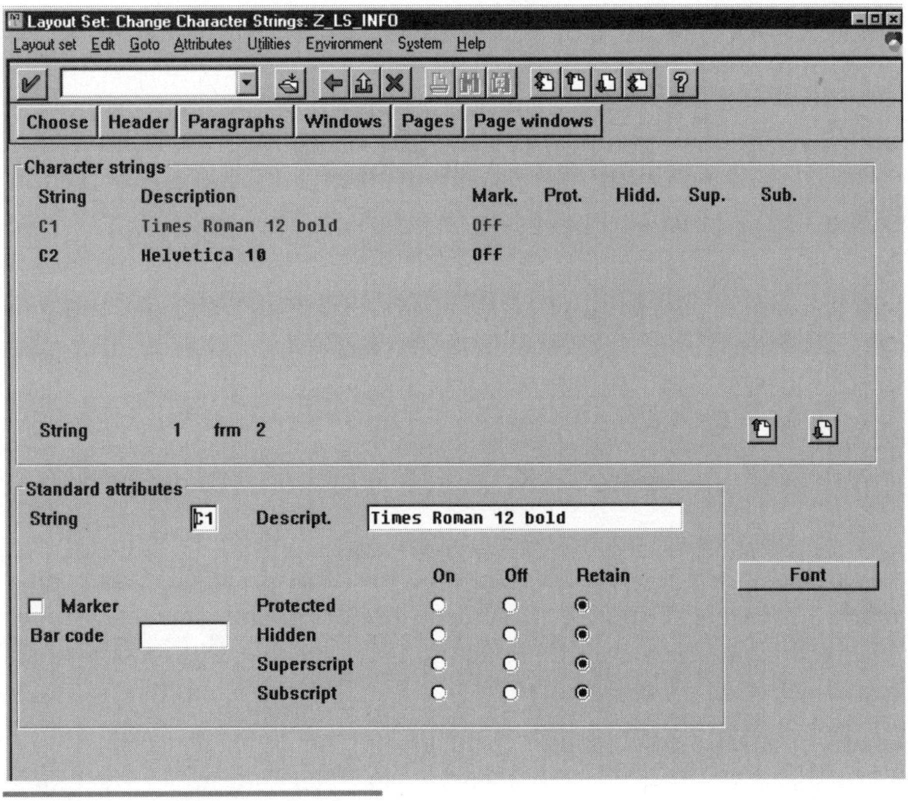

FIGURE 4.9   Character strings
Copyright by SAP AG

Protected—The contents of the character string will not be broken by a page break if the On button is selected. If the Off button is selected, the character string can be broken by a page break. If the Retain button is selected, then the attribute is not changed from the way it is currently set. If the parent paragraph or character string is protected, the character string set to Retain will also be protected.

Hidden—If the On button is selected, the contents of the character string will be hidden when the character string is rendered. If the Off button is selected, then the contents of the character string will always be visible when the image is rendered. If the Retain button is selected then the value of this attribute will remain as set before the character string was started.

Superscript—When superscript is turned On, the characters are rendered in superscript (slightly above the normal line). When it is turned Off the characters are rendered normally no matter what the parent settings. When Retain is selected the value of this attribute will remain as set before the character string was started.

Subscript—When subscript is set On, the characters are rendered in subscript (slightly below the normal line). When subscript is set Off, the characters will not appear in subscript no matter what the settings of the paragraph, the header, or other character strings.

As with the paragraphs, get to the font attributes for the character string by selecting the **Font** button at the standard screen. The lower half of the screen changes to show the font attributes (Figure 4.10).

Family—The font family (Helvetica, Courier etc.).

Font Size—The size of the font (10 CPI, 12 CPI etc.).

Bold—If On is selected, then the characters of the character string always appear in bold. If Off is selected, then the characters always appear regular regardless of whether or not the paragraph, header or other character strings are bold. If Retain is set then the value of this attribute will remain as set before the character string was started.

Italic—If On is selected, then the characters of the character string always appear in italics. If Off is selected, then the characters always appear roman regardless of whether or not the paragraph, header or other character strings are italicized. If Retain is set then the value of this attribute will remain as set before the character string was started.

Underlined—If On is selected, then the characters of the character string always appear underlined. If Off is selected, then the characters always appear normally regardless of whether or not the paragraph, header or other parent character strings are underlined. If Retain is set then the value of this attribute will remain as set before the character string was started. When On is selected click the "➔..." button in the lower right hand of the Font

Attributes screen and set the spacing, thickness and intensity of the character string underline.

Spacing—The spacing between the line and the bottom of the letters that are being underlined.

Thickness—The thickness of the underline.

Intensity—The brightness of the underline (0–100, darkest to lightest respectively).

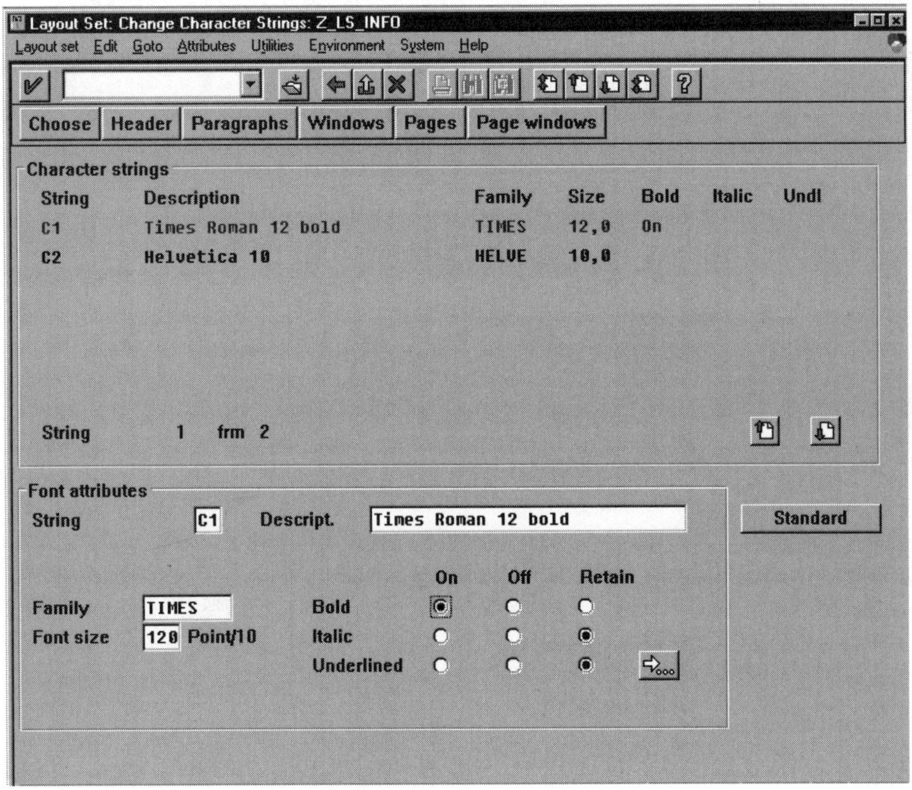

FIGURE 4.10   Character string fonts
Copyright by SAP AG

In Figure 4.10, there are two character strings: C1 and C2. C1 is Times New Roman, 12 CPI and bold is set to On. C2 is Helvetica, 10 CPI with bold set to Off. In page window C3, I have modified the text element to include the lines as shown in Figure 4.11.

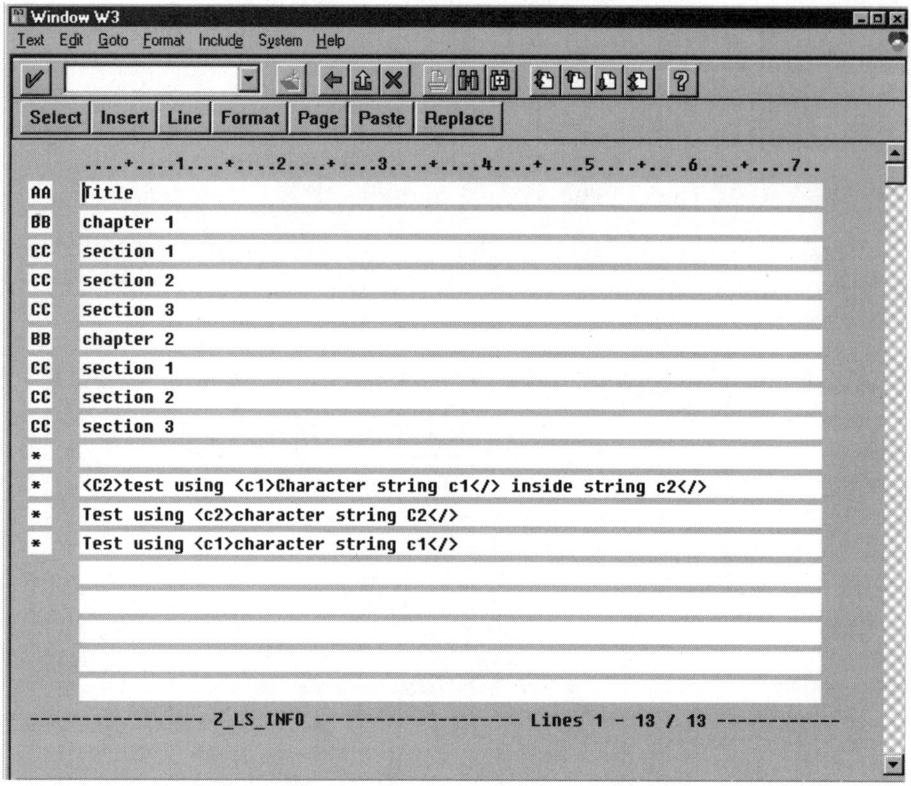

FIGURE 4.11 **Text element to show character strings**
Copyright by SAP AG

The second and third lines show the character strings C2 and C1 being used in a line. The first line shows character string C1 being used inside character string C2. When ZLSINFO is run as a test, the image appears as shown in Figure 4.12.

The characters that appear in bold do so because character string is set to bold On. If the settings for character string C1 are changed so that bold is set to Retain, then character string C1 will use the settings already set, which is Off. Since C1 is set to Retain, C1 will use the settings that C2 uses. C2 is set to Retain, so it will use whatever the default paragraph for the window uses. The default paragraph for Window W3 is blank. So the window defers to the default paragraph setting for the layout set, P1, which also has bold set to Retain. Since the default paragraph is set to Retain, the header settings are consulted. The header settings cannot be set to Retain since there is nothing to retain. Nothing precedes the header settings, and the header is set to bold Off. Hence, C1 would appear with bold Off.

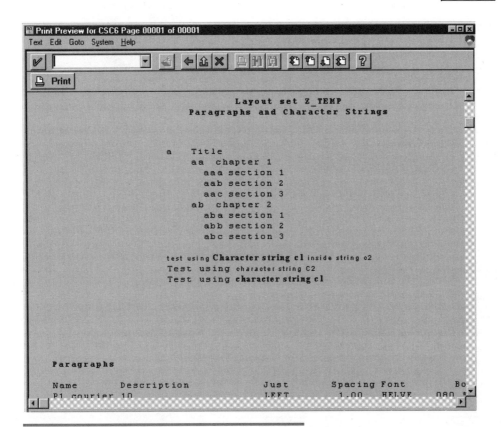

FIGURE 4.12   Character string print preview
Copyright by SAP AG

Windows

Description

As the name implies, a *window* is an area on the page in which to insert text. First windows are created, then the windows are placed on pages. It is possible to put a window on one page but not on others. In fact it is quite common to have a Title window on the first page, but not repeat it on subsequent pages. To get to the Windows Standard Attributes screen in Figure 4.13, select the **Windows** button on the header screen.

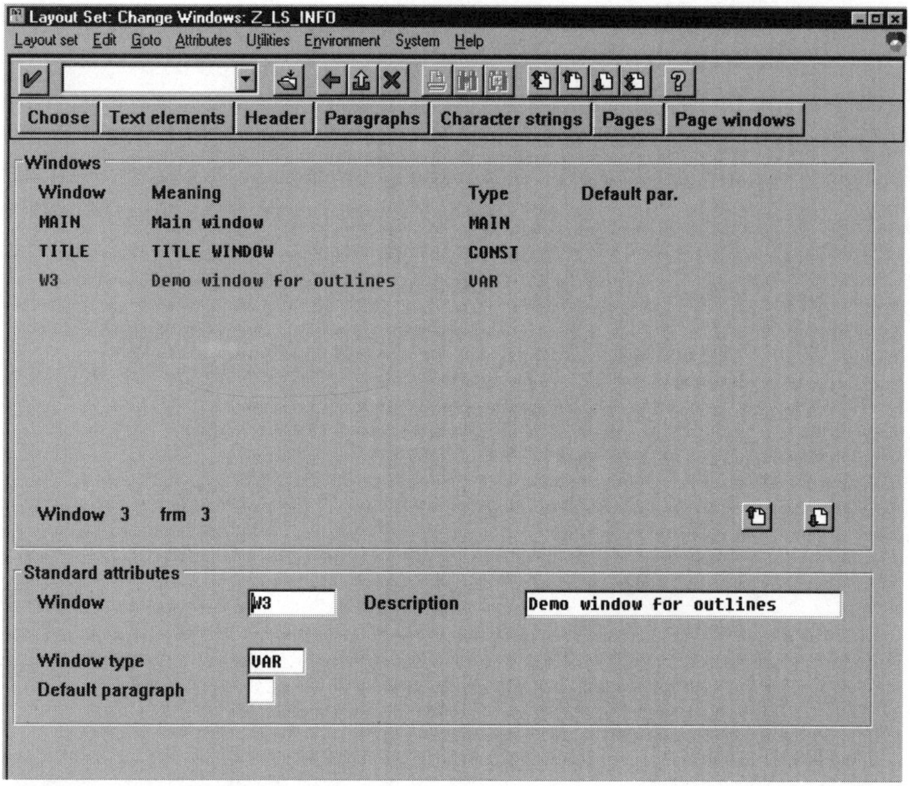

FIGURE 4.13   Windows standard attributes
Copyright by SAP AG

Windows Standard Attributes

Window—This is where to provide a name for the window. I usually use W1, W2, W3 and so on.

Description—A free-form description of the window. This will appear in the Possible Entries list. Use something that helps identify where the window is on the page. If something on the test print has to be changed, the first thing is to figure out in what window it is being generated. This is the text that identifies the Page window also. Post 4.0 versions of R/3 have solved this with a new version of the GUI which shows graphically where the windows are being generated.

Window type—There are three types of windows:

VAR is short for variable. This means that the contents of the window are expected to change from page to page. If there are symbols in the window, it should be VAR.

CONST is short for constant. This means the contents of the window do not change. In Figure 4.13, the Title window is CONST. This is because there is nothing but a simple text title in the window. The Title window prints only on the first page; if it did print on other pages, the contents would not change.

MAIN is a special window best thought of as page independent. MAIN is continued from page to page. For this reason the width of MAIN is not allowed to change from page to page, but its height and vertical location can be controlled. When the Main window is filled up on the first page, the second page is called and the Main window on the second page begins to fill up. In this way the filling up of the Main window controls how many pages are used. If a Main window is not used in Layout set, the easiest way to control it is to call each page from the print program. If a Main window is not used then there is a static number of pages, like a multiple-page balance sheet for example.

Default paragraph—This is the paragraph that will be used if the tag column is set to "*" in the text element.

Pages

Description

Like everything else in the layout set, pages must be defined. To put a window on a page, we must define the page first. The Page window tells the layout set which windows are assigned to which pages.

Pages Standard Attributes

Pages only have standard attributes (Figure 4.14).

Page—The name of the page created.

Next page—When this page is full, this is the next page the layout set should proceed to. Next page can be the same as Page.

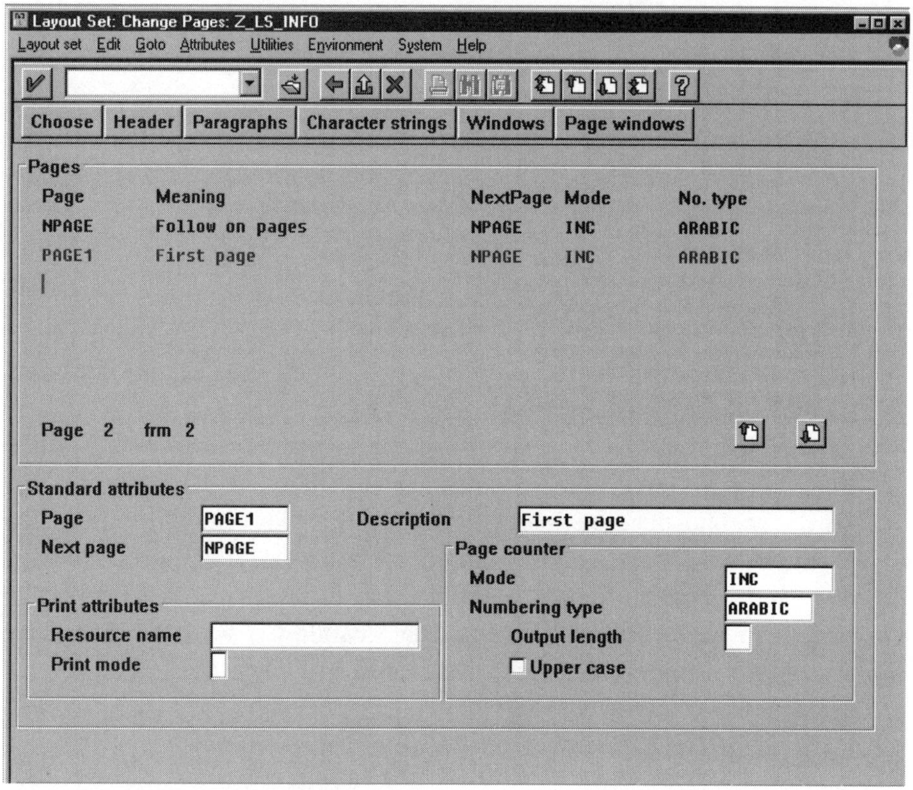

FIGURE 4.14   Pages standard attributes
Copyright by SAP AG

Resource name—The name of the paper tray for the printer to use.

TRY01 means print from paper tray 1.

TRY02 means print from paper tray 2.

TRY03 means print from paper tray 3.

Print mode—There are three modes: simplex, duplex, and tumble duplex.

Simplex—This means print on the front of the page. The value to enter for the attribute is S.

Duplex—This means print on both sides of the page. Assign D to the first page and then leave the attribute blank for subsequent pages.

> **Tumble duplex**—This means print on both sides but print the second side upside down. As with the duplex mode, set the initial page to T and use blank for subsequent pages.

Mode—How the page should be numbered.

> INC means incrementally by 1 (Example: 123456789).

> HOLD means this page will have the same number the last page had.

> START means reset the counter to 1.

Numbering type—The type of page numbering to be used.

> ARABIC means using incremental whole numbers (example: 1, 2, 3, 4, 5, 6, 7, 8, 9...).

> LETTER means incrementing with letters (example: a, b, c, d, e, f, g, h, I, j, k, l...).

> ROMAN means incrementing with Roman numerals (example: i, ii, iii, iv, v, vi, vii, viii, ix...).

Output length—If using Arabic, set the number length. The number will be padded with zeros if necessary to provide the desired length.

Upper case—If using Letter or Roman as the numbering type, set the characters to upper case by checking this box.

Page Windows

Description

Page windows connect the windows with the pages. They are similar to purchasing information records in procurement. The Page windows define the location and content of the window. For each window there is a text element to define the contents of the window. The Text Element button only appears when in the Page Windows screen. In Figure 4.15, there are three Page windows, Main, Title and W3, associated with page1.

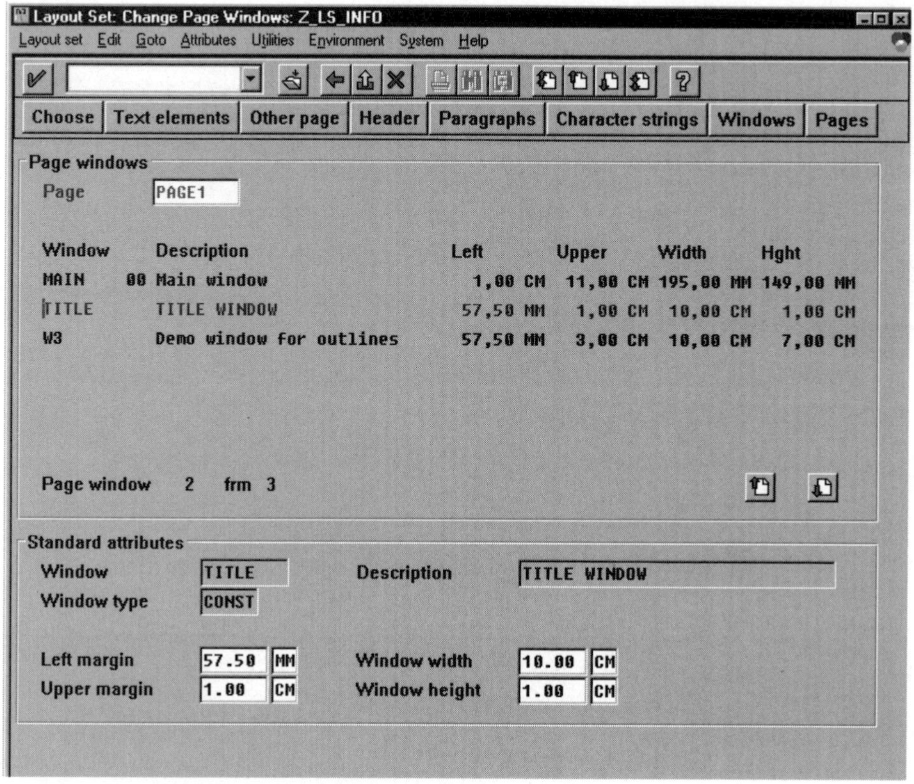

FIGURE 4.15   Page windows for PAGE1
Copyright by SAP AG

If the page in the upper left corner of the screen is changed to NPAGE, the Page windows associated with NPAGE will appear (Figure 4.16). Notice in Figure 4.16 that the Page window TITLE is not included because we only want the title to print on the first page.

Page Window Standard Attributes

Left margin—The distance from the left side of the page to the left side of the window.

Upper margin—The distance from the top of the page to the top of the window.

Window width—The width of the window being defined.

Window height—The height of the window being defined.

Each attribute can use a different unit of measure if necessary.

```
Layout Set: Change Page Windows: Z_LS_INFO                          _ □ X
Layout set  Edit  Goto  Attributes  Utilities  Environment  System  Help

| ✔ |                   ▼ | ⤸ | ⇐ ⬆ ✕ | 📄 🗎 🗎 | 🔁 🗂 🗂 🗂 | ❓ |

| Choose | Text elements | Other page | Header | Paragraphs | Character strings | Windows | Pages |

┌ Page windows ─────────────────────────────────────────────────────────┐
   Page        NPAGE

   Window      Description              Left      Upper     Width       Hght
   MAIN     00 Main window           1,00 CM   11,00 CM  195,00 MM  149,00 MM
   W3          Demo window for outlines   57,50 MM   3,00 CM  10,00 CM    7,00 CM




   Page window    1   frm  2                                      🔁     🔁
─────────────────────────────────────────────────────────────────────────
┌ Standard attributes ──────────────────────────────────────────────────┐
   Window         MAIN          Description      Main window
   Window type    MAIN

   Left margin    1.00   CM     Window width     195.00 MM
   Upper margin   11.00  CM     Window height    149.00 MM
└───────────────────────────────────────────────────────────────────────┘
```

FIGURE 4.16   Page windows for NPAGE
Copyright by SAP AG

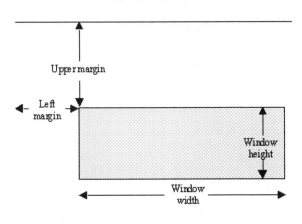

FIGURE 4.17   Window location

Two or More MAIN Page Windows

It is possible to create more than one Main window on a page. Notice that in the Page windows section of the screen in Figures 4.15 and 4.16, the Page window called MAIN has 00 just to its right. If another Main window is added it will also be called MAIN and the number to the right of it will be 01. When MAIN 00 is filled up, then MAIN 01 will begin filling with text. When MAIN 01 is full the next page will start filling MAIN 00.

WARNING

When a test printout is created from the Utility window, it may be necessary to add more "dummy" info to MAIN in order to see subsequent pages. MAIN must fill up on the first page and spill over to the second page in order for the second page to show in the test.

Text Elements

Description

Simply stated, the *text element* is where the text goes. In Chapter 2, "How Standard Texts are Used," we looked at the Standard Text editor. The editor evoked here is basically the same. The text dropdown menu is somewhat different, but navigation is basically the same. Figure 4.18 shows the Text element for the Title page window.

P3 is the paragraph used. That means the text on this line will be Courier 14, centered and bold because paragraph P3 is set that way. The first line incorporates a symbol called itcta-tdform. This field is part of a structure that was populated in the calling print program. (For more information on calling print programs see Chapter 3.) All symbols are surrounded by ampersands. The second line also uses paragraph P3. No symbols are used in the second line. If the down arrow next to the tab column is selected, the list of possible entries for the tag column will be visible (Figure 4.19).

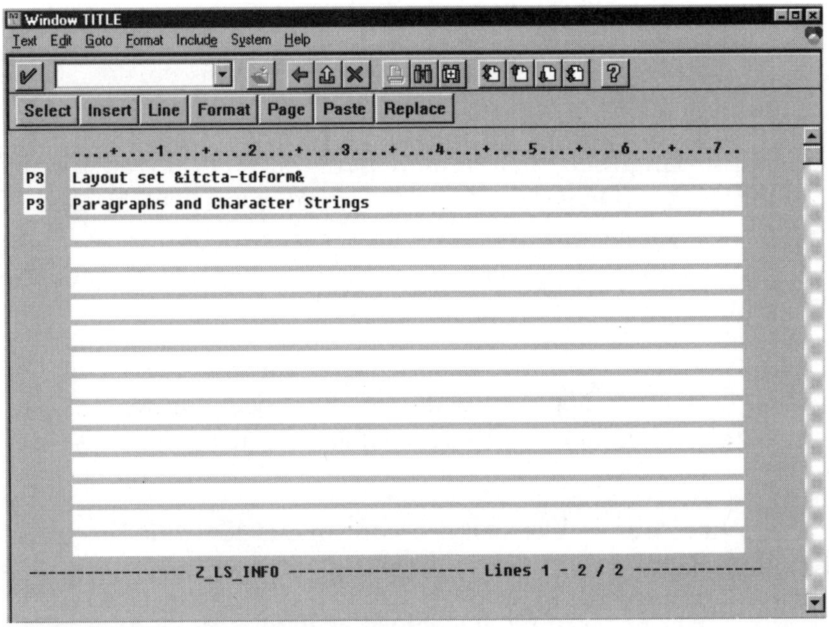

FIGURE 4.18   Text element for Title
Copyright by SAP AG

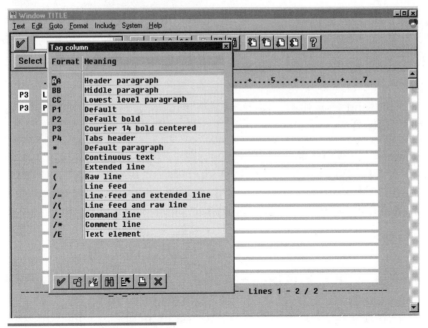

FIGURE 4.19   Tag columns
Copyright by SAP AG

Tag Columns

AA, BB, CC, P1, P2, P3 and P4 are all custom paragraphs created in the paragraphs screen.

*—Use the default paragraph. If a default paragraph is defined for the window (in this case the window is called Title), its attributes will be used. If not, then the default paragraph for the layout set is used. In this example, Title does not have a default paragraph so the default paragraph for the layout set P1, is used.

Blank—This denotes continuous text. If a blank tag column is used, the line will be appended to the line above it, with one space between the two. The line with the blank tag column will have the same attributes as the line above.

=—An extended line; this is like using a continuous text but the blank character is not interjected.

(—Raw line; this appends text to the line above, without a space. It does not interpret any syntax present. To print a line with ampersands as characters, this would be a good choice.

/—Line feed; continue the attributes of the line above, but start on a new line.

/=—The line feed and extended line; this is just like using extended line but with a new line interjected.

/(—The line feed and raw line; this is just like using a raw line but with a new line interjected.

/:—The command line; a command line is not like any of the other tag columns. The command line means use a command instead of text. We have already used the INCLUDE command in previous sections. The command reference section has a complete list of available commands.

/*—The comment line; ignore this line. Used for commenting out lines in the text editor.

/E—The text element. If a Text element is used, it is a way of partitioning the Text element window. In Figure 4.20 the Main window of Z_LS_INFO is shown, but I have added two lines at the top that are not part of any particular text element.

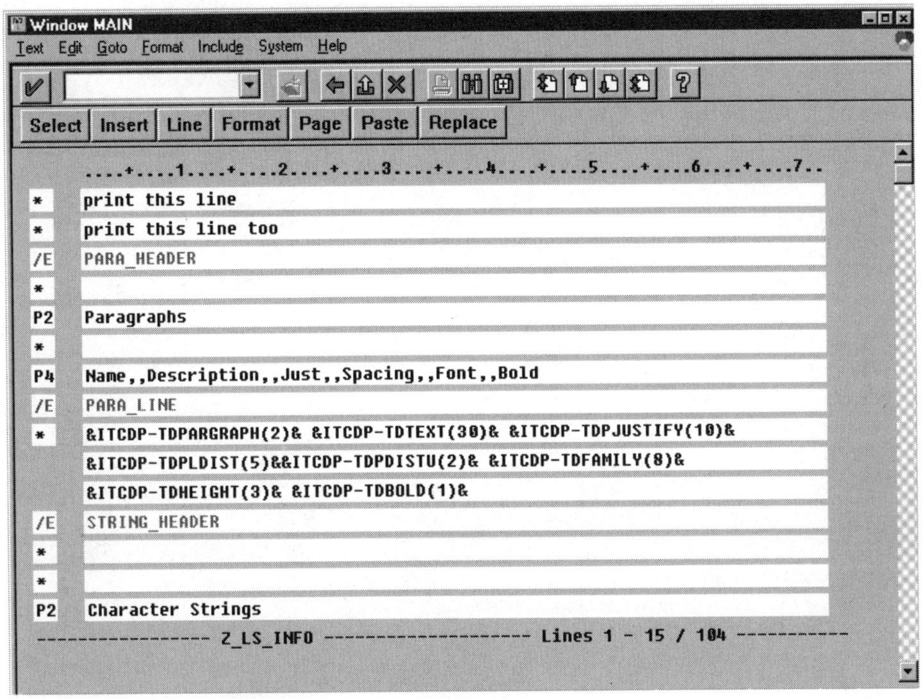

FIGURE 4.20   Text Element tags in MAIN
Copyright by SAP AG

The two lines added to MAIN ("Print this line" and "Print this line too") will print in the Main window as long as one of the text elements in MAIN is called.

In Figure 4.21, the Text element for Page window W3 has been split into two sections. The top part is not under a Text Element tag but the bottom part is, because a text element called TEST is added.

Referring to Figure 4.21, if the TEST text element is called by the print program, the lines above /E TEST will not be printed, nor will the contents of any Text Element tag other than TEST. This is the case because W3 is not a Main window.

```
┌─ Window W3 ────────────────────────────────────────────── _ □ ×
 Text  Edit  Goto  Format  Include  System  Help
┌──────────────┬─────┬───┬──┬─┬────┬─────┬─────┬──┬───┬─┐
│ ✔ │          ▼ │ ◄ │ ⇐ ⇧ ✕ │ ▤ 🔍 🔎 │ ⟳ 📋 📑 📊 │ ? │
├────┬────────┬──────┬────────┬──────┬───────┬─────────┤
│ Select │ Insert │ Line │ Format │ Page │ Paste │ Replace │
└────────┴──────┴────────┴──────┴───────┴─────────┘
     ....+....1....+....2....+....3....+....4....+....5....+....6....+....7..
  AA   Title
  BB   chapter 1
  CC   section 1
  CC   section 2
  CC   section 3
  BB   chapter 2
  CC   section 1
  CC   section 2
  CC   section 3
  /E   TEST
  *    &page&
  *    <C2>test using <c1>Character string c1</> inside string c2</>
  *    Test using <c2>cha
  =    racter string C2</>
  *    Test using <c1>character string c1</>
  ---------------- Z_LS_INFO ------------------ Lines 1 - 15 / 15 -----------
```

FIGURE 4.21   Text Element tags in W3
Copyright by SAP AG

Text Element Example

What follows is a more complex example of a text element. It has been downloaded and printed here in text format so that the entire text element can appear continuously.

```
/: TOP
/: POSITION WINDOW
/: BOX WIDTH 198 MM HEIGHT 13 MM FRAME 20 TW INTENSITY 20
*
/: INCLUDE MAIN_HEADER OBJECT TEXT ID ZARG LANGUAGE &NAST-SPRAS&
*
*
/: ENDTOP
/E ITEM_LINE
/* DEFINE &TEXT_NAME& = ''&VBDPL-MATNR(18)&&VBDKL-VKORG&&VBDKL
=  -ZUKRL(2)&''
/* INCLUDE &TEXT_NAME& NYARAG' OBJECT 'MVKE' ID '0001'
```

```
*
/* DEFINE &TEXT_NAME& := '&VBDPL-MATNR(18)&&VBDKL-VKORG&&VBDKL
=  -ZUKRL(2)&'
/* INCLUDE &TEXT_NAME& OBJECT 'MVKE' ID '0001' LANGUAGE &NAST
=  -SPRAS& PARAGRAPH 'IL'
/* B10147392    NYARAG
IL &vbdpl-posnr(6)& ,,&vbdpl-matnr(18)&,, &vbdpl-arktx(40)&
=     &vbdpl-segr(10)&
IL
/E BATCH_LINE
IL &vbdpl-pickbin(10)&/&vbdpl-charg(10)&/&vbdpl-plot(10)&
= &vbdpl-brgew(15)&
= &vbdpl-us01_vb1b(10)&&'/'vbdpl-usr02_vb1b(10)&
= &'/'vbdpl-usr03_vb1b(10)& &vbdpl-usr04_vb1b(15)&

/E BATCH_TOTAL
/: PROTECT
TO &ULINE(95)&
TO
/: IF &VBDPL-PSTYV& NE TAL
/: INCLUDE ITEM_TOTAL OBJECT TEXT ID ZARG LANGUAGE &NAST-SPRAS&
/: ELSE
/: INCLUDE TAL_ITEM_TOTAL_NS OBJECT TEXT ID ZARG LANGUAGE &NAST
=  -SPRAS&
/: ENDIF
TO &ULINE(95)&
TO
TO
/: ENDPROTECT
/E GRAND_TOTAL
/: PROTECT
TO
TO
TO &ULINE(95)&
/: INCLUDE DELIVERY_TOTAL OBJECT TEXT ID ZARG LANGUAGE &NAST
=  -SPRAS&
TO &ULINE(95)&
/: ENDPROTECT
*
*
*   &VBDPL-LTEXT1&
/: INCLUDE &VBDKL-VBELN(K)& OBJECT VBBK ID Z001 LANGUAGE &NAST
=  -SPRAS&
*
*   &VBDPL-LTEXT2&
```

```
/: INCLUDE &VBDKL-VBELN(K)& OBJECT VBBK ID Z002 LANGUAGE &NAST
= -SPRAS&


/E MERCADER

/: INCLUDE STORAGE_LOCATION OBJECT TEXT ID ZARG LANGUAGE &NAST
= -SPRAS&


/E ORDERNO

/: POSITION WINDOW
/: BOX WIDTH 205 MM HEIGHT '.5' MM INTENSITY 100
*
/: INCLUDE ORDERNO OBJECT TEXT ID ZARG LANGUAGE &NAST-SPRAS&
/: DEFINE &TEXT_NAME& := '&VBDPL-MATWA(18)&&VBDKL-VKORG&&VBDKL
= -ZUKRL(2)&'
/: INCLUDE &TEXT_NAME& OBJECT 'MVKE' ID '0001' LANGUAGE &NAST
= -SPRAS& PARAGRAPH 'IL'
*


/E SHIPPING

/: SET DATE MASK = 'DD MMMM YYYY'
/* &VBDKL-VSTEL_BEZ&, &VBDKL-WADAT&
*   &VBDKL-ort01&, &VBDKL-wadat&
/E SHIPTO

/: POSITION WINDOW
/: BOX WIDTH 205 MM HEIGHT '.5' MM INTENSITY 100
*
/: INCLUDE SHIPTO OBJECT TEXT ID ZARG LANGUAGE &NAST-SPRAS&
/E TEXT1
/: INCLUDE HEADER_TEXT1 OBJECT TEXT ID ZARG LANGUAGE &NAST-SPRAS&
/E V1
*   &VBDKL-J_1ASNR&-&VBDKL-J_1AOFFNUM&
/E X
*   <tn>X</>
/: INCLUDE NO_INVOICE OBJECT TEXT ID ZARG LANGUAGE &NAST_SPRAS&
```

CD-ROM

Text element TE001

The command TOP is used initially to set up a header in the Main window. Anything between TOP and ENDTOP will always print at the top of the Main window on each page. Inside the top section, a shaded box is created and a standard text called MAIN_HEADER is printed in the box.

Under the Text Element tag called ITEM_LINE, the Define command is used. On this line the symbol TEXT_NAME is being defined. TEXT_NAME is created by concatenating parts of three other symbols. Notice that := is used instead of =. This is done so that the symbol is defined immediately, using the source values as they currently exist. If = is used, the new symbol is assigned a value (using the sources) when it is rendered. It is usually necessary to experiment with this to see which way works best. (Set the layout set to Debug mode to see how SAPscript interprets the line.)

Under the BATCH_TOTAL Text Element tag, an IF command is used. Use IF, ELSEIF, ENDIF statements to process lines conditionally. The condition is usually put in the calling program, but sometimes it works better in the text element if it is minor. If the condition relies on some value that only resides in the SAPscript processing, like &PAGE&, then the conditional statement would need to reside in the text element. In this example, the conditional statement could have resided in the calling print program. It was just easier to put it in the text element and avoid a change to the ABAP program.

The GRAND_TOTAL text element uses the Protect command so that it does not get split by a page break. For esthetic purposes the DELIVERY_TOTAL text is encased with lines (ULINE) above and below the text. It looks confusing to the eye when this is spilt on two pages.

Notice that the INCLUDE statements are all qualified with LANGUAGE. This is so because the text elements are language dependent for business reasons.

Building Blocks in Review

1. A basic layout set has certain elements that are essential and therefore mandatory in order to save.

2. Each window contains a Text element that can be split into multiple text elements by using the Text Element tag in the tag column.

3. Windows are assigned to pages along with a size and location. This definition is called a Page window. The window and page must be defined before the Page window can be defined.

4. The layout set must be activated in order for it to be recognized by the print program.

CHAPTER

5

Tools

Creating, Copying, and Deleting Layout Sets

Creating Layout Sets

The are several ways to create new layout set objects. In Chapter 2, we walked through creating an original layout set using the Create button in the layout set request menu. New layout sets can also be created with the Save As feature.

In Chapter 2, we created a layout set called Z_LS_CONTACT_411 (See Figure 5.1). The path to the Layout Set:Request menu is **Tools → Word processing → Layout set**.

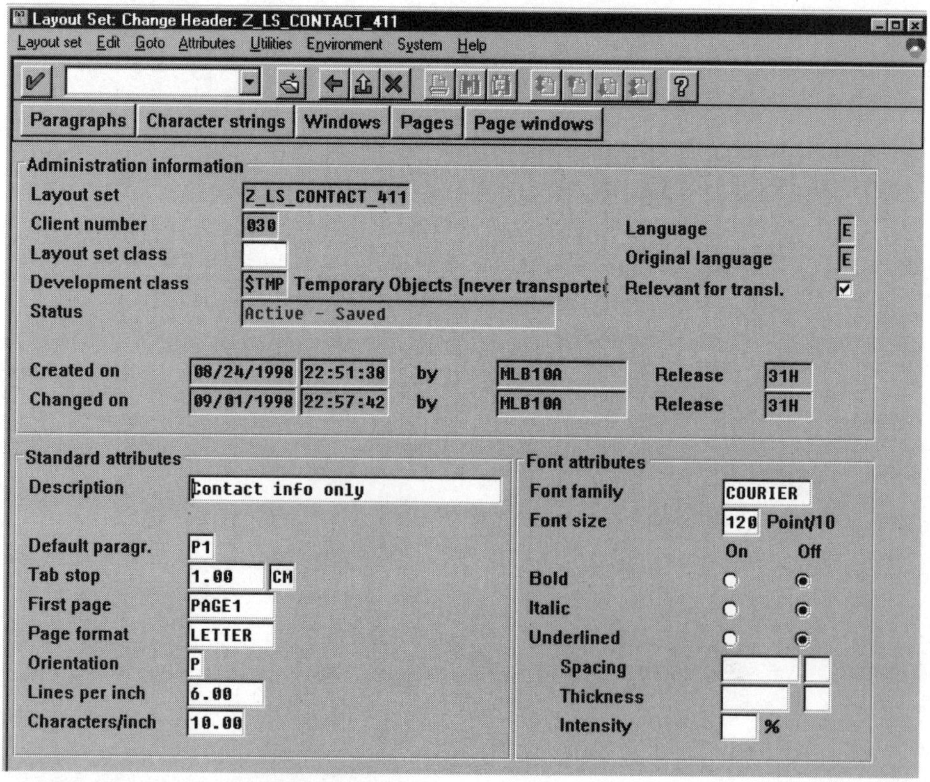

Layout Set: Change Header: Z_LS_CONTACT_411			

FIGURE 5.1   Z_LS_CONTACT_411
Copyright by SAP AG

In this example, we created the layout set by entering the new name at the Layout Set: Request screen and selecting the **Create** button. During completion of the header view, there are several key points to remember.

1. The description must be entered before saving the layout set.
2. The default paragraph must be entered in the header before activating the layout set. A paragraph to be used as the default paragraph must be defined before entering the paragraph name in the Header view.
3. The first page must be entered in the Header screen before activating the layout set. A page to be used as the first page in the header must be defined before entering the "first page" name in the Header view.
4. All defined pages must have at least one Page window attached to them before the layout set is activated. In order to create a Page window, a window to be assigned to the page must be created (or the Main window can be placed somewhere on each page).

WARNING

If an attempt is made to save or activate with a missing component, an error message in the status bar at the bottom of the screen is shown.

When a layout set is created with the same name as another original-language layout set but a different language, a message will appear in the status bar: `Layout set XYZ has original language __`. In this case, the parameters from the original layout set will automatically be copied into the new layout set and only the text elements will be available for change. (See Chapter 2, Using Layout Sets with Different Languages).

When a layout set that is not an original-language layout set is created, the original-language layout set must be active. If it is not, a message will appear saying, `Layout set _____ can not be created. Original language __ being processed`.

Save As

Once a valid layout set has been created the Save As feature can be used to create a new layout set. This feature can be particularly helpful in creation of a new layout set similar to an existing layout set. A few rules apply here:

1. The new layout created with Save As is always an original-language layout set.
2. The Save As feature works only in the Change mode of the original-language layout set.

3. The language itself cannot be changed, only the name, thereby creating an original-language layout set. Notice in Figure 5.2, that the language parameter is not highlighted.

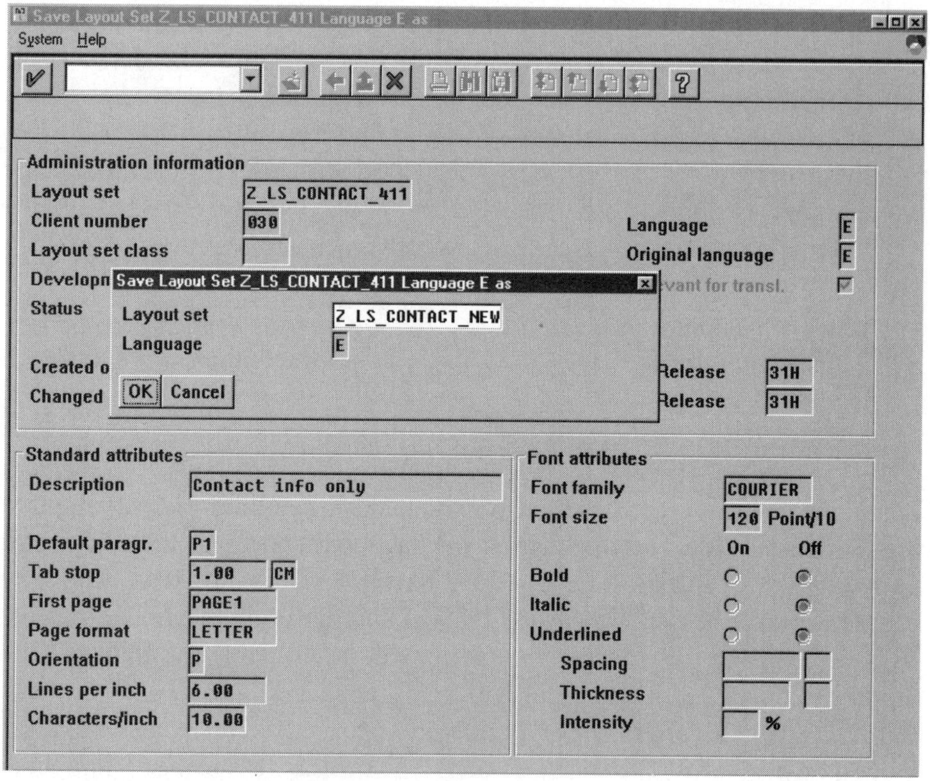

FIGURE 5.2   Layout set: Save As
Copyright by SAP AG

Copy From

The Copy From feature in the layout set pulldown menu can be used to copy all the parameters of an existing layout set. If the target layout set is an original-language layout set, then the source layout set can be any language and any name (see Figure 5.3). If the target layout set is not the original language layout set, then only the original-language layout set can be used as a source.

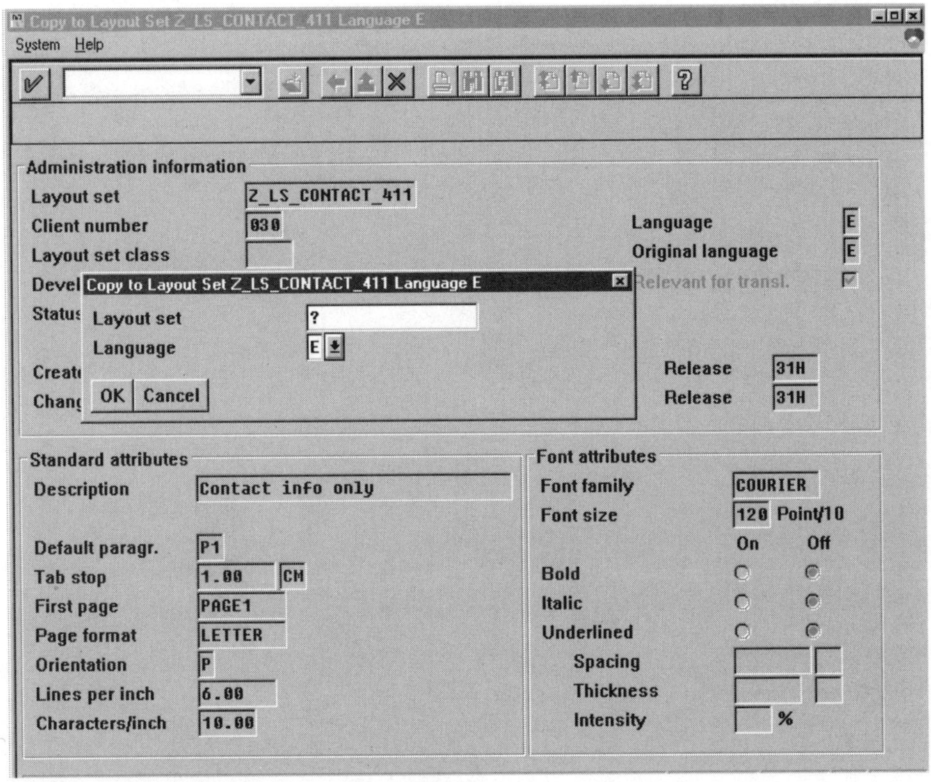

FIGURE 5.3   Layout set: Copy From
Copyright by SAP AG

Deleting Layout Sets

Layout sets can only be deleted in the Change mode. To delete the existing layout set go to **Layout set → Delete**. If an original-language layout set is deleted, then all the languages of that layout set will be deleted (see Figure 5.4). If the layout set being deleted is not an original-language layout set, then only the current language is deleted (see Figure 5.5).

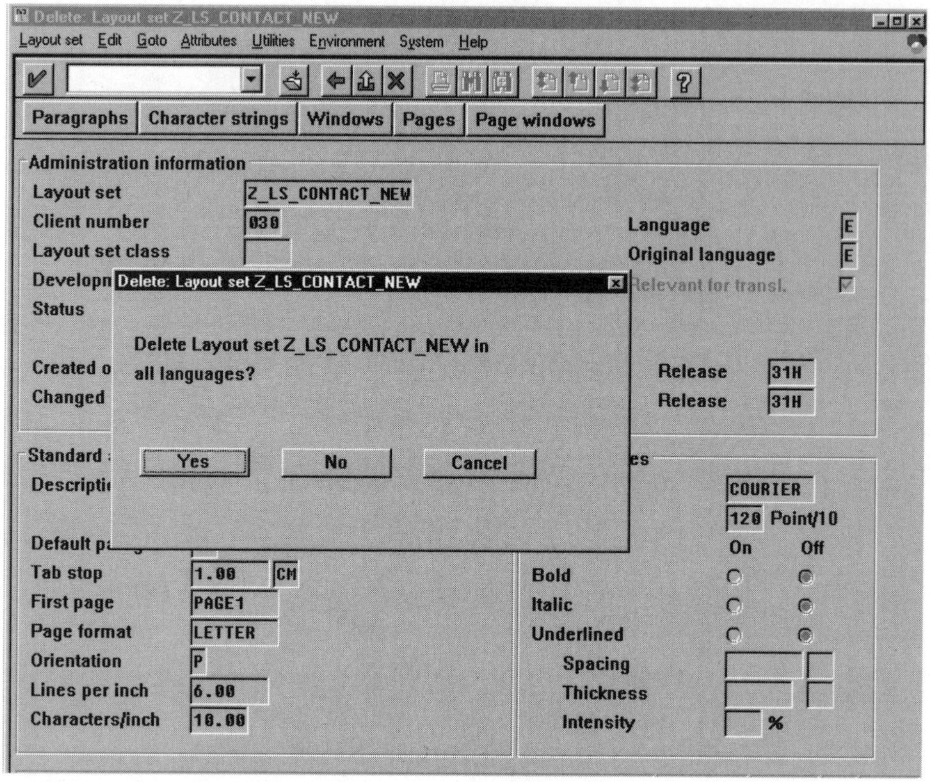

FIGURE 5.4 **Delete original-language Layout set**
Copyright by SAP AG

Creating a Test Printout

Utilities Test Print

To create a test printout in the layout set Change or Display mode, select
Utilities → Test print. At the Print Options screen, choose to print the image
or render it on the screen. The layout set Test Print utility differs from what
will actually appear when the layout set is called from the print program. The
Test Print utility shows text elements and Page windows in their "raw" form.
Inside the Main window the text for all the Text Element tags appear. In non-
Main windows, Text Element tags do not appear. In all windows, symbols are

rendered with Xs. If the symbol is ten characters long in the data dictionary then ten Xs will appear. If the symbol has been defined so that only eight characters appear, then only eight Xs will be shown. The Xs and any literal text appear in the font assigned in the Layout set. If the text does not fit in the window, it will not appear. Figure 5.6 shows a Test Print utility preview of Z_LS_INFO. Compare this to the print preview generated by running the ZLSINFO program shown in Figure 5.7.

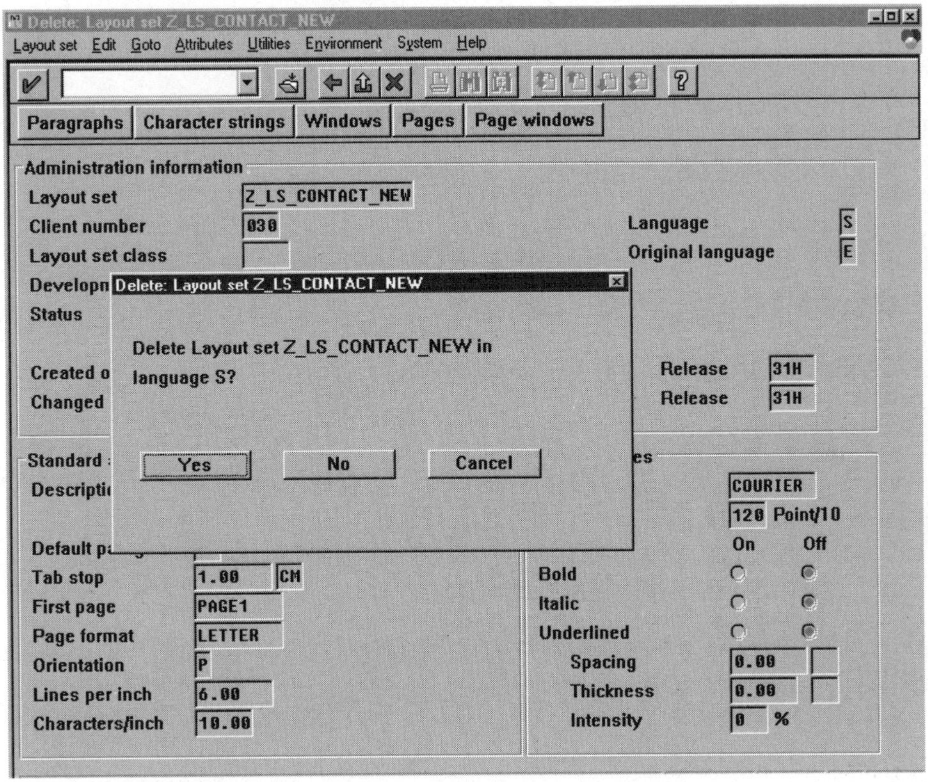

FIGURE 5.5   Delete Layout set with secondary language
Copyright by SAP AG

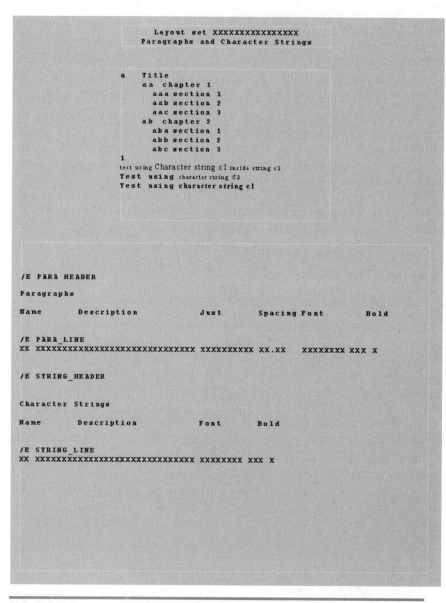

FIGURE 5.6   Z_LS_INFO test print from the Layout Set utility menu

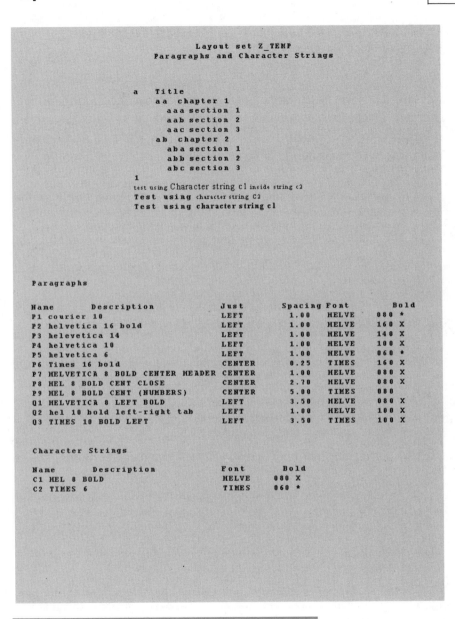

FIGURE 5.7   ZLSINFO print preview (from ABAP)

The Differences between the Print Program and Layout Set Print Tests

The image in Figure 5.7 was rendered by running ZLSINFO and selecting Print Preview. The Test Print utility (within the layout set) will reflect all changes in the layout set, regardless of whether or not they have been saved. In the print program (as in Figure 5.7) to render a test, the layout set must be activated in order for the changes to be recognized.

NOTE

In both cases the printer selection matters. Printers have varying capabilities. When using either of the print preview techniques, use a printer that is the same make and model that will be used in production. In some cases it may be necessary to create separate layout sets for unique printers.

Using Application Data in a Test Printout

In a layout set that is triggered by output determination, the print program cannot be triggered directly. This will be the case in work on a derivative of a standard SAP Layout set. In this case the print program is always triggered by output determination. Output determination passes essential parameters to the print program so that it knows what to print. If a custom copy of a standard SAP layout set has been created and changes are contemplated, then tests for the changes must be set up by repeating the application-data output. For more information on output determination, see the section called, "Output Determination and Layout Sets" in Chapter 2. Most application areas work similarly to SD with respect to repeating outputs. They each have some way of administering the application-document outputs.

Although outputs are maintained in the spool file, they cannot be used for testing layout sets. When items from the spool file are reprinted, the result is always exactly what was printed the first time. In reprints from the application area, the print program and layout set are reacquired and the application data are passed to them for reprocessing. In reprints from the spool file this does not happen; the original output sent to the printer is forwarded to the printer of choice. This does not help in testing layout-set or print-program modifications.

Example: Sales and Distribution (SD) Billing Outputs

The SD module generates many different types of outputs: sales documents, billing documents, delivery documents, and others. Once an application document has been triggered using a new layout set, that output can be reprocessed. If the layout set has been changed and activated, then the changes will be reflected when the output is reprocessed. If changes have been made to the print program and work saved, these changes will also be reflected when the output is reprocessed.

NOTE
If a new layout set or print program has been created, output determination must be changed to reflect the new object name, otherwise the new layout set and/or print program will be ignored. (For more information, see the section "Output Determination and Layout Sets" in Chapter 2.)

To reprint SD billing documents select **Logistics → Sales/Distribution → Billing → Output → Billing Documents**. This will trigger the screen in Figure 5.8.

At the Output from Billing screen enter a valid output type. In our case the output medium is going to be "1" for "printer". If the reprocess box is selected, only the outputs previously *processed* will be selected. Provided previous outputs exist, a screen similar to that shown in Figure 5.9 should appear.

Select the output of choice and then select **Goto → Preview**, to evoke the Print Options screen. From there, select **Print Preview** to see the output on the screen.

Debugging Layout Sets

Check Layout Sets

When the layout set is activated, a check is performed for any problems in the layout set. If problems exist, the activation will not occur and a message in the status bar will show the nature of the problem. If the activation is successful, the message in the status bar will state this.

This same check can be performed without activating the layout set by selecting **Layout set → Check**. If there are no problems with the layout set the status bar will display the message, No errors found in Layout set _____. The Check utility examines the layout set regardless of whether or not it has been saved. Stated another way—the check utility examines the buffered version of the layout set. The buffered version may or may not be the same as the saved or activated version.

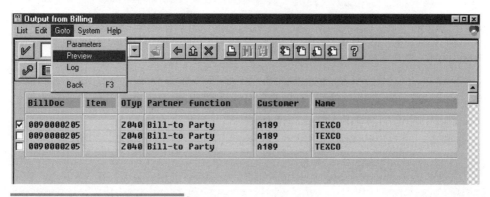

FIGURE 5.8   Billing documents output selection
      Copyright by SAP AG

FIGURE 5.9   Billing Outputs
      Copyright by SAP AG

Triggering the Layout Set Debugger

As in ABAP, Layout sets can be debugged. The debugger is engaged in the Layout: Request screen as shown in Figure 5.10. After selection of Activate Debugger, the status bar will read, `SAPscript layout set debugger was activated`. Once it is activated the debugger is evoked every time a layout set is used online. This includes the use of the layout set Test Print utility.

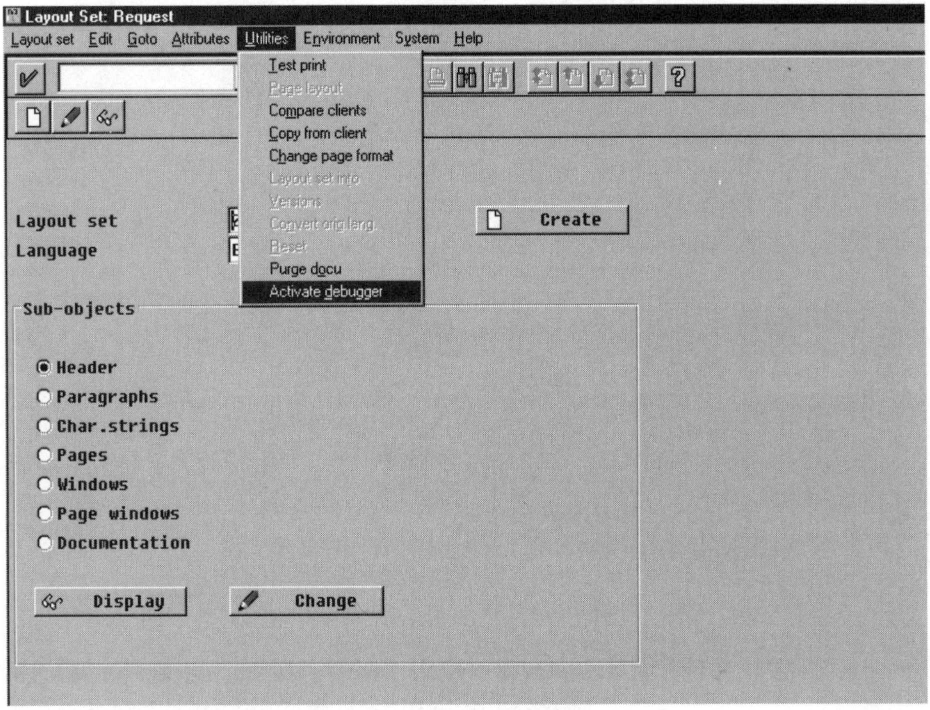

FIGURE 5.10   Starting the layout set debugger
Copyright by SAP AG

In our example, when ZLSINFO is executed, the screen in Figure 5.11 will offer breakpoint options for examining the layout set.

Referring to Figure 5.11:

Warning messages—If this box is checked the debugger will stop each time a warning message is called.

Includes—If this box is checked the debugger will stop each time an INCLUDE statement is encountered.

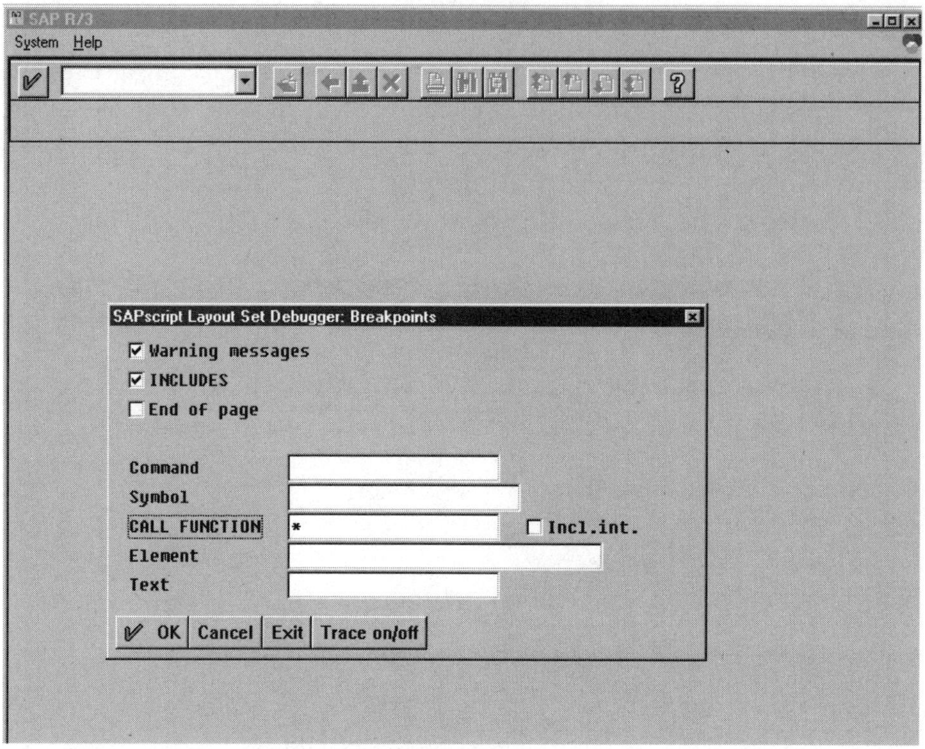

FIGURE 5.11 Layout set breakpoints
Copyright by SAP AG

End of page—When this is selected, a breakpoint is set at the end of each page.

Command—It is possible to specify which command the debugger should stop on. The debugger will stop every time the command is encountered.

Symbol—The debugger will stop when a matching symbol is encountered. Use the name of the symbol as shown in the text element, not the literal value expected at runtime.

Call Function—The default is "*". This means that the debugger will stop each time one of the layout set function modules is called. (These are the same function modules identified in Chapter 3.) This value can be replaced with a specific function-module name like WRITE_FORM.

Element—The debugger will stop when a match to the text element is found. If PARA_LINE is entered while running ZLSINFO the debugger will stop when the element PARA_LINE is started as shown in Figure 5.12.

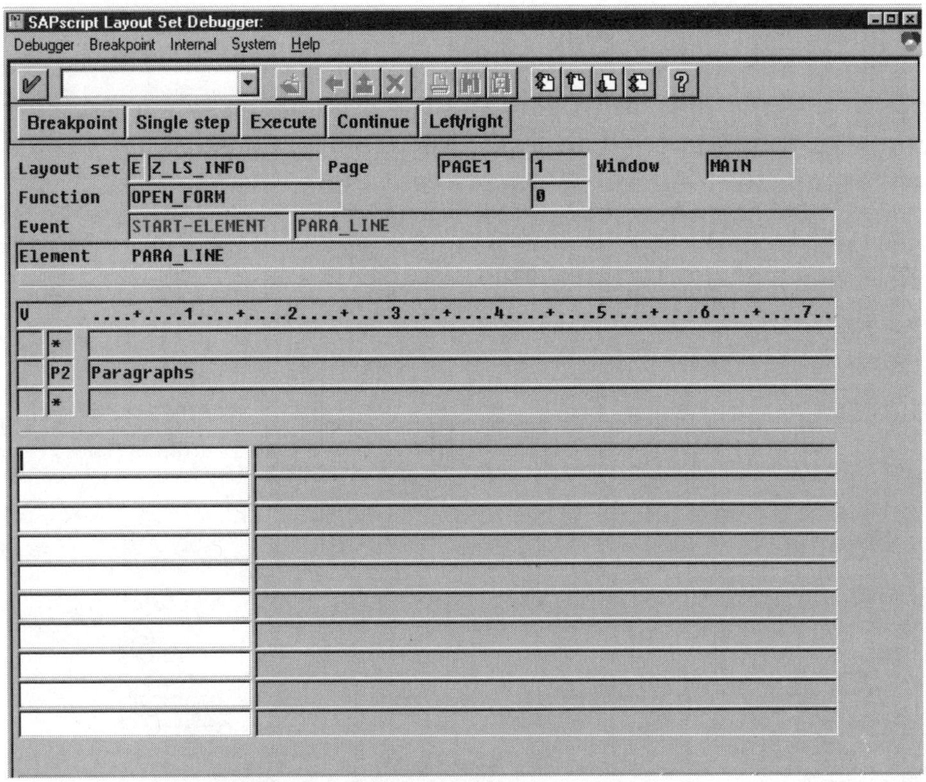

FIGURE 5.12   Debugger halted at PARA_LINE
Copyright by SAP AG

Text—A literal value can be entered here. The debugger will stop whenever this value is used in a line. If Font is entered for the text value, the debugger will stop in the PARA_HEADER text element where Font is used (Figure 5.13). If the Continue button in the Debugger window is selected, the debugger will continue until Font is encountered again, this time in the STRING_HEADER text element (Figure 5.14).

The Debugger Window

The top of the layout set debugger displays all the administrative information about location in the layout set as well as specific information about which event within each line is being evaluated. The middle of the screen shows the part of the text element (in ITF format) currently being evaluated. The bottom part of the screen provides the symbol names and their current values. Each field in the screen is defined as follows:

Layout set—The first part shows the language of the layout set being evaluated (not the original language). The second part is the name of the layout set.

Page—This indicates the current page name and number of pages that have been generated within the current form.

Window—The window that is currently being evaluated.

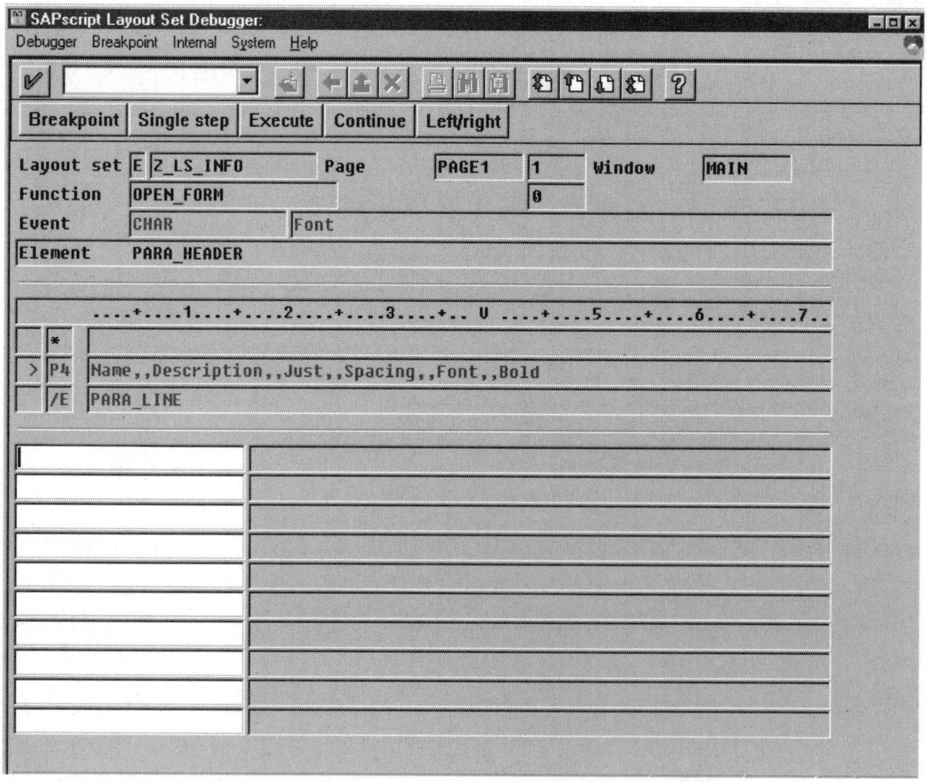

FIGURE 5.13   Debugger halted at Font in PARA_HEADER
Copyright by SAP AG

```
SAPscript Layout Set Debugger:                                    _ □ ✕
Debugger  Breakpoint  Internal  System  Help

 ✔ [                    ▼]  ◄  ←  ↥  ✕   ▦ ▦ ▦   ▨ ▨ ▨ ▨   ?

 Breakpoint | Single step | Execute | Continue | Left/right

Layout set  E Z_LS_INFO        Page    PAGE1   1    Window    MAIN
Function     OPEN_FORM                          0
Event        CHAR              Font
Element      STRING_HEADER

        ....+....1....+....2.. U ....3....+....4....+....5....+....6....+....7..
    *
  > P4  Name,,Description,,Font,,Bold
    /E  STRING_LINE
```

FIGURE 5.14   Debugger halted at Font in STRING_HEADER
Copyright by SAP AG

Function—The layout set debugger is activated by triggering the layout set. The layout set is always triggered by a function module in the ABAP program. The name of the function module that triggered the current debugging session is given here.

Event—An event is something SAPscript needs to do, like write a word or issue a command. Some of the events are CHAR (writing literal character), TEXT_SYMBOL (interpreting a symbol) and COMMAND (issuing a command).

NOTE

Just below the event, the current Text Element tag is given. If the window is not split up into different Text Element tags, then only the word Element appears.

Ruler—In the middle section of the screen, a ruler is shown just above the line that is currently being evaluated. There is a V on the line where the current event is. In Figure 5.15, the current event being processed is TEXT-SYMBOL. The symbol being interpreted is ITCDP-TDFAMILY. Notice that the V appears just at the start of the symbol.

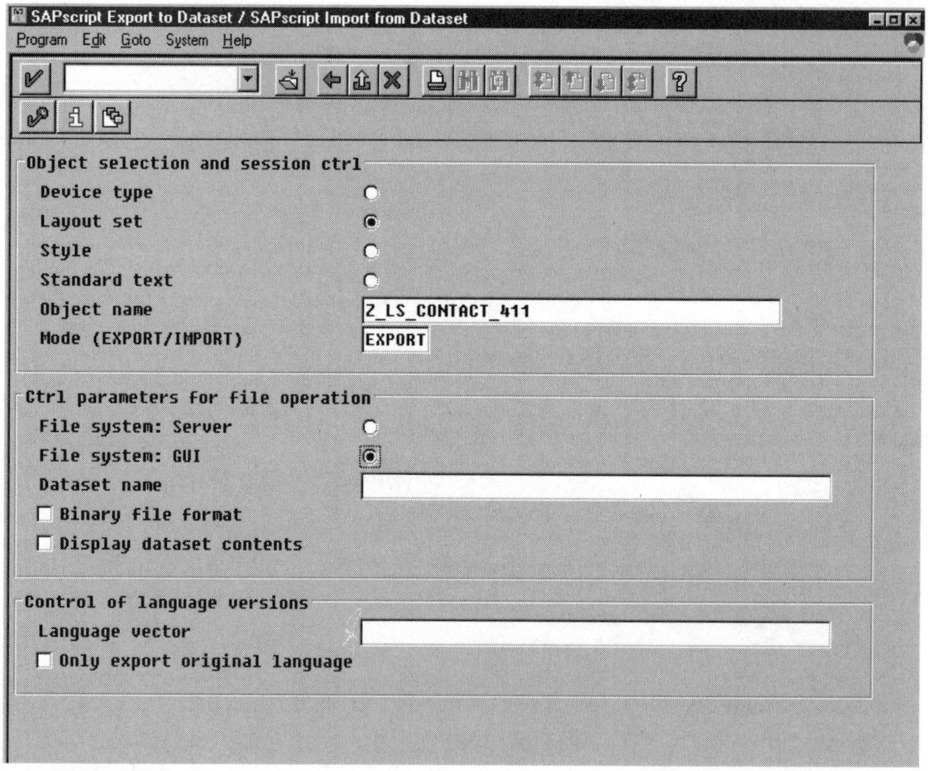

FIGURE 5.15   Downloading a layout set
Copyright by SAP AG

Current Line—On the left of the lines, the character > designates the current line being processed.

Breakpoints—Specific breakpoints can be set by double clicking on the line or selecting **F2**. When a breakpoint is set, an asterisk appears in the field to the right of current line indicator.

Symbol values—The current symbol values are shown in the bottom part of the screen. The symbol is on the left and its value is on the right. The symbols are placed here as they are interpreted by the debugger. When all the lines fill up, the list starts at the top again. To get specific values, copy and paste the symbol into the field. Do not double click the symbol as in ABAP. Double clicking the symbol will put a breakpoint on the line.

Execute button—The Execute button on the debugger screen will execute the whole line and move to the next line.

Single step—The Single Step button will execute the current event and move to the next event.

Left/right—The Left/Right button will move to the right side (not shown) of the text line. If selected again it will return to the left side of the line.

How to Turn Off the Layout Set Debugger

Select the **Exit** button in the SAPscript Layout Set Debugger: Breakpoints screen shown in Figure 5.11. This will process the current layout set with Debug mode off. Subsequent layout sets will also be processed with debug mode off.

Uploading and Downloading Layout Sets

Like ABAP programs, layout sets can be downloaded and uploaded. Depending on the version of the system it may or may not be possible to download the layout set to the local work station. The example provided derives from a 3.1H system. Some earlier versions are only capable of downloading to the application server. In that case there must be some method of accessing the application server file system. The active version of the layout set is downloaded, regardless of whether or not the layout set has been saved.

NOTE

When downloading/uploading to and from an application server it is advisable to use a file system common to all the application servers. Check with the basis team, who will most likely have a shared mount point for interfaces.

Downloading Layout Sets

To download a layout set, run program RSTXSCRP in transaction SE38. The initial screen is shown in Figure 5.15. Z_LS_CONTACT_411 is used here as an example.

The figure indicates that RSTXSCRP can be used to download other SAPscript objects as well. To download a layout set, select the **Layout Set** radio button and enter the name of the layout set object as shown. Type the word EXPORT in the Export/Import field. If the File system: GUI radio button is selected, the file will be downloaded to the workstation. When downloading to a server, fill in the data set name (path and file name on the application server). When down loading to a GUI (local workstation) leave the data set name blank. The program will permit selecting the path of any file name graphically at run time (see Figure 5.16).

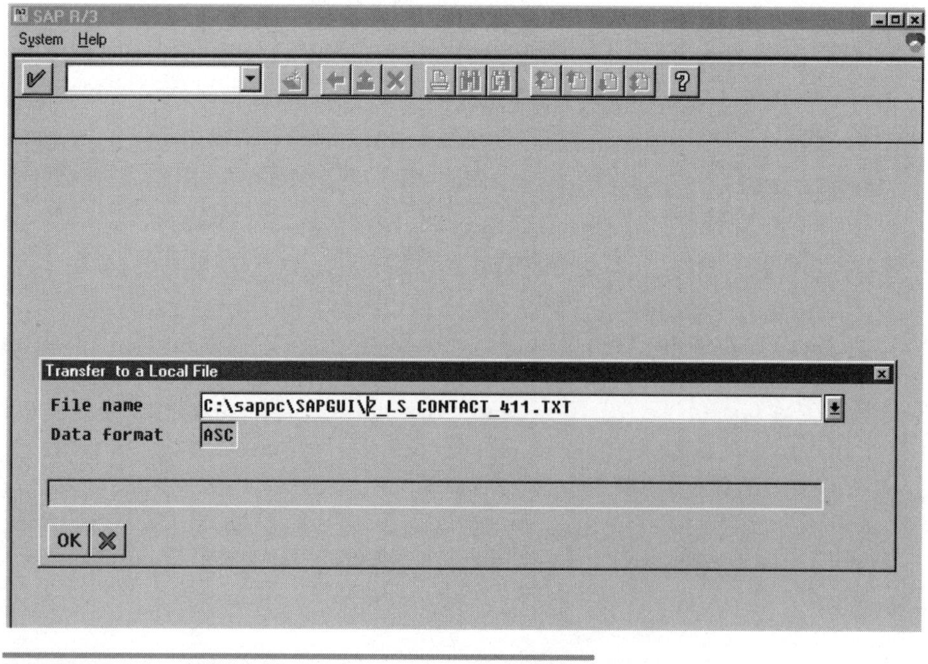

FIGURE 5.16   GUI path for layout set download
Copyright by SAP AG

In Figure 5.16, the down arrow on the right of the File Name field enables selection of a file name. In the example, the data format is ASCII; other formats are available by using the select option.

The contents of the text file after downloading (Z_LS_CONTACT_411.TXT):

```
SFORMZ_LS_CONTACT_411
HFORMZ_LS_CONTACT_411
     OLANE
     HEADFORM       Z_LS_CONTACT_411SAP
DEF EContact info only                    Z_LS_CONTACT_411
00028MLB10A       31H 19980824225138MLB10A       31H
1998100109335413200008 E0
030
     LINE/:FORM CPI 10; LPI 6; TAB-STOP 1 CM; START-PAGE PAGE1;
          FORMAT LETTER PORTRAIT;
     LINE/:FORM PARAGRAPH P1;
     LINE/:PARAGRAPH P1 LINE-SPACE 1 LN; FONT COURIER; FONT-SIZE
          14; BOLD ON;
     LINE/:WINDOW MAIN
     LINE/:WINDOW WIN1 TYPE CONST; PARAGRAPH P1;
     LINE/:PAGE PAGE1
     LINE/:PAGE PAGE1 MAIN 0 37.50 MM 100 MM 140 MM 150 MM;
     LINE/:PAGE PAGE1 WINDOW WIN1 37.50 MM 50 MM 140 MM 40 MM;
     END
     HEADFORM       Z_LS_CONTACT_411SAP
TXT EContact info only                    Z_LS_CONTACT_411
00029MLB10A       31H 19980824225138MLB10A       31H
1998100109335413200007 E0
030
     LINE/:FORM TEXT 'Contact info only';
     LINE/:PARAGRAPH P1 TEXT 'Courier 14 bold';
     LINE/:WINDOW MAIN TEXT 'Main window';
     LINE/:WINDOW WIN1 TEXT 'window for contact info';
     LINE/:PAGE PAGE1 TEXT 'Page for text';
     LINE/WWIN1
     LINE/:INCLUDE Z_CONTACT_INFO OBJECT TEXT ID ST
     END
     ACTVSAP
E
```

CD-ROM

Z_LS_CONTACT_411 FE002

Uploading Layout Sets

To upload a layout set, execute RSTXSCRP. Fill in the parameters the same way they were filled in before (for the export) but this time use Import for the mode (see Figure 5.17). Just as in exporting, the program will permit graphically selecting a file from the local workstation file system.

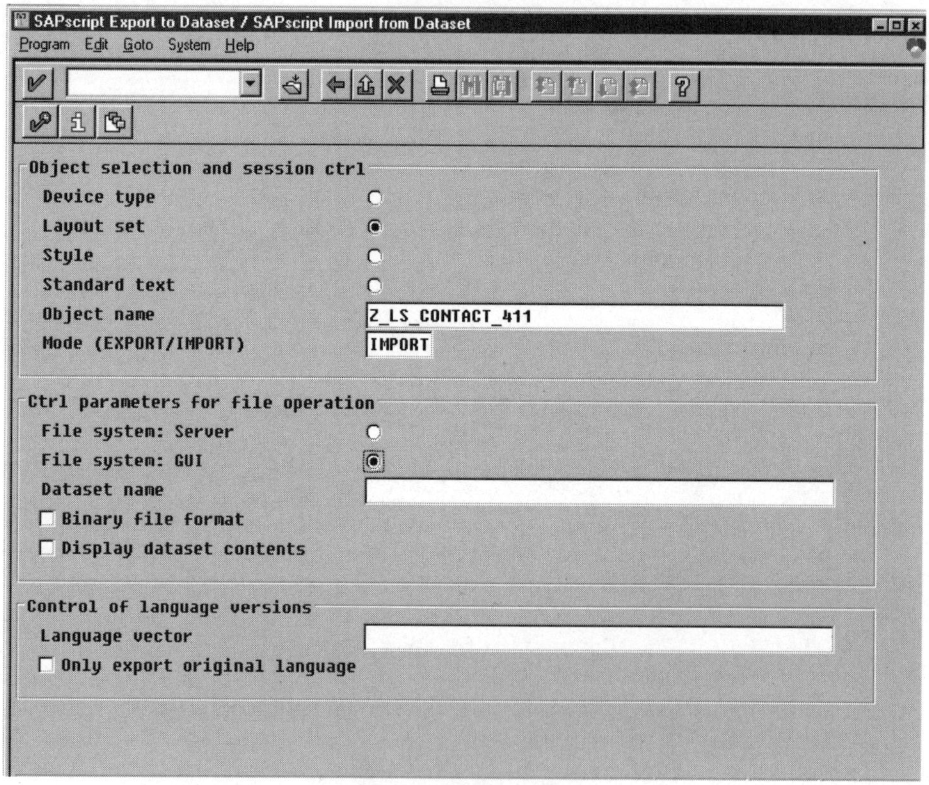

FIGURE 5.17   **Importing a layout set from GUI**
Copyright by SAP AG

The layout set must be imported using the same object name used for exporting. In this example the object name is Z_LS_CONTACT_411. If a different object name were used, an error would occur. However, the correct object name was used and the layout set has been imported as expected. The result is shown in Figure 5.18. If there were any errors or warnings they would appear here as well.

```
SAPscript Export to Dataset / SAPscript Import from Dataset          _ □ ×
List  Edit  Goto  System  Help                                         ●

  ✔ |                  |▼|  ☑ | ←⇧×| ▣⚙⚙ | ⚙⚙⚙⚙ | ?|


SAPscript Export to Dataset / SAPscript Import from Dataset        1 ▲

**************************** Start SAPscript Transporter RSTXR3TR ******
Transport object FORM Z_LS_CONTACT_411 is being processed
Language vector used: DE
Original language was set to E
Definition E imported
Original language E imported
Object imported and activated
```

FIGURE 5.18   Import layout set results
Copyright by SAP AG

When a layout set that already exists is imported, the active version of the layout set will be replaced. If the layout set does not exist, it will be created on import.

WARNING

If a layout set is being edited and the same layout set is imported in another instance, the active version will be replaced. If the version being edited is then activated, it will overwrite what was imported.

It is wise to export work. This is a way of making sure to have a personal copy. It does not happen often, but sometimes objects get overwritten. If a copy of the layout set has been exported, it will not be necessary type it all back in.

Layout Set Information

Another way to capture information about the layout set is to display the layout set information on the screen in a list format and then download the list. It is not possible to upload the layout information in this format, though the information is much more readable. This is a good way to capture layout set information for an appendix to technical documentation.

In the Display or Change mode, select **Utilities ➜ Layout set info** to get to the layout set information on the screen in text format. Figure 5.19 shows the first page of the layout set information for Z_LS_CONTACT_411. To pull this

list down to the local workstation select **System → List → Save → Local file**
(**System → List → Download** in some earlier versions).

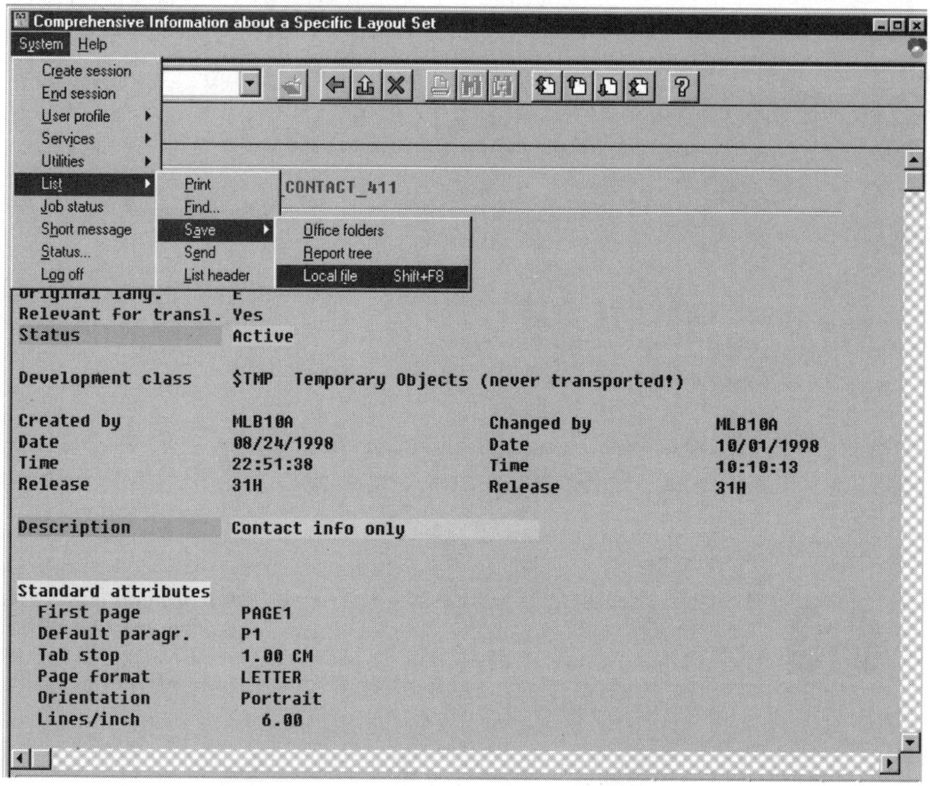

FIGURE 5.19   Layout set info
Copyright by SAP AG

Depending on the version of SAP that is running, downloading can be done
in various formats. All versions are capable of downloading in the text or
unconverted format. The following is the layout set Z_LS_CONTACT_411
information, as it would appear on the local workstation:

```
-------------------------------------------------------------
Layout set          Z_LS_CONTACT_411
-------------------------------------------------------------
Client              030
Language            E
Original lang.      E
Relevant for transl. Yes
```

```
Status                Active
Development class     $TMP  Temporary Objects (never transported!)
Created by            MLB10A             Changed by    MLB10A
Date                  08/24/1998         Date          10/01/1998
Time                  22:51:38           Time          10:10:13
Release               31H                Release       31H
Description           Contact info only
Standard attributes
  First page          PAGE1
  Default paragr.     P1
  Tab stop            1.00 CM
  Page format         LETTER
  Orientation         Portrait
  Lines/inch            6.00
  Characters/inch     10.00
Font attributes
  Font family         COURIER
  Font size           12.0 Point
  Bold                No
  Italic              No
  Underlined          No
-----------------------------------------------------------------
Paragraphs    Attributes
-----------------------------------------------------------------

  P1          Courier 14 bold
              Standard attributes
                Line spacing    1.00 LN
                Alignment       Left-aligned
              Font attributes
                Font family     COURIER
                Font size       14.0 Point
                Bold            Yes
-----------------------------------------------------------------
Windows       Attributes
-----------------------------------------------------------------

  MAIN        Main window
                Window type     MAIN
  WIN1        window for contact info
                Window type     CONST
                Default par.    P1
-----------------------------------------------------------------
Pages         Attributes
-----------------------------------------------------------------

  PAGE1       Page for text
              Page counter
```

```
        Mode                    INC
        Numbering type          Arabic numerals
    Page window
        MAIN                    Left margin         37.50   MM
                                Upper margin       100.00   MM
                                Window width       140.00   MM
                                Window height      150.00   MM
        WIN1                    Left margin         37.50   MM
                                Upper margin        50.00   MM
                                Window width       140.00   MM
                                Window height       40.00   MM
--------------------------------------------------------------
Text elements for following windows:
--------------------------------------------------------------
WIN1
/:  INCLUDE Z_CONTACT_INFO OBJECT TEXT ID ST
```

Info for Z_LS_CONTACT_411 IE001

Text Element—Include Utilities

In creating text elements a few utilities provide shortcuts that make building text elements a little easier. All these utilities can be accessed from the Include menu in the Text Element editor. (They can also be accessed when creating standard text.) Figure 5.20 shows the Text Element editor and the path to these utilities. The window in the Text editor is the WIN1 window of layout set Z_LS_2CNDCON_411, which is a copy of Z_LS_CONTACT_411.

Z_LS_2CNDCON_411 FE003

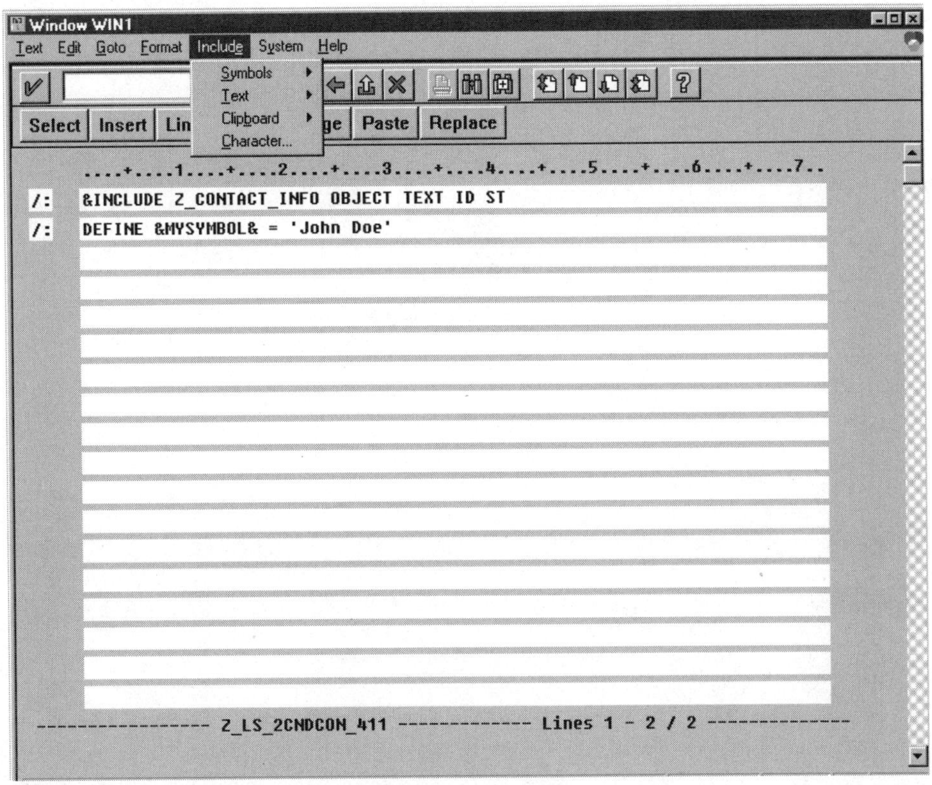

FIGURE 5.20   Text element Include utilities
Copyright by SAP AG

Include Symbols

The Include Symbols utility works like a mini applications generator. It helps interject a symbol into a Text element. The four types of symbols basically all work the same way.

Text Symbols

Text symbols are the symbols that have been defined. (The program symbols list here also because SAPscript does not know what program is calling it until run time.) Also, it is possible to define the symbol in a standard text and then include the standard text in the text element. In Figure 5.20, I have added a Define statement for MY_SYMBOL for an example. With a symbol identified, and the cursor in a position where a symbol is needed, select **Include → Symbols → Text** to get the listing of available symbols. In the example, MY_SYMBOL is the only available text symbol (see Figure 5.21).

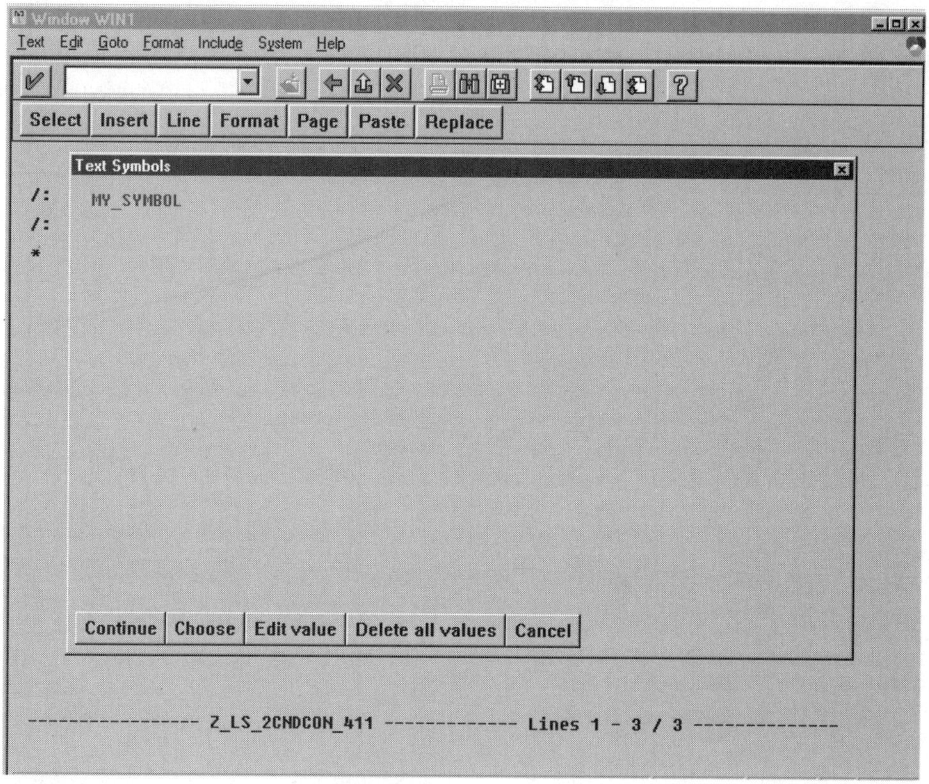

FIGURE 5.21   Include text symbols
Copyright by SAP AG

To add a new symbol select **Include → Symbols → New**. (This does not define the symbols, it only creates the syntax that refers to an existing symbol.)

In Figure 5.21 there are various buttons at the bottom. For layout set editing, Continue and Cancel basically have the same effect: they both go back to the editor with no change. If we select the Edit Value button we can assign a temporary value to the symbol. This value is good only until we exit the editor. Since there is no print preview selection inside the editor, it is pointless to assign a value. This option will work if there is a text with a bunch of program symbols and work is done in the Standard Text editor. In this case it is possible to assign values to the symbols and run a print preview from the Text pulldown menu to render an image with values in the place of the symbols. In our example, any value that we assign will be replaced by "John Doe" at run time. (John Doe was set as the value in Figure 5.20.)

If the cursor is on MY_SYMBOL and the **Choose** button is selected, formatting options can be provided for the symbol. In the example, I have chosen to fix the output at ten characters (see Figure 5.22). Selecting **Continue** will interject the symbol (as formatted) into the text element. The result is shown in Figure 5.23.

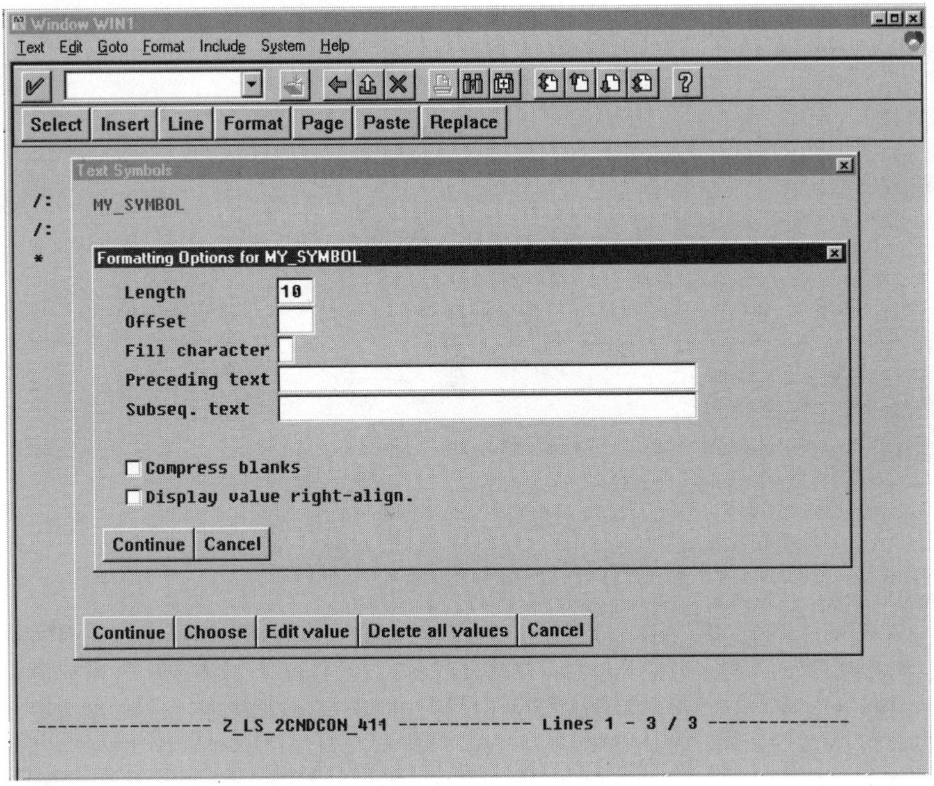

FIGURE 5.22 **Assign formatting options to a text symbol**
Copyright by SAP AG

This utility can be handy if there is a complex Main window with, many repeated symbols. The Include utility will give a simple list and permit interjecting the symbol quickly with no typos.

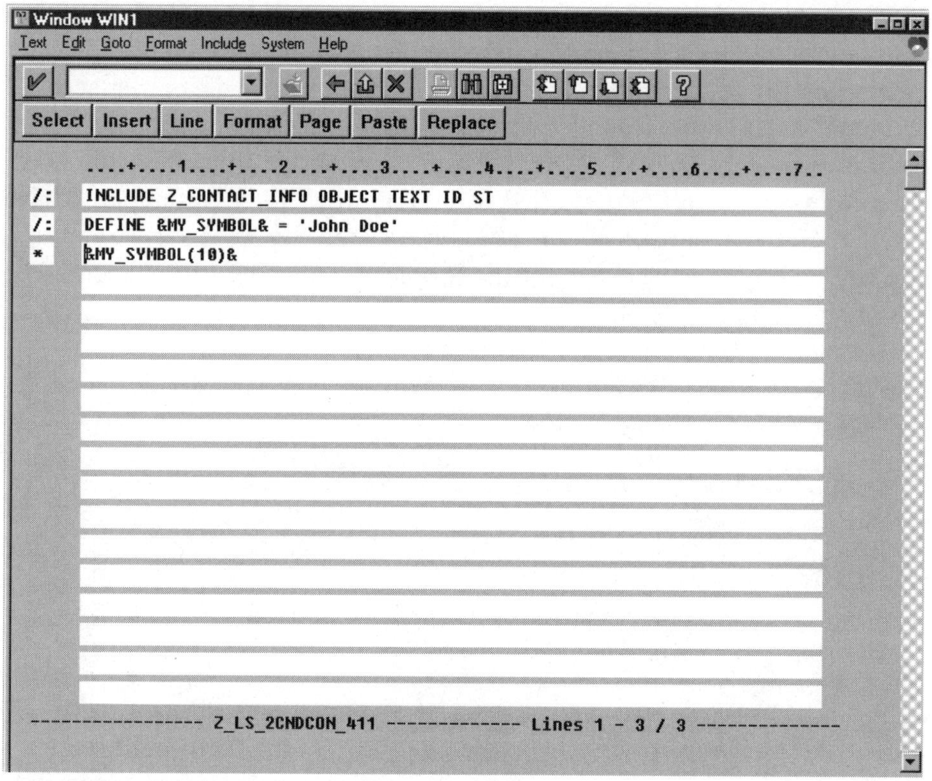

FIGURE 5.23 Include text symbol results
Copyright by SAP AG

Program, Standard and System Symbols

Program, standard and system symbols all work just as text symbols do, only there is no option to change the value. In the program symbols the SAPscript and Syst structure fields will always be available to the layout set at run time. The standard symbols supply a list of commonly used text strings. If a standard phrase like "Dear Sir or Madam...", will be used, it may be in the list of standard symbols. System symbols are those that are populated by SAPscript. &PAGE&, for example, is a system symbol. It is dependent upon the type of printer used. System symbols are variables that will not be populated until the layout set is called.

Include Text

We have used the Include command in several examples in previous chapters. It is basically used to interject a standard text into a Text element. With the

Include Text utility an Include statement can be generated, or the actual text in the standard text can be interjected. Here are examples of each of the two ways to use this utility:

I have created a standard text called `Z_MY_TEXT`. The text ID is `ST`. The language is `E`. The text looks like this in ITF format:

```
*    Remit to:
*    Company XYZ Inc.
*    123 Main Street Richmond, VA 12345
```

Using `Z_LS_2CNDCON_411` as an example again, if we select **Include →
Text → Standard**, we get an Include Text selection screen as shown in Figure
5.24. If the down arrow button is selected, we get a list of available standard
texts.

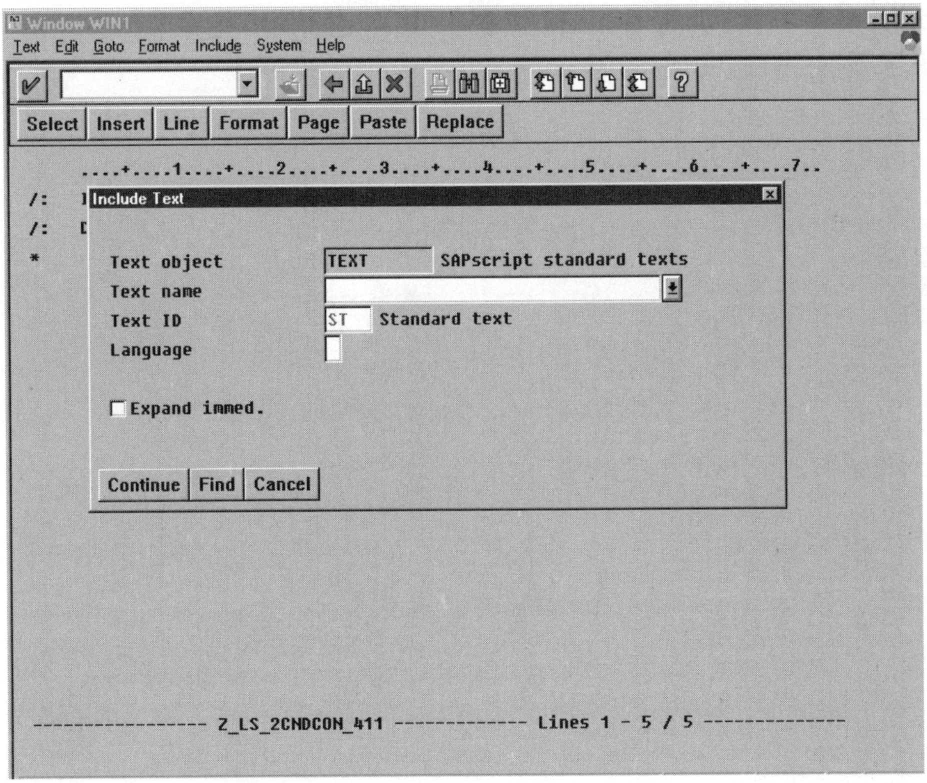

FIGURE 5.24   Insert Include command
Copyright by SAP AG

If `Z_MY_TEXT` is entered as the standard text, a command line will be added to the Text element as shown in Figure 5.25. Notice that the `/:` was automatically used as the tag column because we are inserting a command instead of text.

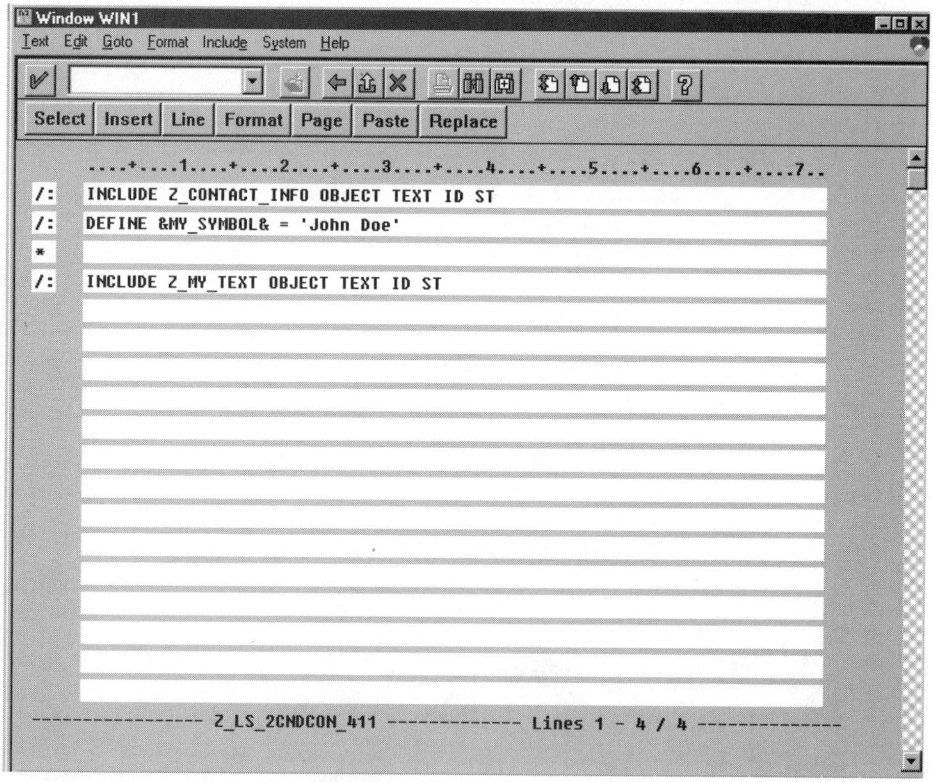

```
Window WIN1                                                    _□×
Text  Edit  Goto  Format  Include  System  Help

 ✔  [              ▼]   ⬛  ⬅🔼✖  🗎🔍🔍  🔳🗇🗇🗇  ❓

 Select | Insert | Line | Format | Page | Paste | Replace

   ....+....1....+....2....+....3....+....4....+....5....+....6....+....7..
/:   INCLUDE Z_CONTACT_INFO OBJECT TEXT ID ST
/:   DEFINE &MY_SYMBOL& = 'John Doe'
*
/:   INCLUDE Z_MY_TEXT OBJECT TEXT ID ST




-------------------- Z_LS_2CNDCON_411 ------------- Lines 1 - 4 / 4 ---------------
```

FIGURE 5.25   Include text result
Copyright by SAP AG

In Figure 5.24 there is a check box called "Expand immed.". If this box is checked, the actual text of the standard text will be interjected into the Text element as shown in Figure 5.26. As in the other instance, the tag column is automatically set. In this case we are interjecting text so the tag column is *.

If an Include command line has been inserted and it must be changed to the expanded text, select the Include line and select **Edit → Selected area → Expand INCLUDE**. This will change the Include statement to the actual text referred to in the statement.

```
┌─────────────────────────────────────────────────────────────────────────┐
│ ▣ Window WIN1                                                     _□×      │
│ Text  Edit  Goto  Format  Include  System  Help                       ◉   │
│ ┌───────────────────────────────────────────────────────────────────────┐ │
│ │ ✔ │              ▼│ ◁ │ ←│⬆│✕ │ ▤│▥│▦ │ ▤▤▤▤ │ ? │                      │
│ ├───────────────────────────────────────────────────────────────────────┤ │
│ │ Select │ Insert │ Line │ Format │ Page │ Paste │ Replace │             │ │
│ └───────────────────────────────────────────────────────────────────────┘ │
│      ....+....1....+....2....+....3....+....4....+....5....+....6....+....7..│
│  /:  INCLUDE Z_CONTACT_INFO OBJECT TEXT ID ST                             │
│  /:  DEFINE &MY_SYMBOL& = 'John Doe'                                       │
│  *                                                                         │
│  *   Remit to:                                                             │
│  *   Company XYZ Inc.                                                      │
│  *   123 Main Street Richmond, VA 12345                                    │
│                                                                            │
│ --------------------- Z_LS_2CNDCON_411 ------------- Lines 1 - 6 / 6 ----- │
└─────────────────────────────────────────────────────────────────────────┘
```

FIGURE 5.26   Include "expanded" text result
Copyright by SAP AG

Include Clipboard

Include clipboard pastes the contents of various clipboards into the text element.

User clipboards are "permanent" clipboards. The contents of a user clipboard remains until it is overwritten, like a notepad that follows a log on. The user clipboard is in ITF format.

Line editor clipboards (X, Y, and Z) can be used to paste text from the ABAP editor. The text must be copied to the X, Y, or Z editor within the ABAP editor; it can then be pasted to the text element with the Include utility. The tag element / ((raw element, line feed) is applied to the inserted text.

Just as with common word processors, characters from the system character set can be inserted. Select **Include → Character** to get the screen shown in Figure 5.27. Now select a displayable or nondisplayable character and interject it into the text element.

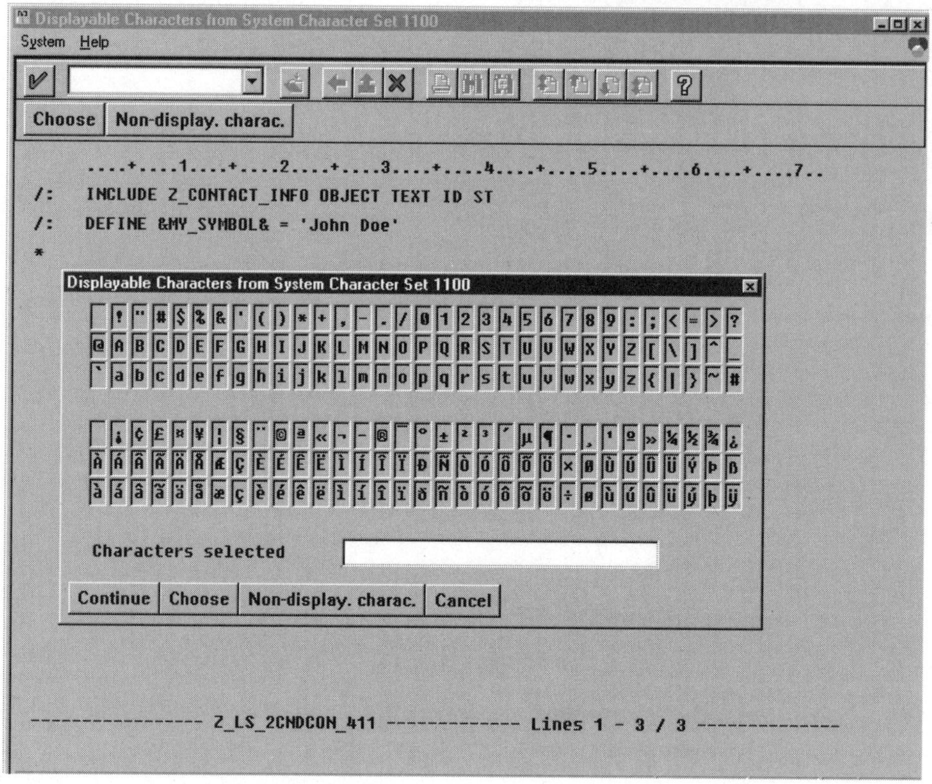

FIGURE 5.27   Insert character
Copyright by SAP AG

Tools in Review

1. If a layout set is deleted in the original language all of the other languages will be deleted.
2. To test a layout set, run the print program (in some cases start a transaction that starts the print program) or use the Test Print utility.
3. The debugger can show what SAPscript sees at runtime.
4. To copy layout sets use: **Copy from** or **Save as**.

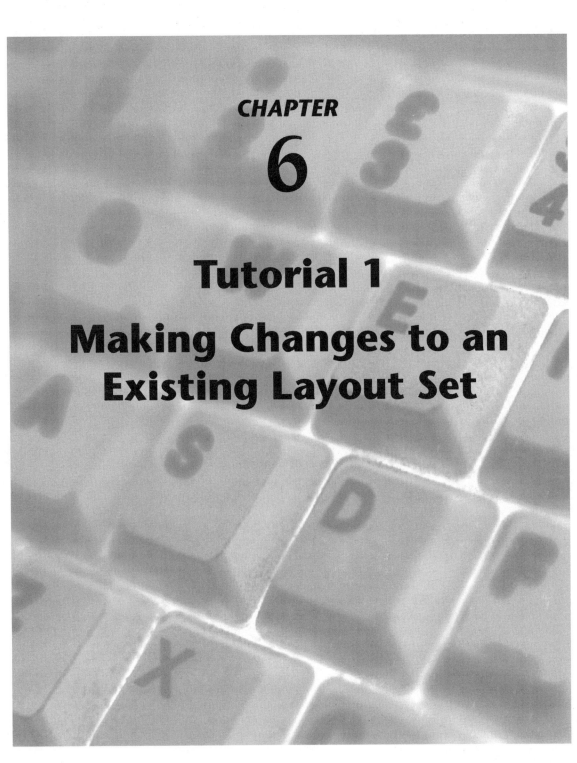

CHAPTER

6

Tutorial 1

Making Changes to an
Existing Layout Set

The Requirement

In Chapter 1, we looked at an example of a layout set called Unearned Discount Invoice shown in Figure 6.1. This correspondence is fairly typical. It has a Title window, a header, a body, and a footer window on each page. The name of this layout set is Z_EX_UNDIS_INV. It is triggered by a custom ABAP program which gathers the invoice information and calls the layout set for printing. In this tutorial we will change only the layout set; the ABAP program is not affected.

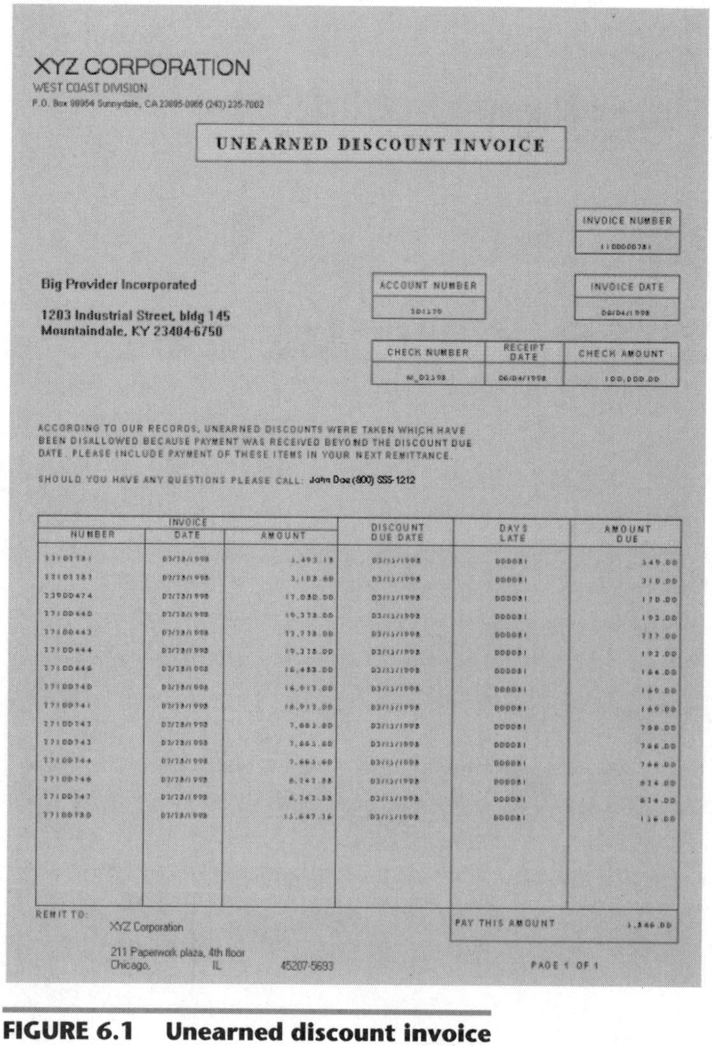

FIGURE 6.1   Unearned discount invoice

The Changes

For example's sake, suppose that the client wants to make the following changes to the correspondence shown in Figure 6.1:

1. Change the name, address and phone number to:
   AB Incorporated
   East Coast Division
   P.O. Box 12345 New York, NY 33344-5555 (800) 555-1212
2. Enlarge the font of address (shown above) to Helvetica 8.
3. Change the column called "Discount Due Date" to "Due Date."
4. Change the name in the Remit To section so that it reflects the new name but do not change the address.

Preparations

If text changes need to be made in a standard layout set, follow along with this tutorial. If not, upload the sample layout set Z_EX_UNDIS_INV as a starting point.

> **NOTE**
>
> See the section in Chapter 5 "Uploading and Downloading Layout Sets" if uploading the layout set.

In our example, we know which layout set needs to be changed because the layout set name is given implicitly in the calling ABAP. To make a change to standard SAP correspondence, remember that the standard SAP print programs do not name layout sets implicitly, rather they refer to configuration settings made in the application area. Refer to the section in Chapter 2 "Output Determination and Layout Sets" to help determine the correct layout set name. Obviously we would not want to change an existing standard SAP layout set directly. Instead, either open the original version and copy to a new version or create a new layout set and copy from the original. In our example we will create a new layout set and copy from the original.

Creating a New Layout Set

To create a layout set select **Tools → Word processing → Layout set** (transaction SE71). At the Layout Set: Request screen, enter the name of the new layout set. Our new version of Z_EX_UNDIS_INV will be called Z_E2_UNDIS_INV. Enter the language in which to create the layout set. In our example we enter "E."

NOTE Since this is a new layout set, it does not matter which subobject is selected. SAPscript will recognize that the layout set name is new and proceed to the Header screen regardless of which subobject is selected.

Select the **Create** button. The information screen shown in Figure 6.2 tells us that the layout set is not available in our client. This makes sense because we are creating a new layout set. The message is confirming that the object name is new.

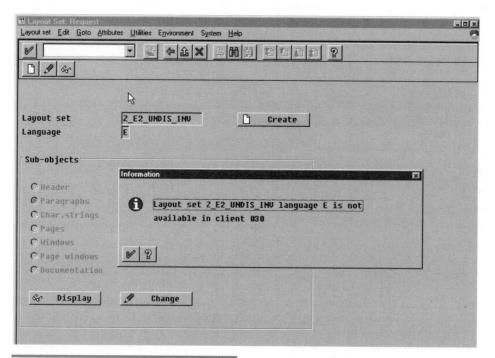

FIGURE 6.2   Create Z_E2_UNDIS_INV
Copyright by SAP AG

Click the green check mark or press the **Enter** key to clear the message. From here we come to the Header screen. The status of the new layout set will be "New-not saved." At this point we are forced to enter a temporary description. The example shows "copy of Z_EX_UNDIS_INV" as the description. (It does not matter what description is entered, it will get overwritten in the "copy from" step.)

Copying from the Old Layout Set

With a description entered, select **Layout set → Copy from**. Enter the name of the original layout set and language as shown in Figure 6.3 and select the **OK** button.

The contents of Z_EX_UNDIS_INV will be copied to Z_E2_UNDIS_INV, as shown in Figure 6.4. Having successfully created a working version of the layout set, we are now prepared to make the necessary changes.

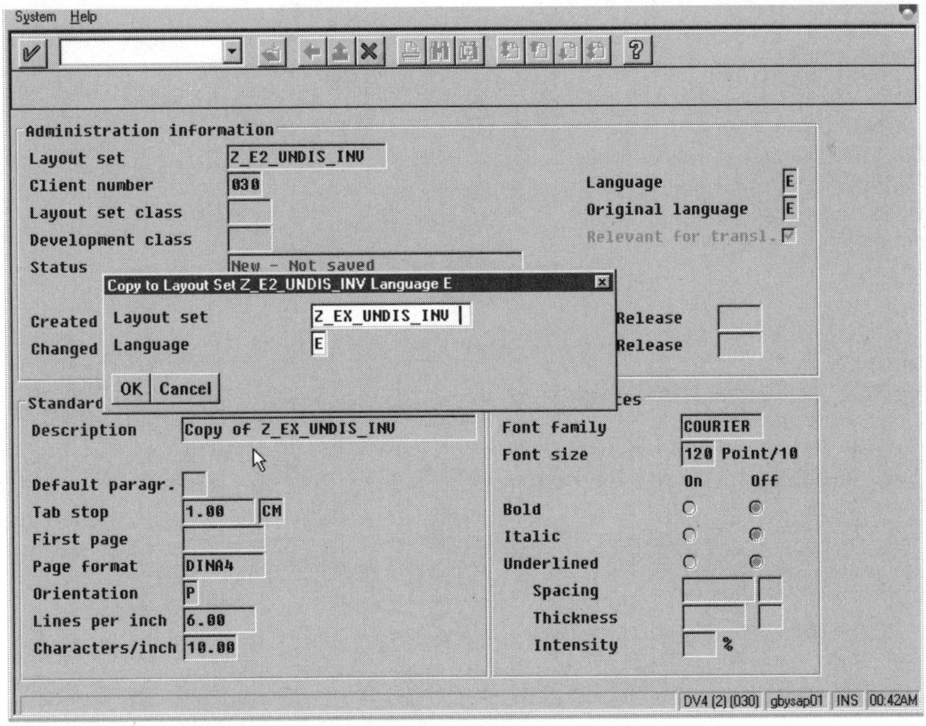

FIGURE 6.3   Copy from Z_EX_UNDIS_INV
Copyright by SAP AG

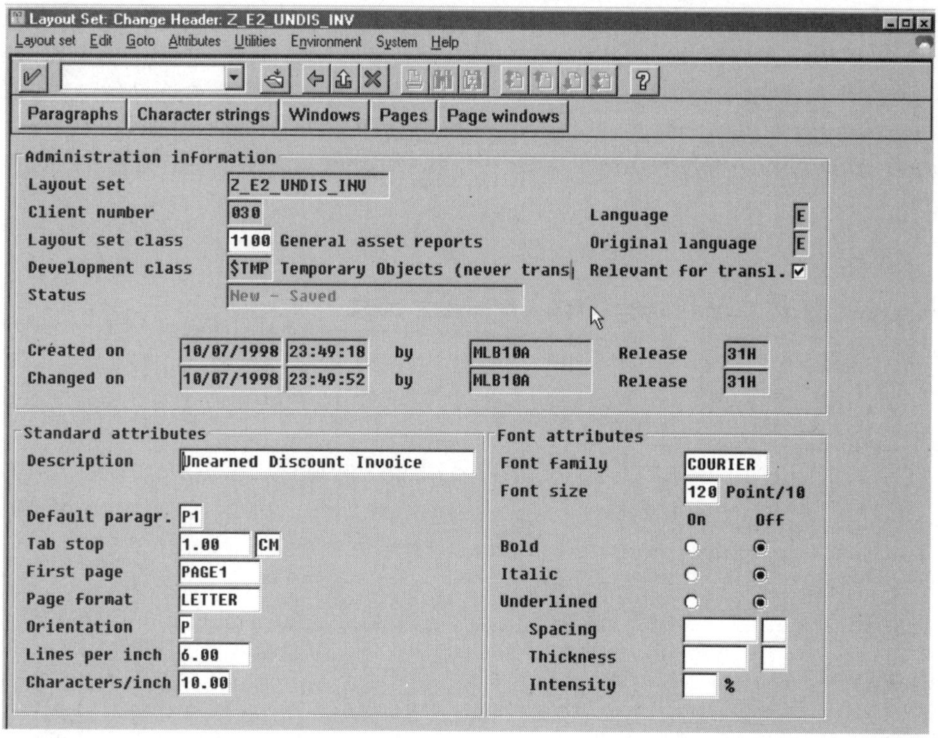

FIGURE 6.4   Z_E2_UNDIS_INV
Copyright by SAP AG

Creating a Test Printout to Show the Relative Locations of the Windows

The first task is to change the address in the upper left corner of the page. We need to find out what window holds the text. We can get help from the SAPscript Test Print utility. To look at a test printout select **Utilities → Test print**. At the Print Parameters screen, supply a printer name and select the Print Preview button as shown in Figure 6.5.

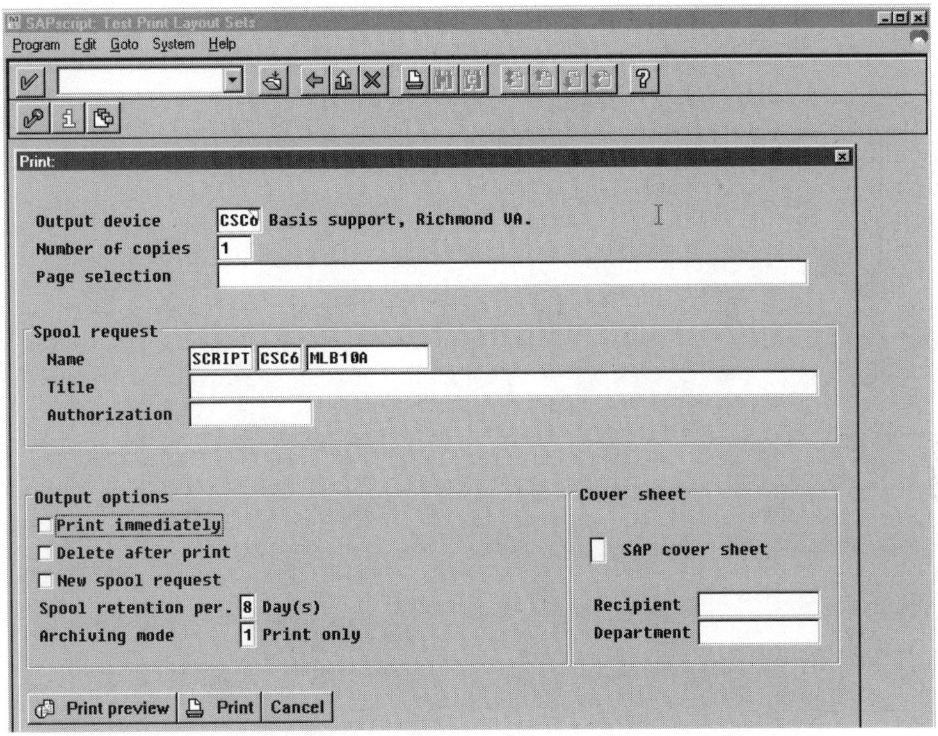

FIGURE 6.5   Print parameters for print preview of Z_E2_UNDIS_INV
Copyright by SAP AG

In the print preview shown in Figure 6.6, the windows are highlighted with a line slightly lighter than the background. The windows are highlighted like this only in the Test Print utility. These lines will not appear in the actual correspondence. Some windows include borders (the window with Unearned Discount Invoice for example). The windows with borders do not show a highlight because the dark border has overwritten it.

From the print preview in Figure 6.6, we can see that the name of the company is enclosed in a window all by itself and is located in the uppermost left corner. The next task is to go to the Page Windows screen and look for a window that fits this description.

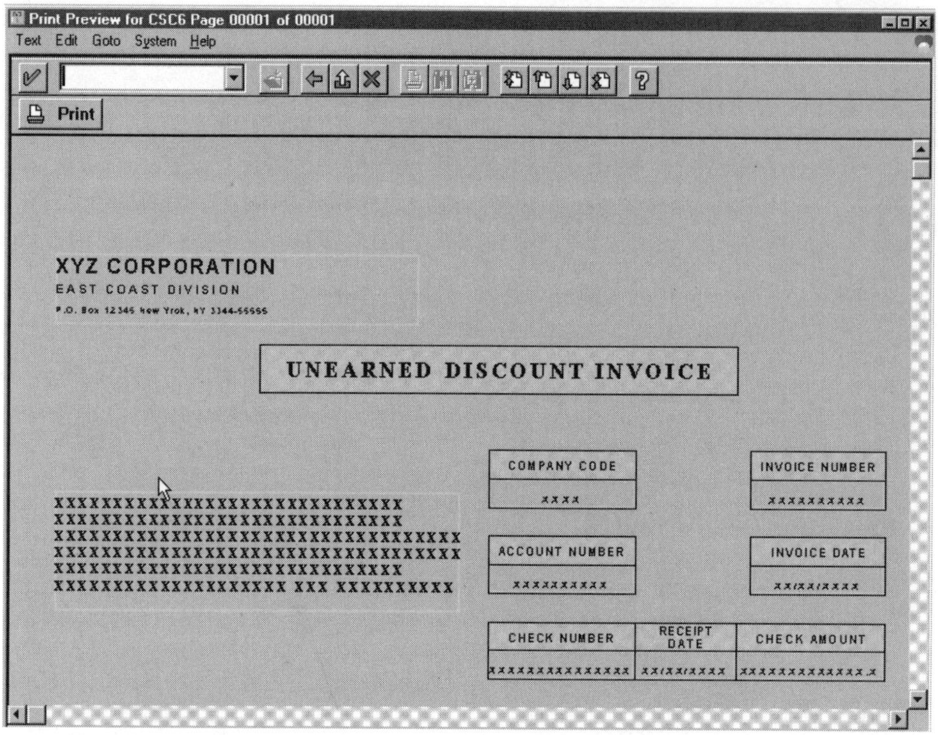

FIGURE 6.6   Print preview test print of Z_E2_UNDIS_INV
Copyright by SAP AG

Making Changes to the Name and Address Window

Selecting the Page Window

To exit from the print preview select **Text → Exit**. Then, to get to the Page Windows screen select the **Page Windows** button.

Notice in the Page Windows screen in Figure 6.7, that only six windows are listed. Below the listing we see "Page window 10 frm 26." From this we know that our cursor is on item "10" and there are 26 windows in the layout set. Use the Page Up and Page Down buttons on the tool bar to view other windows associated with this page that are not currently shown. (There are also Page Up and Page Down buttons just below the listing on the right side.) In Figure 6.7, I have selected Page window "W1." The description is "title." We can see from the left margin (1 cm) and the upper margin (2.5 cm), that the W1 window is in the approximate position we are looking for. Sometimes we need to look in a few windows before finding the correct one. The description "title" helps, but something like "Company information" might have been better.

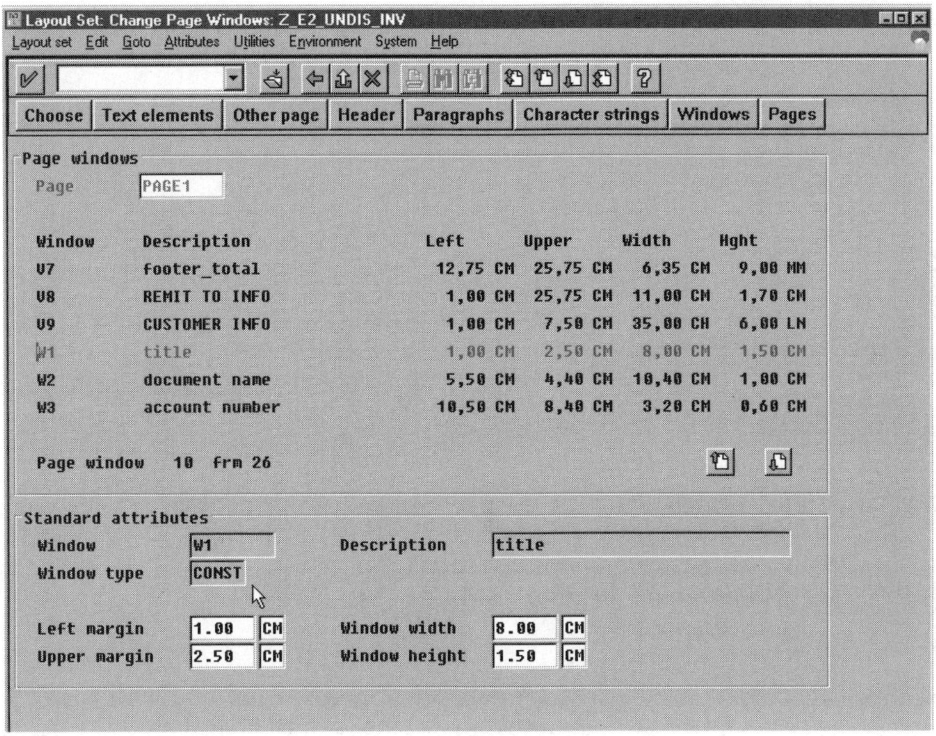

FIGURE 6.7   Page windows for Z_E2_UNDIS_INV
Copyright by SAP AG

Changing the Text

To see what is contained in the window, select **Edit → Text** elements. From Figure 6.8, we can see that we have selected the correct window. Window W1 contains the text that we want to change.

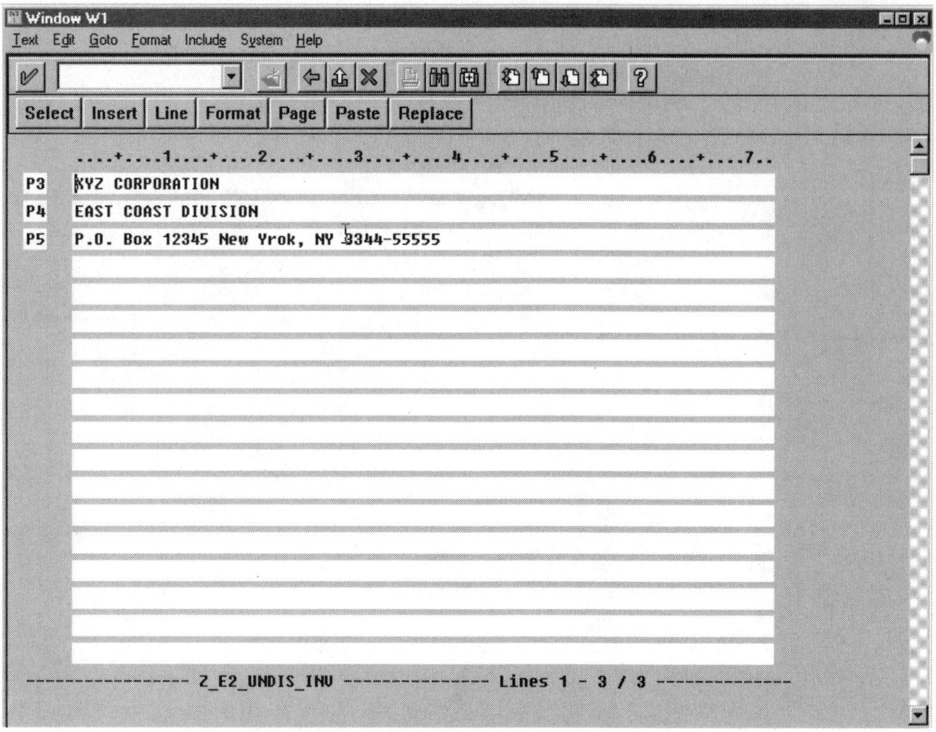

```
Window W1                                                    _ □ ×
Text  Edit  Goto  Format  Include  System  Help

 ✓  [              ▼]  🔙  ⇦ ⇧ ✕   📄 🔍 🔍   🔖 🔖 🔖 🔖   ?

 Select │ Insert │ Line │ Format │ Page │ Paste │ Replace

      ....+....1....+....2....+....3....+....4....+....5....+....6....+....7..
 P3   XYZ CORPORATION
 P4   EAST COAST DIVISION
 P5   P.O. Box 12345 New Yrok, NY 33344-55555




 ------------------ Z_E2_UNDIS_INV ------------- Lines 1 - 3 / 3 ------------
```

FIGURE 6.8   Text element for Page window W1
Copyright by SAP AG

To affect the change, we replace the respective text in each line with the new company name, address and phone number as shown in Figure 6.9.

The changes completed so far are sufficient to correct the name, address and phone number, but we still have not dealt with the requirement to change the font size on the address line.

Changing the Font Size

The address line uses the paragraph setting P5. The font setting of paragraph P5 dictates how our line will look. If paragraph P5 is set to Helvetica 6, then our address line will be printed in Helvetica 6. If paragraph P5 is set to Helvetica 8, then our line will print using Helvetica 8 and so on. It is possible that we could simply change the setting for paragraph P5 and effect our font change that way. This will work as long as no other texts use paragraph P5. If they do, the font for these lines will be changed as well.

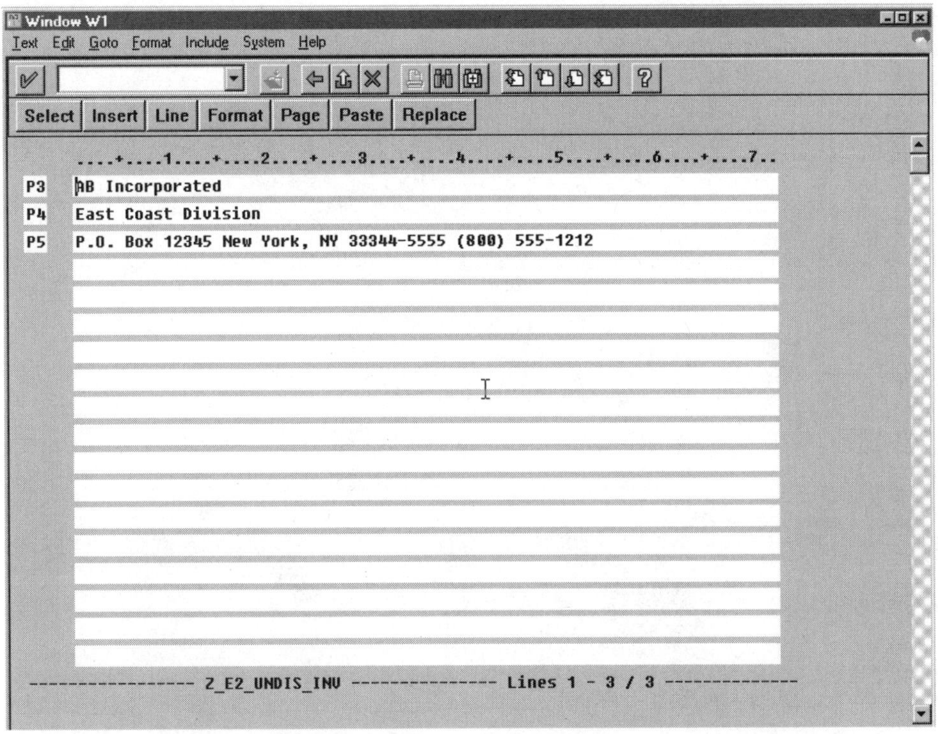

FIGURE 6.9 Replace the text with the new company information
Copyright by SAP AG

Before changing paragraph P5, we will use the layout set Info utility to make sure that no other texts in our layout set use paragraph P5. To get to the layout set Info utility, close the Text Element window with **F3** (or the green arrow) and select **Utilities → Layout set info**. The information will appear on the screen much as it looks in Figure 6.10.

We will need to scroll down toward the bottom of the listing to look at the Text elements associated with each window. This is the same information we get if we go to each window and open the Text Element editor to see what paragraphs are being used for each line. However, opening each window is time consuming. With the layout set information listed on the screen, we can scroll through all the Text Element tags quickly.

If we scroll up and down to see the text elements of the other windows, we notice that there are no other lines that use paragraph P5. Now we know it is safe to change paragraph P5 and we will not inadvertently affect the font of another line. To get to the Paragraphs screen, select **F3** (or the green arrow) and then the **Paragraphs** button (or **Goto → paragraphs**). Initially the Paragraph screen will appear as it does in Figure 6.11.

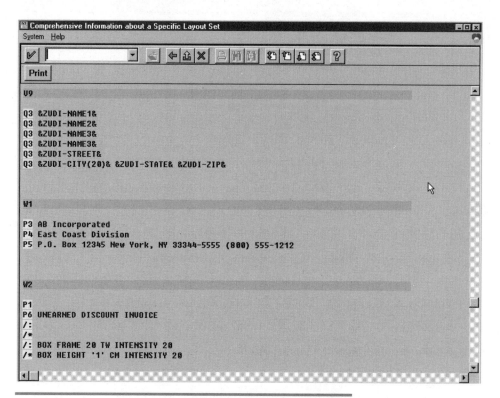

FIGURE 6.10   Z_E2_UNDIS_INV Layout set information
Copyright by SAP AG

In Figure 6.11 paragraph P5 is listed along with other paragraphs. To modify paragraph P5, highlight the line with P5 by double clicking it, and then press the **Font** button. When we select the Font button, the font attributes for P5 are shown in the lower portion of the screen (see Figure 6.12). Notice that the font settings are highlighted and available for change. First, position the cursor in the Description field and change the description to Helvetica 8.

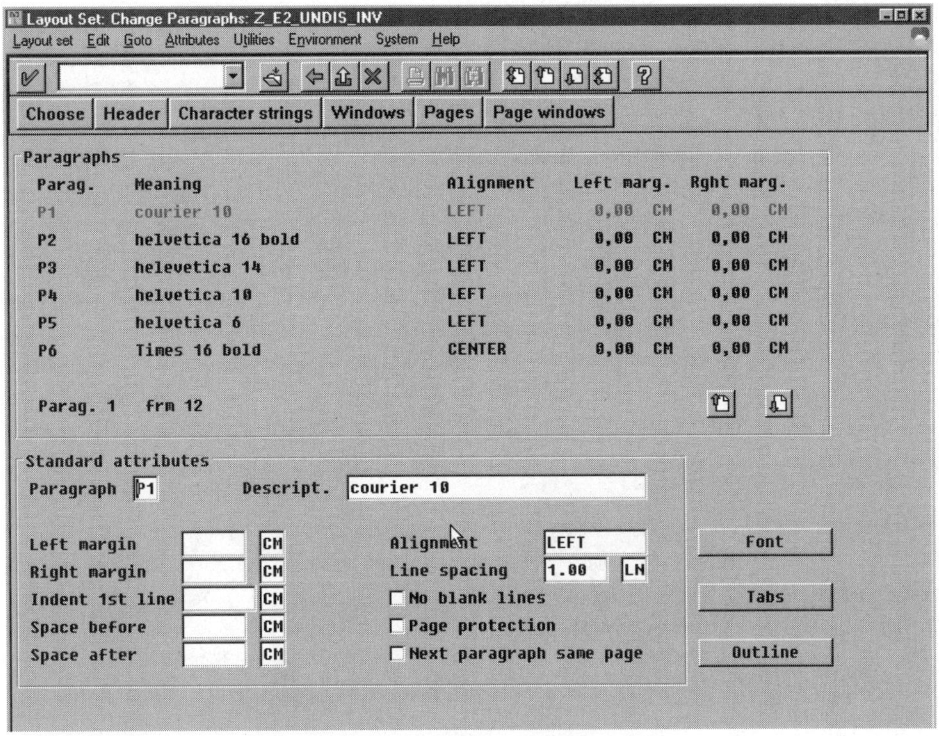

![Layout Set: Change Paragraphs: Z_E2_UNDIS_INV screen]

FIGURE 6.11 Z_E2_UNDIS_INV Paragraph screen
Copyright by SAP AG

NOTE

The paragraph description can be anything. It is good to use something that helps identify the paragraph in a unique way. The only thing unique about this paragraph is the font. Hence the description—Helvetica 8.

To change the font size, simply move the cursor to the Font Size field and use the down arrow (select **Options**) to select **8** from the list of available font sizes (see Figure 6.12). By using the down arrow, we can be sure to select a size that is available to the font family.

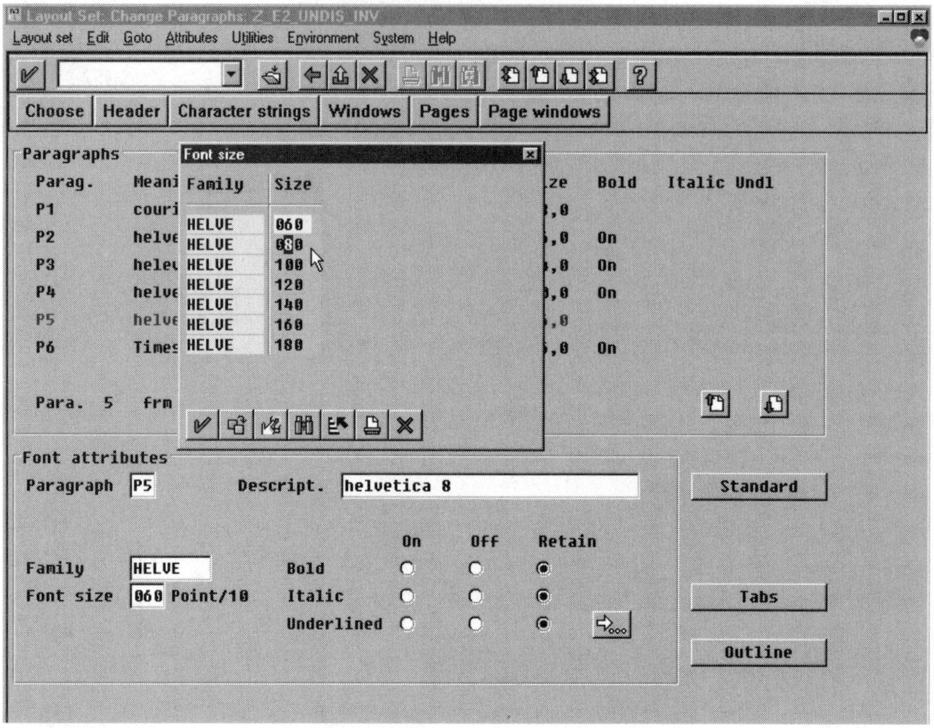

FIGURE 6.12   Changing the Font size for paragraph P5
Copyright by SAP AG

Having made these changes, we will run the Test Print utility to see how it looks. We can initiate a test printout directly from the Paragraph screen by selecting **Utilities → Test print**. Our test printout is shown in Figure 6.13. The name, address and phone number have been changed and the font of the address line has been enlarged. However, part of the phone number no longer fits in the window and does not appear.

To remedy the problem with the phone number we can widen the window slightly to allow for the extra line length we need. From our test printout, we can see that we have room to widen the window without causing any ill effect to the rest of the document.

To widen the window, back out of the Print Preview screen (**F3** or green arrow) and select the Page window button (or **Goto → Page windows**). Find the W1 window, "Title," and select it by double clicking on the line. Once the W1 Page window is highlighted, move the cursor to the Window Width field and change it to 9.00 cm. Another centimeter in width should be sufficient to render the phone number. The W1 Page window attributes should appear as they do in Figure 6.14. A test printout (print preview) with the corrected window width is shown in Figure 6.15.

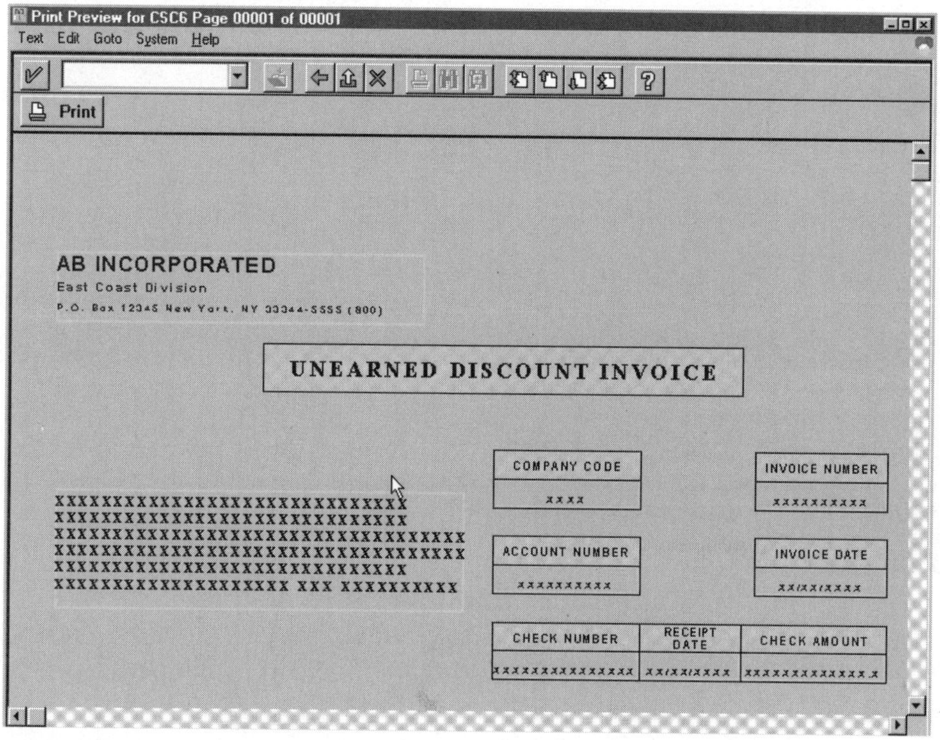

FIGURE 6.13   Z_E2_UNDIS_INV Test printout after changes
Copyright by SAP AG

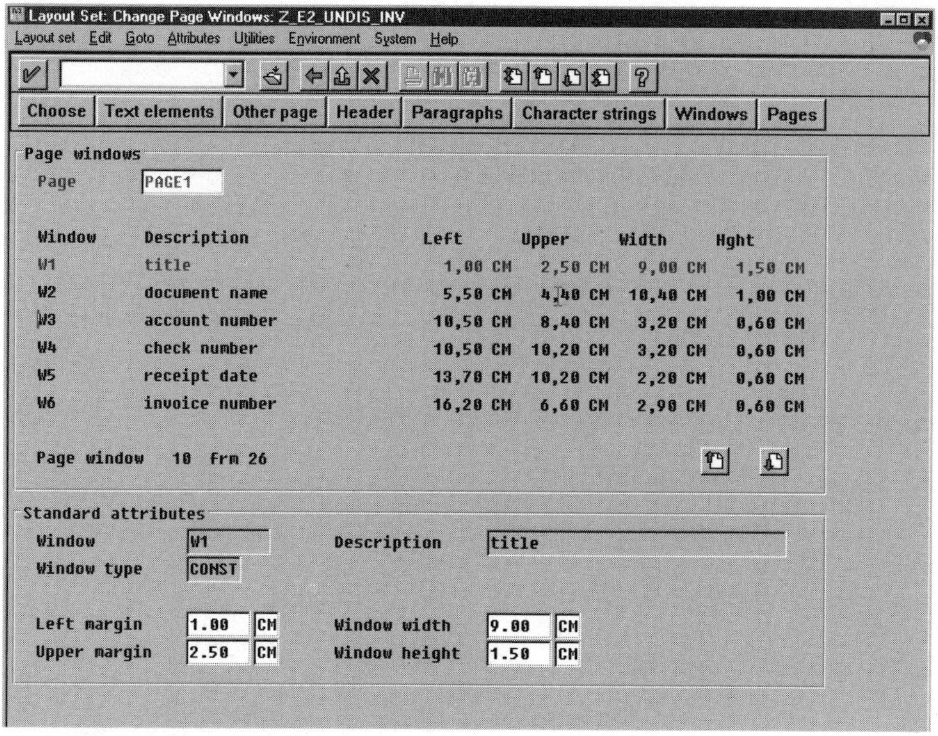

FIGURE 6.14   Page window attributes for "W1"
Copyright by SAP AG

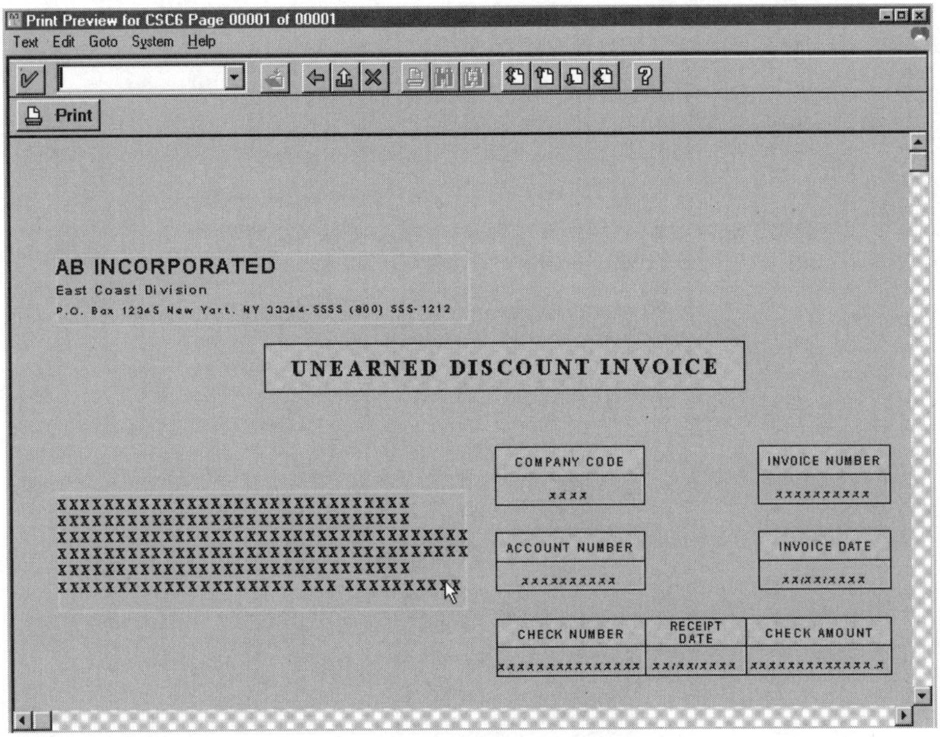

FIGURE 6.15   Test printout with window expanded
Copyright by SAP AG

Changing the Column Header

Finding the Window

The next requirement on the list is to adjust the header which reads Discount Due Date, so that it reads Due Date. The first task is to find the window with the header. Usually the column headers can be found either in the Main window or in a window by themselves just above the main window. If a column header is located in the Main window, the Top and Endtop commands normally embrace the header information to ensure that it is only printed at the top of each page. A quick review of the Main window shows that nothing that fits this description (see Figure 6.16).

```
 Window MAIN                                                          _ □ ×
 Text  Edit  Goto  Format  Include  System  Help

 ✔ [            ▼] ◁  ←⬆✗  🖨🔍🔁  🔂🔃🔄🔀  ❓

 Select │ Insert │ Line │ Format │ Page │ Paste │ Replace

 ....+....1....+....2....+....3....+....4....+....5....+....6....+....7..
 /E   NEW_INVOICE
 /:   NEW-PAGE PAGE1
 P9   ,, &ZUDI-CUST_INUN(14)& ,, &ZUDI-C_INV_DATE& ,, &ZUDI-INV_AMOUNT& ,,
      &ZUDI-DUE_DATE& ,, &ZUDI-DAYS_LATE(Z)& ,, &ZUDI-DIS_AMOUNT&
 /E   SAME_INVOICE
 P9   ,, &ZUDI-CUST_INUN(14)& ,, &ZUDI-C_INV_DATE& ,, &ZUDI-INV_AMOUNT& ,,
      &ZUDI-DUE_DATE& ,, &ZUDI-DAYS_LATE(Z)& ,, &ZUDI-DIS_AMOUNT&
 /*   ,, 21612698 ,, 11/30/94 ,, 21,946.65 ,, 12/15/94 ,, 22 ,, 419.69
 /*   ,, 21612698 ,, 11/30/94 ,, 21,946.65 ,, 12/15/94 ,, 22 ,, 419.69
 /*   ,, 21612698 ,, 11/30/94 ,, 21,946.65 ,, 12/15/94 ,, 22 ,, 419.69
 /*   ,, 21612698 ,, 11/30/94 ,, 21,946.65 ,, 12/15/94 ,, 22 ,, 419.69
 /*   ,, 21612698 ,, 11/30/94 ,, 21,946.65 ,, 12/15/94 ,, 22 ,, 419.69
 /*   ,, 21612698 ,, 11/30/94 ,, 21,946.65 ,, 12/15/94 ,, 22 ,, 419.69
 /*   ,, 21612698 ,, 11/30/94 ,, 21,946.65 ,, 12/15/94 ,, 22 ,, 419.69
 /*   ,, 21612698 ,, 11/30/94 ,, 21,946.65 ,, 12/15/94 ,, 22 ,, 419.69
 /*   ,, 21612698 ,, 11/30/94 ,, 21,946.65 ,, 12/15/94 ,, 22 ,, 419.69
 /*   ,, 21612698 ,, 11/30/94 ,, 21,946.65 ,, 12/15/94 ,, 22 ,, 419.69
 /*   ,, 21612698 ,, 11/30/94 ,, 21,946.65 ,, 12/15/94 ,, 22 ,, 419.69
 ------------------ Z_E2_UNDIS_INV -------------- Lines 1 - 18 / 32 -----------
```

FIGURE 6.16   Main window of Z_E2_UNDIS_INV
Copyright by SAP AG

NOTE The commented out lines in the Main window are used for testing purposes. To run repetitive tests of multiple pages, this is a good way to fill up the main window without having to re-generate test data each time.

Since we now know that the column header is not in MAIN, we look at other possibilities. In a search for a window just above MAIN, the upper dimension should be slightly less than MAIN at 15.75 cm. Window V6, "Discount Details" is a likely candidate at 15.10 cm. An examination of the text element shows us that this window is indeed the one that holds the "Discount Due Date" text.

Changing the Column Text

Modifying the text itself is simple. In Figure 6.17 the Text element for window V6 has two lines which print the texts that appear as column headers on the right half of the Main window in Figure 6.1. To effect the change, retype the text as it appears in Figure 6.18.

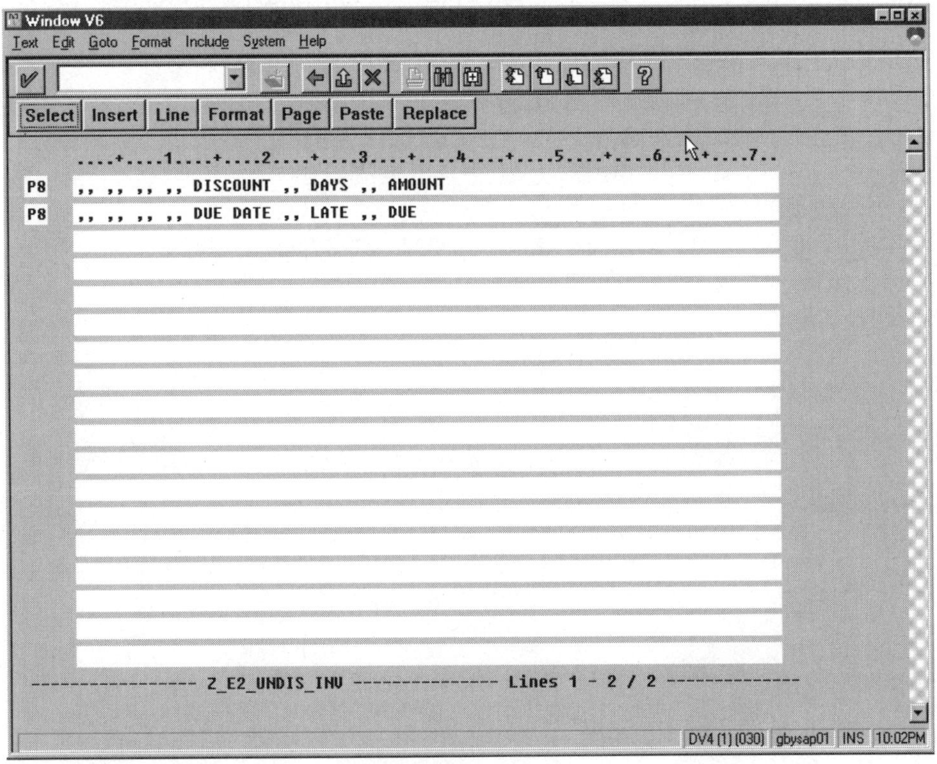

FIGURE 6.17   Text element for window V6
Copyright by SAP AG

What Are the Commas For?

Notice that there are pairs of commas in front of and between the texts in Figures 6.17 and 6.18. These are tab marks. On the first line of the window, SAPscript will initiate four tabs before writing the word "Due." Then it will tab again and write the next word "Days" and so on.

With a typical word processor and typing a letter, the tab marks can be set where required. The same is true with SAPscript. To see where the tabs are set we have to look at the paragraph associated with the line. In this case both these lines are using paragraph P8. If we look at the tab settings for paragraph P8 in Figure 6.19, tab number four is set at 10.12 cm. This means that the fourth tab will stop 10.12 cm from the left side of the window. The fourth tab is also set to center as are all of the other tabs. 10.12 cm from the left, positions our text exactly in the middle of the desired column in our layout set. Since Center is selected, the text will always appear centered about our tab (in the middle of the column).

```
Window V6                                                                    _ □ ×
Text  Edit  Goto  Format  Include  System  Help
 ✔ │                    ▼ │ ◄ │ ⇐ ⬆ ✕ │ 🗐 🔍 🔁 │ 🗇 🗇 🗇 🗇 │ ？
Select │ Insert │ Line │ Format │ Page │ Paste │ Replace
     ....+....1....+....2....+....3....+....4....+....5....+....6....+....7..
P8   ,, ,, ,, ,, DUE ,, DAYS ,, AMOUNT
P8   ,, ,, ,, ,, DATE ,, LATE ,, DUE




                              I




----------------- Z_E2_UNDIS_INV ----------------- Lines 1 - 2 / 2 -----------------
                                            DV4 (1) (030)  gbysap01  INS  10:05PM
```

FIGURE 6.18   Text element in window V6 after change
Copyright by SAP AG

WARNING

If using tabs to line up columns on a page, be careful that none of the texts is large enough that it extends over the other tabs. If it does, the tabs will not line up as expected. If the texts are given by symbols, be sure that the maximum length of the symbol will not overwrite an adjacent tab.

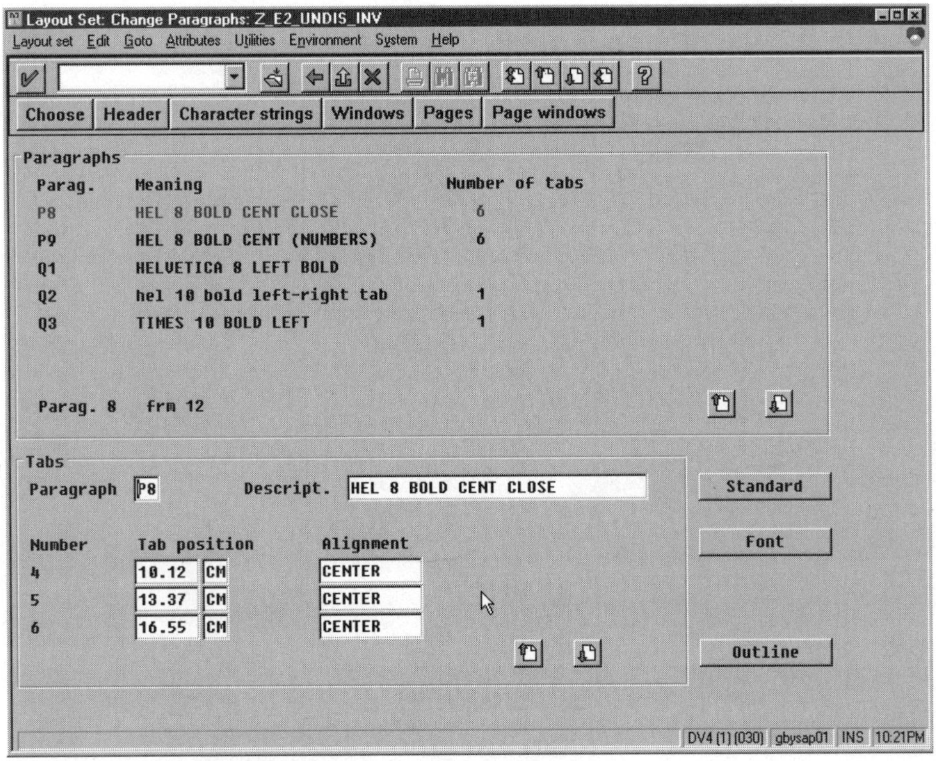

FIGURE 6.19 **Tab settings for paragraph P8**
Copyright by SAP AG

The Test Print utility in Figure 6.20 shows how the Due Date lines up in the middle of the column, although it does not appear to do so when viewed in the Text Element editor.

Changing the Footer

The final task is to change the company name that appears at the foot of the page. Changing this window is just like changing any other. The fact that this window appears below the Main window has no significance.

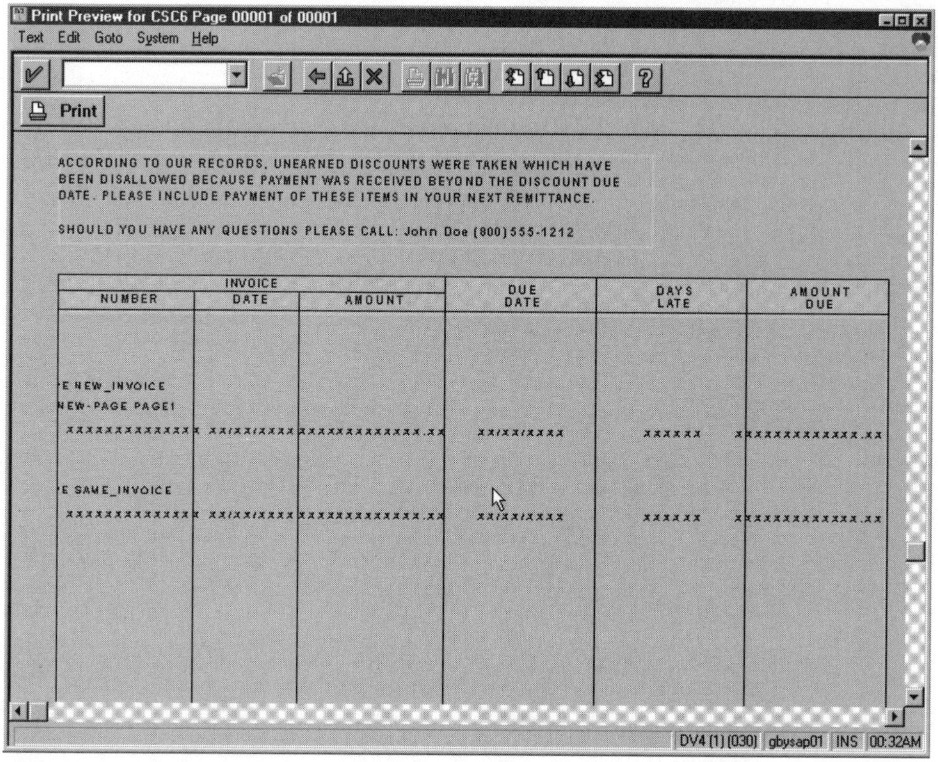

FIGURE 6.20 Test Print utility showing the column header
Copyright by SAP AG

Locating the Window

Finding this window is easy. Window V8 is called Remit To Info (see Figure 6.21). The upper margin of the Main window is 15.75 cm and its height is 9.9 cm. This means the bottom of main is 25.65 cm (15.75 + 9.9) from the top of the page. The window V8 starts just under the bottom of MAIN at 25.75 cm (1 mm below MAIN).

Changing the Text

The unchanged Text window is shown in Figure 6.22. As before, the new company name replaces the old. Notice that in this instance a single tab is used to line up the Remit To name and address information. Notice also that the character string format C1 is used to render the text Remit To:. The changed text element is shown in Figure 6.23.

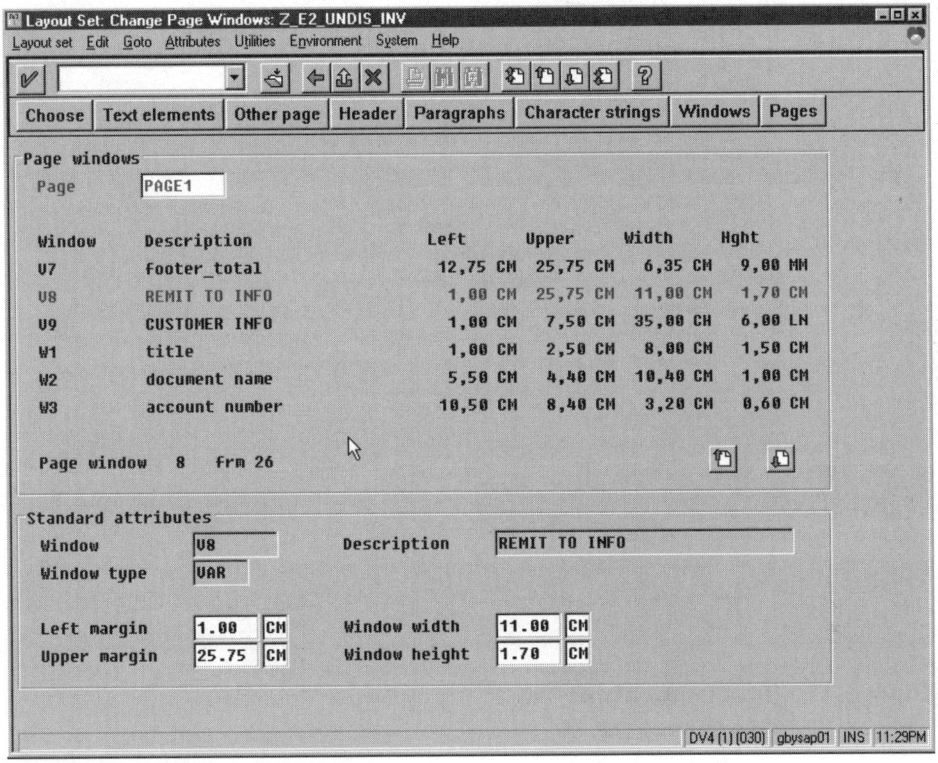

FIGURE 6.21   Page window V8
Copyright by SAP AG

Notice that there is a Text Element tag on the first line of the text element called Remit_To. This means that all the text below the tag (all of the text shown) is part this text element. If this tag were not present, all the lines would always appear in this window. Since the tag is present, the text will appear only if the text element Remit_To is specifically called from the print program. Text in a non-Main window that falls under the umbrella of a Text Element tag does not appear when the Test Print utility is used. If there were no Text Element tag, the text would appear when the Test Print utility was used. This allows the print program to control when the Remit To information is printed.

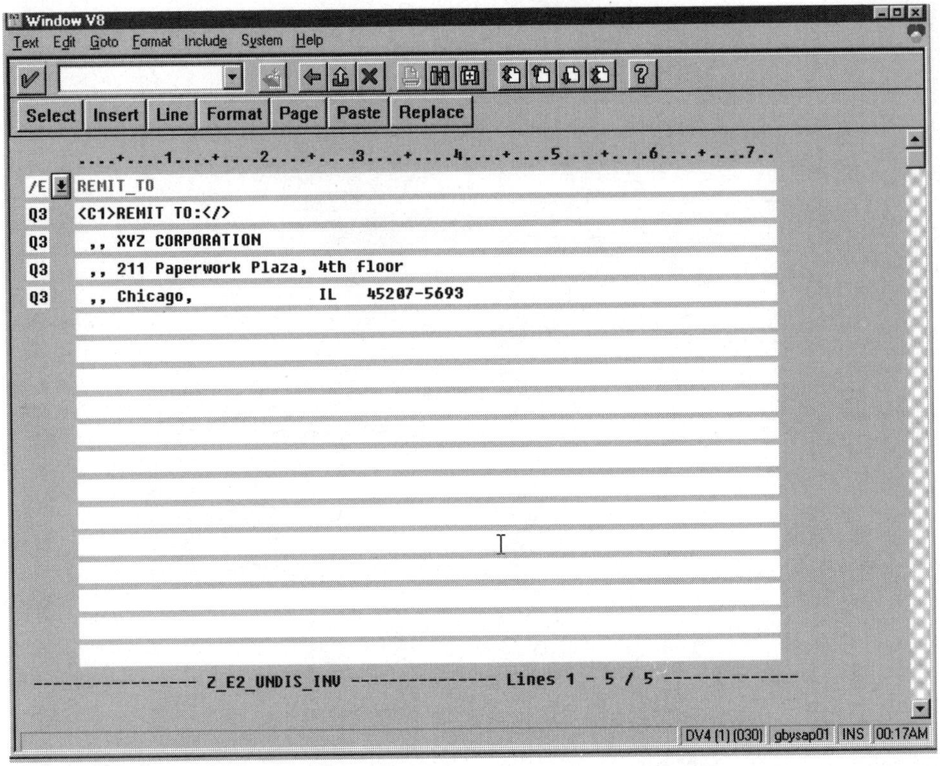

FIGURE 6.22   **Text element for V8**
Copyright by SAP AG

Tutorial 1 in Review

1. Finding the window in which the text prints can be a large part of the challenge.
2. It is possible to change many attributes of a correspondence without changing the print program.
3. The Test Print utility will show the relative location of each window.

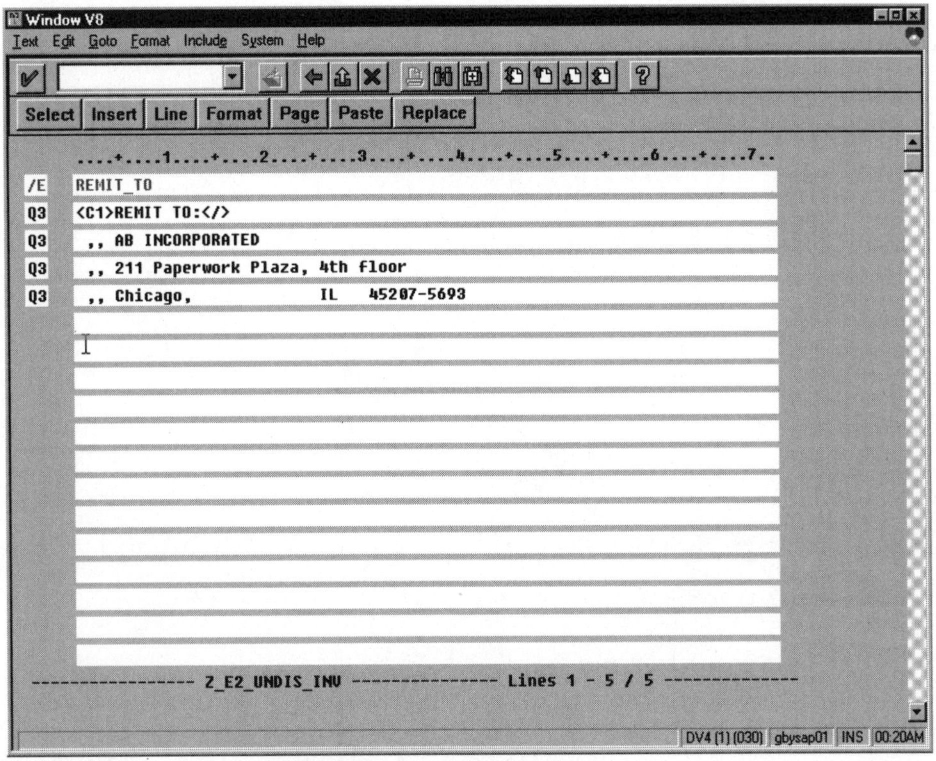

```
Window V8                                                              _ □ ×
Text  Edit  Goto  Format  Include  System  Help                          ●

 ✔  [              ▼] ◄ ← ⬆ ✕  ⎙ 🔍 🔲  🔲 🔲 🔲 🔲  ?

 Select │ Insert │ Line │ Format │ Page │ Paste │ Replace

      ....+....1....+....2....+....3....+....4....+....5....+....6....+....7..
 /E   REMIT_TO
 Q3   <C1>REMIT TO:</>
 Q3   ,, AB INCORPORATED
 Q3   ,, 211 Paperwork Plaza, 4th floor
 Q3   ,, Chicago,          IL    45207-5693


           I










------------------ Z_E2_UNDIS_INV --------------- Lines 1 - 5 / 5 ---------------

                                           DV4 (1) (030)  gbysap01  INS  00:20AM
```

FIGURE 6.23   Text element for V8 with change
            Copyright by SAP AG

Tutorial 2

Changing an
ABAP Report So That
It Calls a Layout Set

The Requirement

In this tutorial we will change a standard ABAP report to one that calls a layout set. Creating custom reports in ABAP is a common task. Many times, the requirement to use features in the report that necessitate the use of a layout set comes after the report is already written. Here we will build the layout set and change the ABAP report so that it calls the new layout set instead of issuing a series of Write statements.

The Changes

In this example tutorial I have created a standard ABAP report which produces a "Training Plan Confirmation" as shown in Figure 7.1. Presume that we have been asked to change the look of the report so that it appears as shown in Figure 7.2. The following changes are necessary:

1. Put the Title and Detail Line header in shaded boxes.
2. Change the Courses Offered line so that there are two columns and use Courier 8 as the font.

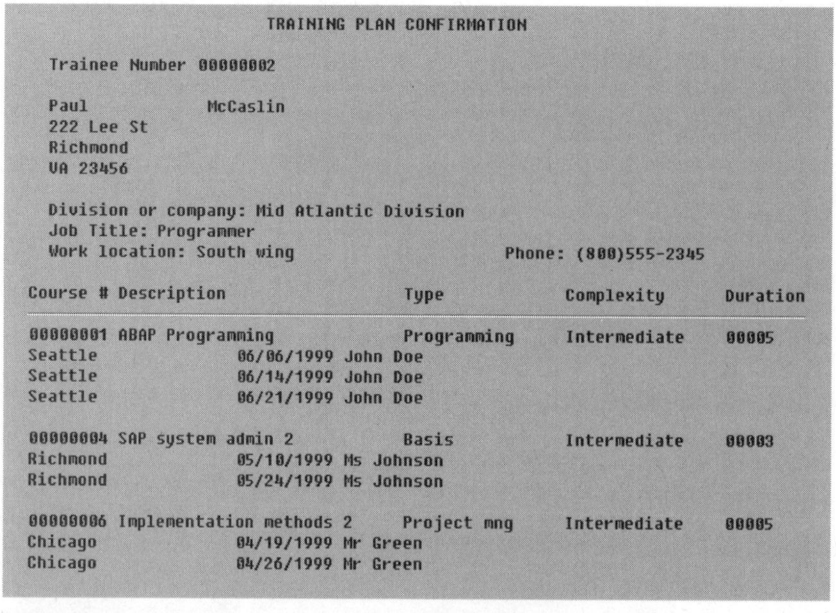

```
                         TRAINING PLAN CONFIRMATION

  Trainee Number 00000002

  Paul           McCaslin
  222 Lee St
  Richmond
  VA 23456

  Division or company: Mid Atlantic Division
  Job Title: Programmer
  Work location: South wing                          Phone: (800)555-2345

Course # Description                   Type            Complexity      Duration
-------------------------------------------------------------------------------
00000001 ABAP Programming              Programming     Intermediate    00005
Seattle              06/06/1999 John Doe
Seattle              06/14/1999 John Doe
Seattle              06/21/1999 John Doe

00000004 SAP system admin 2            Basis           Intermediate    00003
Richmond             05/10/1999 Ms Johnson
Richmond             05/24/1999 Ms Johnson

00000006 Implementation methods 2      Project mng     Intermediate    00005
Chicago              04/19/1999 Mr Green
Chicago              04/26/1999 Mr Green
```

FIGURE 7.1 Training Plan Confirmation in ABAP only

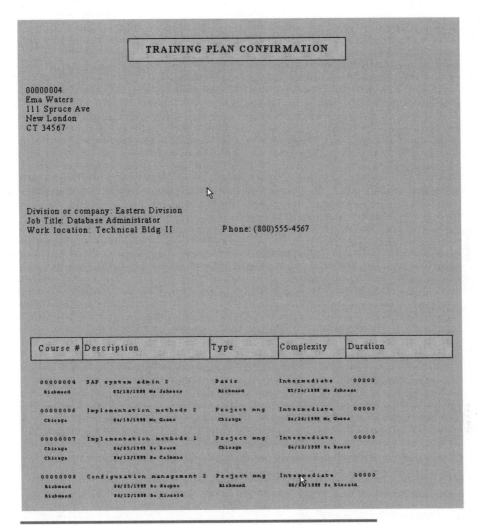

FIGURE 7.2   Training Plan Confirmation using layout set

The Program

The Program and Tables Used

The program name for the "Training Plan Confirmation" report is ZTRNCONF. Basically, the user enters a trainee number range via Select–Options and the program returns a confirmation report for each trainee found. Four custom tables are used to create this example:

ZCOURSES—Listing of courses

Field	Data element	Type length	Description
COURSE_NUM (key)	SETTXTNUM	Char 8	Course number
DESCRIP	UKRSBE	Char 30	Course description
COURSE_TYP	TEXT15	Char 15	Type of course
COMPLEXITY	TEXT15	Char 15	Complexity of course
DURATION	STAT_PLDUC	Numc 5	Duration in days

Sample contents:

COURSE_NUM	DESCRIP	COURSE_TYP	COMPLEXITY	DURATION
00000001	ABAP Programming	Programming	Intermediate	00005
00000002	Unix system administration 1	System admin	Intermediate	00003
00000003	Database 101	Database admin	Intermediate	00003
00000004	SAP system admin2	Basis	Intermediate	00003
00000005	SAP system admin 1	Basis	Intermediate	00003
00000006	Implementation methods 2	Project mng	Intermediate	00005
00000007	Implementation methods 1	Project mng	Intermediate	00003

ZOFFERINGS—Course offerings (course scheduled dates and instructor)

Field	Data element	Type length	Description
COURSE_NUM (key)	SETTXTNUM	Char 8	Course number
LOCATION (key)	CCBEZ	Char 20	Location of course
START_DATE (key)	CO_GSTRS	Dats 8	Course start date
INSTRUCTOR (key)	ISTXT_T	Char 40	The course instructor

Sample contents:

COURSE_NUM	LOCATION	START_DATE	INSTRUCTOR
00000001	Seattle	06/06/1999	John Doe
00000001	Seattle	06/14/1999	John Doe
00000001	Seattle	06/21/1999	John Doe
00000002	Detroit	06/07/1999	Mary Smith
00000002	Detroit	06/14/1999	Mary Smith
00000002	Detroit	06/21/1999	Mary Smith
00000003	Atlanta	05/10/1999	Dr Jones

ZTRAINEE—List of employees/trainees

Field	Data element	Type length	Description
TRAINE_NUM (key)	BDEPERNR	Char 8	Trainee ID number
FIRST_NAME	FL_FNAME	Char 15	Trainee first name
LAST_NAME	NAME	Char 35	Trainee last name
DIV_CMPNY	KOFMA	Char 26	Division or Company
TRN_TITLE	STLTX	Char 25	Title of trainee
STREET_ADD	XUSTRAS	Char 30	Trainee street address
CITY	CCBEZ	Char 20	Trainee city
STATE	AKLAS_VA	Char 2	Trainee state
ZIP_CODE	PLZ	Char 10	Trainee zip code
WORK_LOC	STRASSE	Char 30	Trainee work location
PHONE	RSX_08	Char 13	Trainee phone

Sample contents:

TRAINE_NUM	FIRST_NAME	LAST_NAME	DIV_CMPNY	TRN_TITLE
STREET_ADD	CITY	STATE	ZIP_CODE	WORK_LOC
PHONE				
00000001	John	Cormack	Eastern Division	Programmer
123 Elm st	Boston	MA	12345	Technical Bldg
(800)555-1234				
00000002	Paul	McCaslin	Mid Atlantic Division	Programmer
222 Lee St	Richmond	VA	23456	South wing
(800)555-2345				
00000003	Lucas	Harper	Mid Atlantic Division	Project Manager
333 Harper St	Richmond	VA	45678	South wing
(800)555-3456				

ZTRNPLAN—Trainee vs course number

Field	Data element	Type length	Description
TRAINE_NUM (key)	BDEPERNR	Char 8	Trainee ID number
COURSE_NUM (key)	SETTXTNUM	Char 8	Course number
COMPLETED	QKZQMSM	Char 1	Completed? Y/N
DATE_COMP	SWL_AED	Dats 8	Date course complete
PRIORITY	PRIO_TERHK	Char 1	Priority of course
DATE_REQ	SIN_DAT_AC	Dats 8	Date required by

continued on next page

Sample contents:

TRAINE_NUM	COURSE_NUM	COMPLETED	DATE_COMP	PRIORITY	DATE_REQ
00000001	00000001	X	06/10/1998	2	08/01/1999

TRAINE_NUM	COURSE_NUM	COMPLETED	DATE_COMP	PRIORITY	DATE_REQ
00000001	00000004		00/00/0000	2	08/01/1999
00000001	00000006		00/00/0000	2	08/01/1999
00000001	00000008		00/00/0000	2	08/01/1999
00000001	00000009		00/00/0000	2	08/01/1999
00000001	00000010		00/00/0000	2	08/01/1999
00000002	00000001		00/00/0000	2	08/01/1999
00000002	00000004		00/00/0000	2	08/01/1999

Source Code

The source code for ZTRNCONF looks like this :

```
1   ************************************************
2   *--------------------------------------*
3   Report  ztrnconf
4   Author: M, Buchanan
5   *--------------------------------------*
6   *
7   *
8   *--------------------------------------*
9   REPORT ZTRNCONF
10     NO STANDARD PAGE HEADING
11     LINE-SIZE  80
12     LINE-COUNT 65(0).
13  ************************************************
14  *Tables
15  TABLES:
16  ZCOURSES,    "courses
17  ZOFFERINGS,  "courses offerings
18  ZTRAINEE,    "trainees
19  ZTRNPLAN.    "training plans
20
21  DATA: I_TRNPLAN LIKE ZTRNPLAN OCCURS   0 WITH HEADER LINE.
22  DATA OLD_TRAINE_NUM LIKE ZTRNPLAN-TRAINE_NUM.
23
24  SELECT-OPTIONS P_TRAINE FOR ZTRAINEE-TRAINE_NUM DEFAULT
25  '00000001' TO '00000007'.
```

```
26  *---------------------------------------*
27  *select
28
29  SELECT * FROM  ZTRNPLAN
30         WHERE  TRAINE_NUM IN P_TRAINE.
31     MOVE-CORRESPONDING ZTRNPLAN TO I_TRNPLAN.
32     APPEND I_TRNPLAN.
33  ENDSELECT.
34
35  *---------------------------------------*
36  *process selection
37
38  CLEAR OLD_TRAINE_NUM.
39  SORT I_TRNPLAN.
40
41  LOOP AT I_TRNPLAN.
42     IF I_TRNPLAN-TRAINE_NUM NE OLD_TRAINE_NUM.
43         PERFORM NEW_TRAINEE.
44     ENDIF.
45     PERFORM WRITE_PLAN_ITEM.
46     PERFORM WRITE_OFFERINGS.
47     MOVE I_TRNPLAN-TRAINE_NUM TO OLD_TRAINE_NUM.
48  ENDLOOP.
49
50  *&-------------------------------------*
51     PERFORMS
52  *&-------------------------------------*
53  *&-------------------------------------*
54  *& Form NEW_TRAINEE
55  *&-------------------------------------*
56
57  FORM NEW_TRAINEE.
58     SELECT SINGLE * FROM ZTRAINEE
59         WHERE TRAINE_NUM = I_TRNPLAN-TRAINE_NUM.
60     IF SY-SUBRC NE 0.
61         WRITE 'Trainee information not found.'.
62     ENDIF.
63     NEW-PAGE.
64     WRITE: 27 'TRAINING PLAN CONFIRMATION',
65     /,/05 'Trainee Number', I_TRNPLAN-TRAINE_NUM,
66     /,/05 ZTRAINEE-FIRST_NAME, ZTRAINEE-LAST_NAME,
67     /05 ZTRAINEE-STREET_ADD,
68     /05 ZTRAINEE-CITY,
69     /05 ZTRAINEE-STATE, ZTRAINEE-ZIP_CODE,
70     /,/05 'Division or company:', ZTRAINEE-DIV_CMPNY,
```

```
71    /05 'Job Title:', ZTRAINEE-TRN_TITLE,
72    /05 'Work location:', ZTRAINEE-WORK_LOC, 'Phone:',
         ZTRAINEE
73    -PHONE,
74    /,/03 'Course #',
75       12 'Description',
76       41 'Type',
77       57 'Complexity',
78       73 'Duration'.
79    ULINE AT /3.
80
81 ENDFORM.
82
83 *&-------------------------------------*
84 *& Form WRITE_PLAN_ITEM
85 *&-------------------------------------*
86 FORM WRITE_PLAN_ITEM.
87    SELECT SINGLE * FROM  ZCOURSES
88       WHERE  COURSE_NUM  = I_TRNPLAN-COURSE_NUM.
89
90       WRITE: /03 ZCOURSES-COURSE_NUM,
91       12 ZCOURSES-DESCRIP,
92       41 ZCOURSES-COURSE_TYP,
93       57 ZCOURSES-COMPLEXITY,
94       73 ZCOURSES-DURATION.
95
96 ENDFORM.      "WRITE_PLAN_ITEM
97
98 *&-------------------------------------*
99 *& Form  WRITE_OFFERINGS
100 *&-------------------------------------*
101 FORM WRITE_OFFERINGS.
102
103    SELECT * FROM  ZOFFERINGS
104          WHERE  COURSE_NUM  = I_TRNPLAN-COURSE_NUM.
105       WRITE: /03 ZOFFERINGS-LOCATION,
106          ZOFFERINGS-START_DATE,
107          ZOFFERINGS-INSTRUCTOR.
108    ENDSELECT.
109    WRITE /.
110 ENDFORM.      "WRITE_OFFERINGS
```

CD-ROM

CE008 ZTRNCONF

Process Description

ZTRNCONF includes only what is needed to illustrate the point. Error handling and other elements that might be expected in a production report have not been included. The processing steps are as follows.

Step 1. Lines 29–33. Select the records from ZTRNPLAN that have a trainee number within the range entered by the user and move them to internal table I_TRNPLAN. ZTRNPLAN basically holds the trainee number and the courses the trainee needs to attend.

Step 2. Lines 42–43. For each new user, a new page is issued and the header information about the user is printed.

Step 3. Line 45. Write a Detail record using the course information.

Step 4. Line 46. In ZOFFERINGS, select course offerings that match the course number from Step 3. Write out the scheduled course (offerings) information. (There may be more than one.)

Steps two through four are within a loop, so a separate report is generated for each trainee.

The New Layout Set

Using Structures to Pass Information

As it exists currently, the program ZTRNCONF writes directly from fields that have been returned by select statements (i.e. ZTRAINEE-FIRST_NAME) and fields within an internal table (i.e. I_TRNPLAN-TRAINE_NUM). Although we *could* refer to the selected transparent table fields in our layout set, this is rarely done in practice. Typically values are passed via structures. Usually we can find a working structure that will suit this purpose.

To provide continuity in our example four structures for passing values to the layout set have been created: ZSCOURSES, ZSTRAINEE, ZSOFFERINGS, and ZTRNPLAN. All values to be printed will be moved to these structures by the print program before calling the layout set (with WRITE_FORM). The layout set will refer to the field in the structure as its symbol.

Creating the New Layout Set

To create the layout set go to **Tools → Word processing → Layout set** (transaction SE71). Enter the layout set name, ZFTRNCONF, and E for the language, as shown in Figure 7.3.

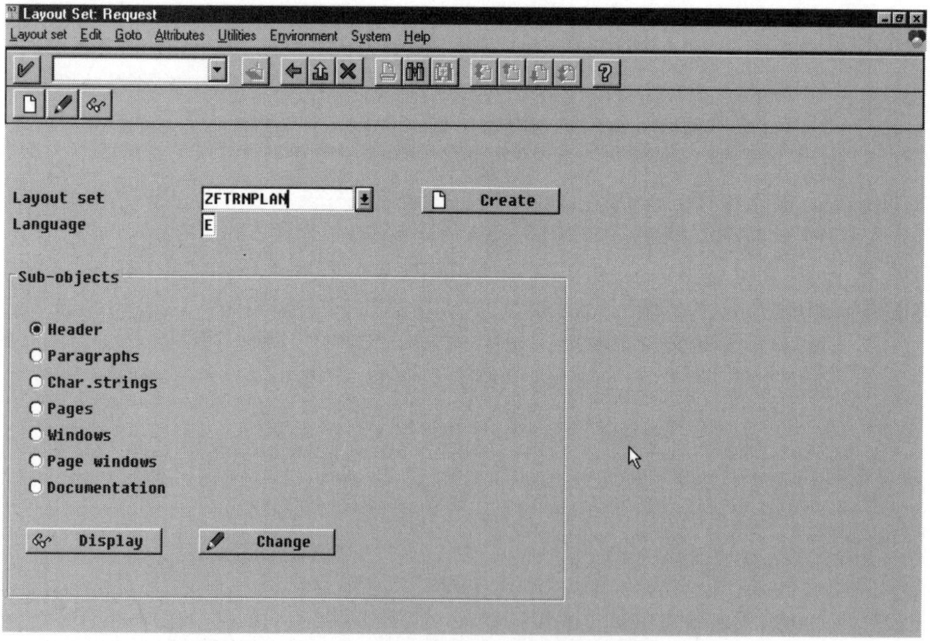

FIGURE 7.3   Creating a layout set called ZRFTRNCONF
     Copyright by SAP AG

Layout sets (form objects) must be named within the customer name range (thus the Z). The rest is personal preference. I used the F because it is a Form object and TRNCONF to associate it with the program.

Press the **Create** button and get a message indicating that the object does not exist in the client. Acknowledge this with **Enter** (or green check icon), which will proceed to the Change Header screen.

At the Change Header screen enter a description as shown in Figure 7.4 and press the **Save** icon.

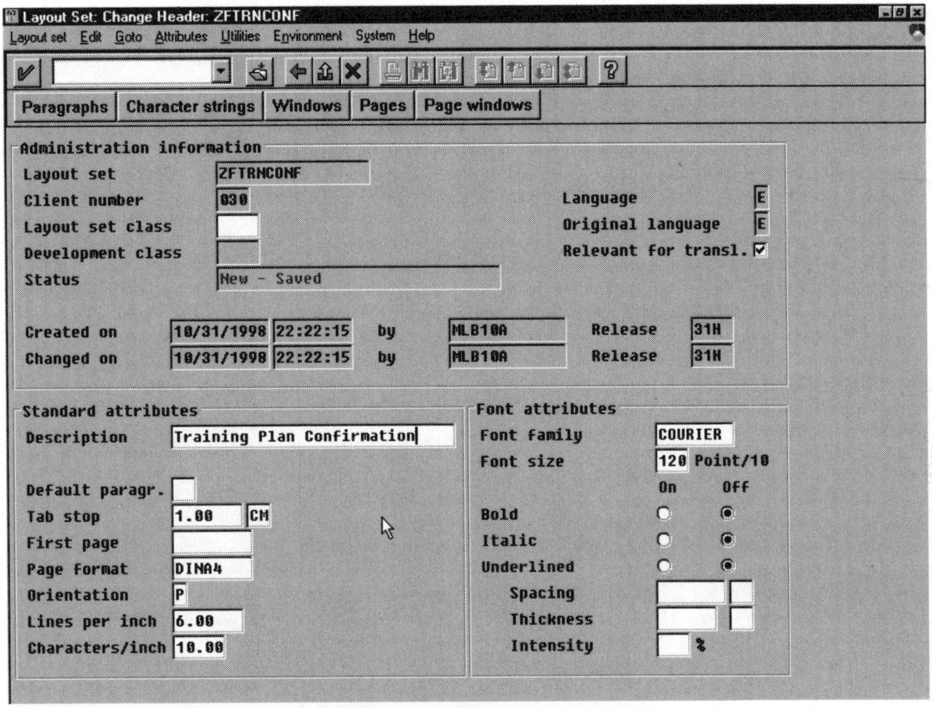

FIGURE 7.4 Layout set ZFTRNCONF Header screen
Copyright by SAP AG

Creating Paragraphs

After saving the header, select **Goto → Paragraphs** (or press the **Paragraph** button) to get to the Change Paragraphs screen shown in Figure 7.5.

The Change paragraphs screen is empty because we have not yet created any paragraphs (or paragraph elements). When we define a paragraph element, we are defining the characteristics of a hypothetical paragraph, not the actual paragraph text. Once a paragraph is defined, it can be associated with the actual text when the text elements are created.

To create the first paragraph element, select **Edit → Create element**. A window will appear requesting a paragraph name and description. Paragraph names are two characters. The first character of the name must be a letter and there must be some type of description included. Enter the P1 and a description as shown in Figure 7.6.

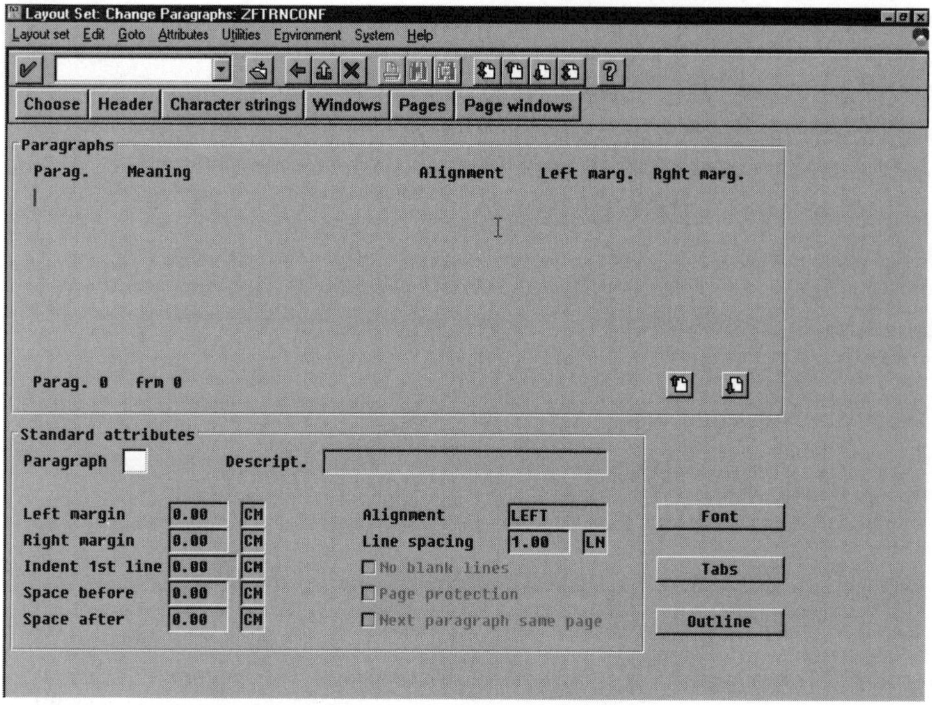

Layout Set: Change Paragraphs: ZFTRNCONF

Layout set | Edit | Goto | Attributes | Utilities | Environment | System | Help

| Choose | Header | Character strings | Windows | Pages | Page windows |

Paragraphs

Parag.   Meaning   Alignment   Left marg.   Rght marg.

Parag. 0   frm 0

Standard attributes

Paragraph [ ]   Descript. [   ]

Left margin   0.00   CM   Alignment   LEFT   [Font]
Right margin   0.00   CM   Line spacing   1.00   LN
Indent 1st line 0.00 CM   ☐ No blank lines   [Tabs]
Space before   0.00   CM   ☐ Page protection
Space after   0.00   CM   ☐ Next paragraph same page   [Outline]

FIGURE 7.5   Change paragraphs for ZFTRNCONF
            Copyright by SAP AG

After identifying the name and description, we need to define a font associated with the paragraph. To do this, select the **Font** button shown in the lower right corner of Figure 7.6. This will change the lower portion of the screen to show the font attributes of the paragraph. Currently there are none. To enter a font, position the cursor in the Font field and select the dropdown arrow to get the possible entries for the field. Select **Times 120** as shown in Figure 7.7 by double clicking.

If all the fonts needed are not visible, select the icon with the green plus sign at the bottom of the select options screen shown in Figure 7.7.

NOTE

Because this is the paragraph we will use to render the document title, we will select bold letters by clicking the **Bold** on radio button. Also click the **Standard** button and change Alignment from Left to Center and Line Spacing to 0.75 LN. This will allow the report title to fit squarely in the center of our box. These adjustments to the standard attributes are not necessary for the other paragraphs.

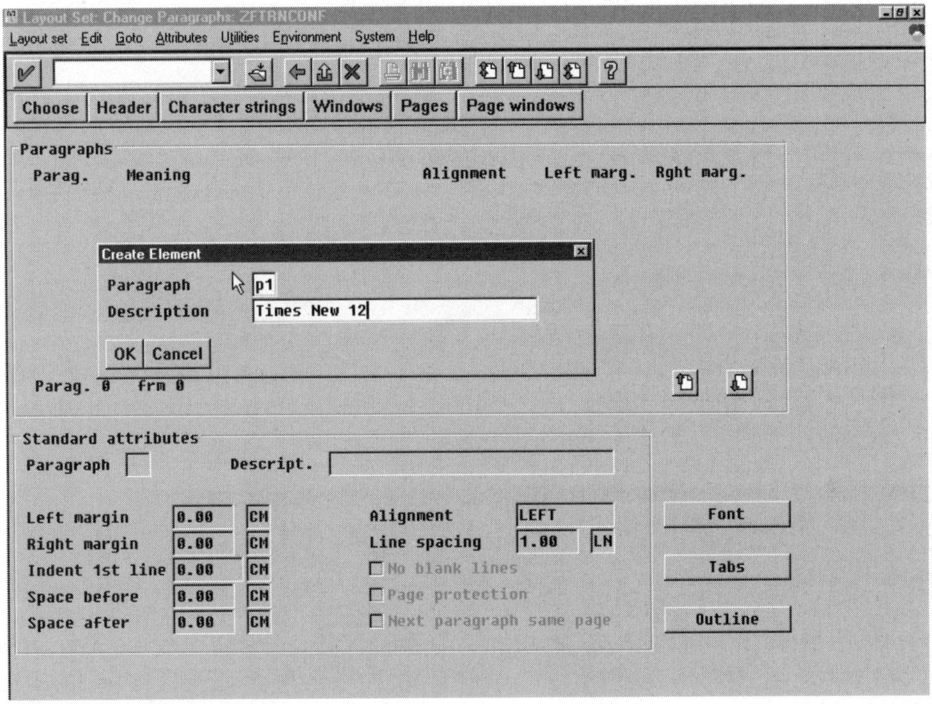

FIGURE 7.6   Creating a new paragraph
Copyright by SAP AG

Create two more paragraphs P2 and P3, in the same manner, P2 should be Courier 080 and P3 should be Times 140. The Paragraph screen should now look like the one in Figure 7.8.

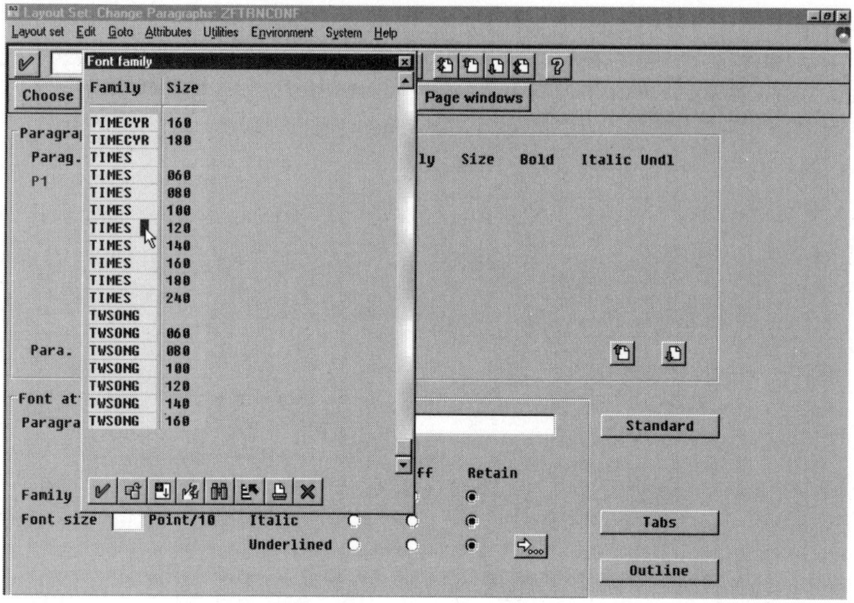

FIGURE 7.7   Selecting a font
Copyright by SAP AG

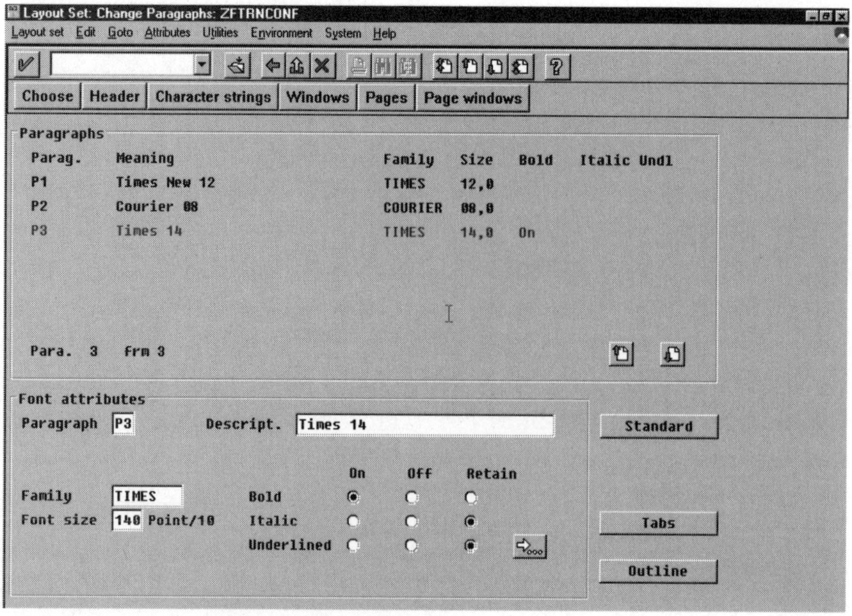

FIGURE 7.8   Paragraphs P1, P2 and P3
Copyright by SAP AG

Pages

One or more pages must be defined in every layout set. In our case two types of pages will be needed for the "Training Plan Confirmation." The first will include the trainee's name, address, phone number and other information as shown in Figure 7.2. It is not necessary to include anything other than the name on subsequent pages. Subsequent pages would be needed if a trainee had enough courses in the training plan to fill the first page of the report and more. We will call our two types of pages FPAGE (for first page) and NPAGE (for n subsequent pages).

To create a page select **Goto → Pages**. This will open the Change Pages screen and position our cursor on the Name field. Enter NPAGE for the page name and press **Enter**. Next enter a Description and a Next Page. The next page should be NPAGE. This means that if we have filled up a subsequent page the next type of page we want to use is NPAGE (the same type of page). Press the **Save** button.

Add another page definition in the same way but this time call it FPAGE. Next page should be NPAGE. The Change Pages screen should now appear as it does in Figure 7.9.

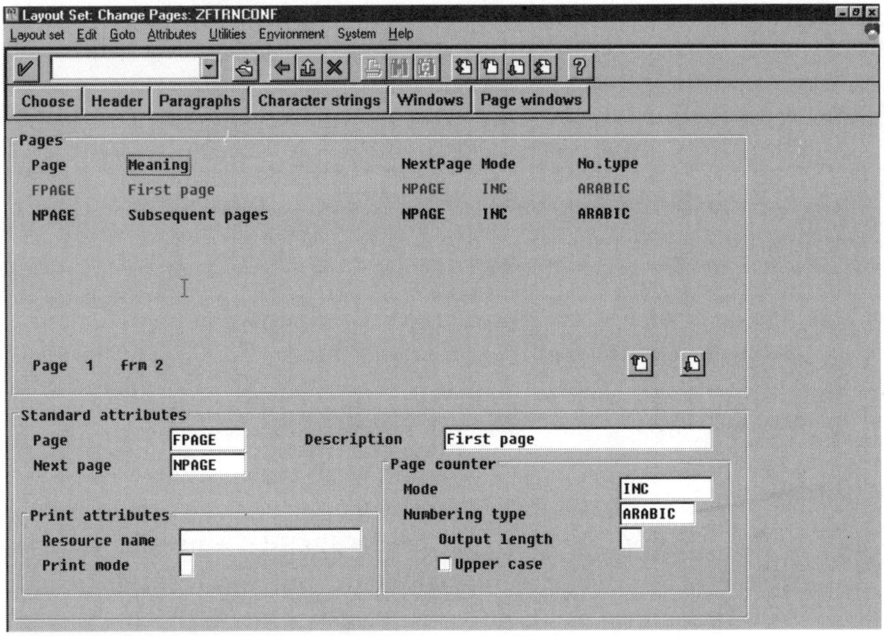

FIGURE 7.9   Pages for ZFTRNCONF
Copyright by SAP AG

Default Values

Return to the Header by selecting **Goto → Header** and enter P1 as the Default paragraph and FPAGE as the first page. Unless another specification is made, P1 will always be used as the default paragraph. The report will start with FPAGE.

Change the page format to suit the printer. In my case this is Letter. When complete, the header screen will appear as it does in Figure 7.10.

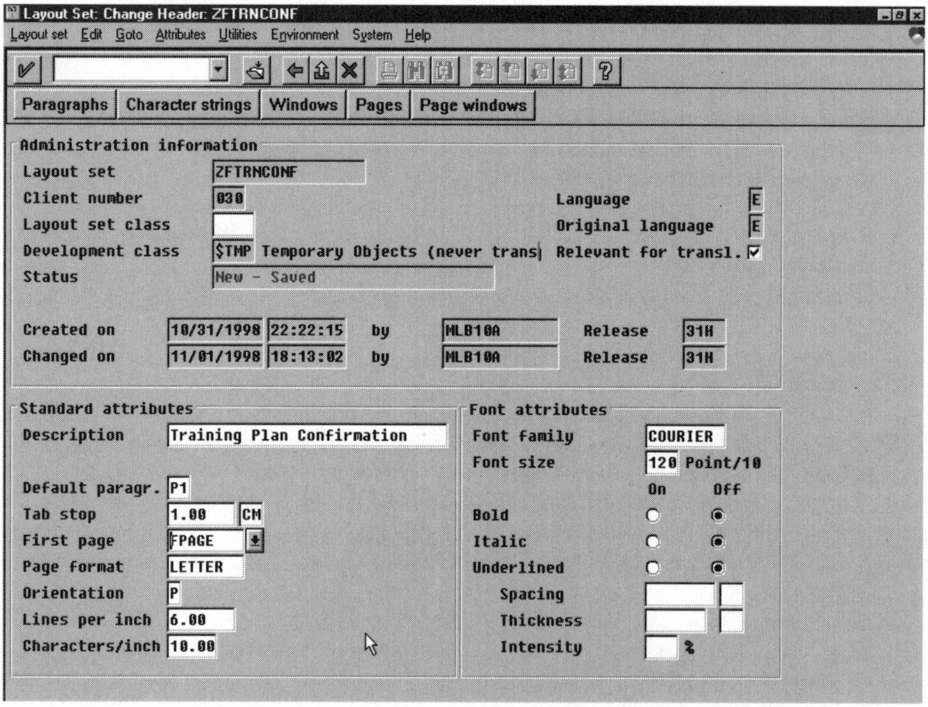

FIGURE 7.10   Header with default paragraph, first page and page format
Copyright by SAP AG

Windows

We will need five windows for our first page (FPAGE). Subsequent pages (NPAGE) will use some of the same windows but omit detail header information not needed on the continuing pages. Our first page will be arranged as shown in Figure 7.11.

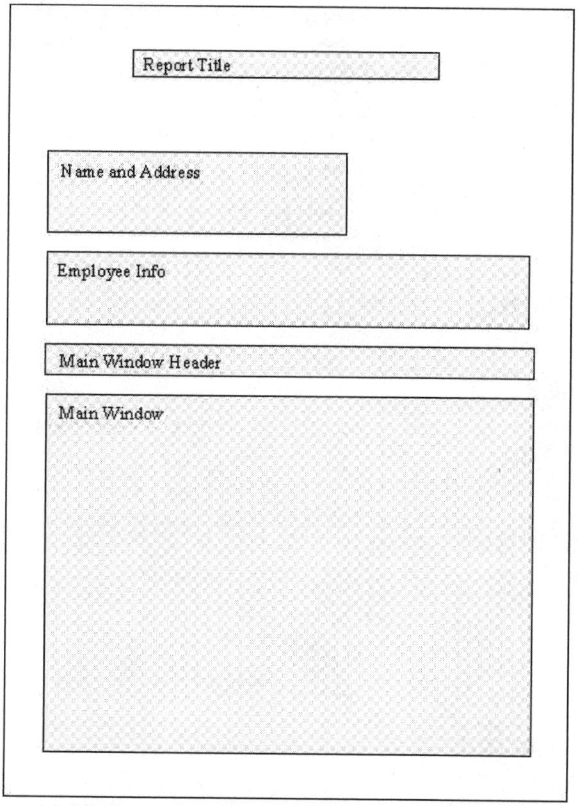

FIGURE 7.11   Report layout for ZFTRNCONF

Subsequent pages will look the same but with the main window raised and the address and employee information omitted.

To create the first window select **Goto → Windows**. This will bring us to the Change Windows screen. The Main window has already been added for us by default. Select **Edit → Create element** to add the first of our windows. Enter a name and description. I have called it TITLE for report title, shown in Figure 7.11. In the Report Title window, we will use our large font so make the default paragraph P3. The window type should be CONST because the value in the Title window does not change. In the other windows we will have information that changes so we will use VAR in the remaining windows.

Do the same for the other windows. Use P1 as the default paragraph. Create an additional window identical to NAME called NAME2. This will be used on NPAGE as the "smaller" name window. When complete, the Change Windows screen should appear as it does in Figure 7.12.

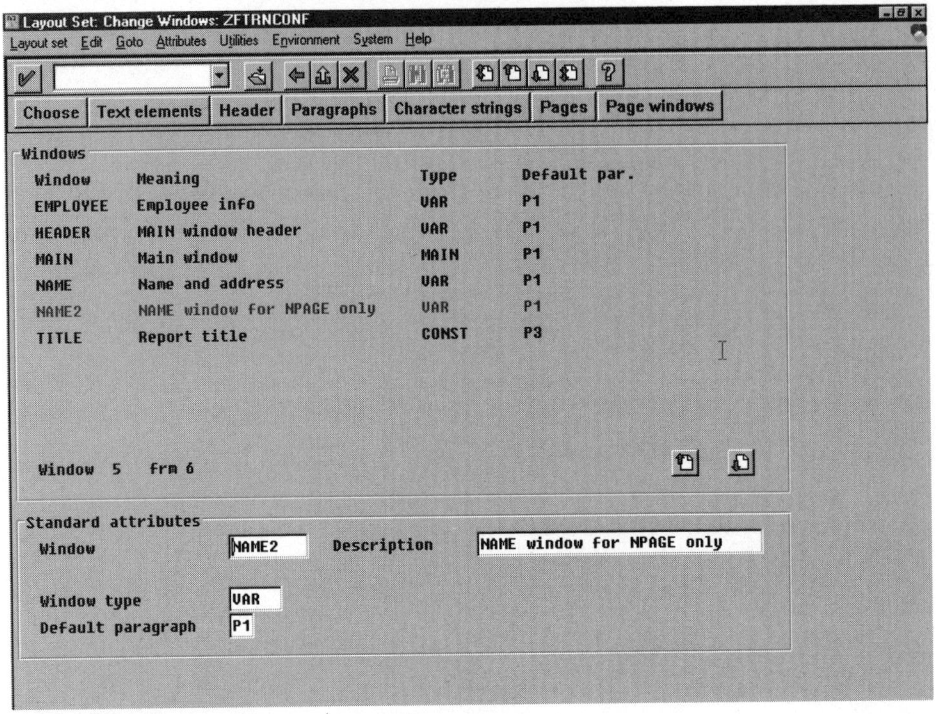

Window 5   frm 6

Standard attributes

Window   NAME2   Description   NAME window for NPAGE only

Window type   VAR
Default paragraph P1

FIGURE 7.12 Windows for ZFTRNCONF
Copyright by SAP AG

Since P1 is the default paragraph for the entire layout set, we could have left the Default Paragraph field blank for those that are defaulted to P1.

NOTE

Page Windows

In creating Page windows, we are defining which windows go with which pages and where to put them. To get to the Change Page Windows screen select **Goto → Page windows**. Once in the Change Page Windows screen select **Edit → Create element**. There will then be a prompt to select from the list of windows defined (see Figure 7.13). Start by selecting TITLE.

Once the window has been selected (TITLE), we have to enter the location and size of the window. Make the following entries:

Left margin	5.75	cm
Upper margin	1	cm
Window width	10	cm
Window Height	1	cm

We want the Titlebox to appear 1 cm from the top of the page. It will be 1 cm high, 10 cm wide and begin 5.75 cm from the left side of the page (see Figure 7.14).

NOTE Why 5.75 cm? Because we know the page width is 215 mm (transaction SPAD). Subtract the intended box width (10) from the page width (21.5 cm), which leaves 11.5 cm. Half of that (half for each side) is 5.75 cm.

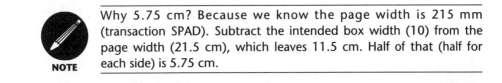

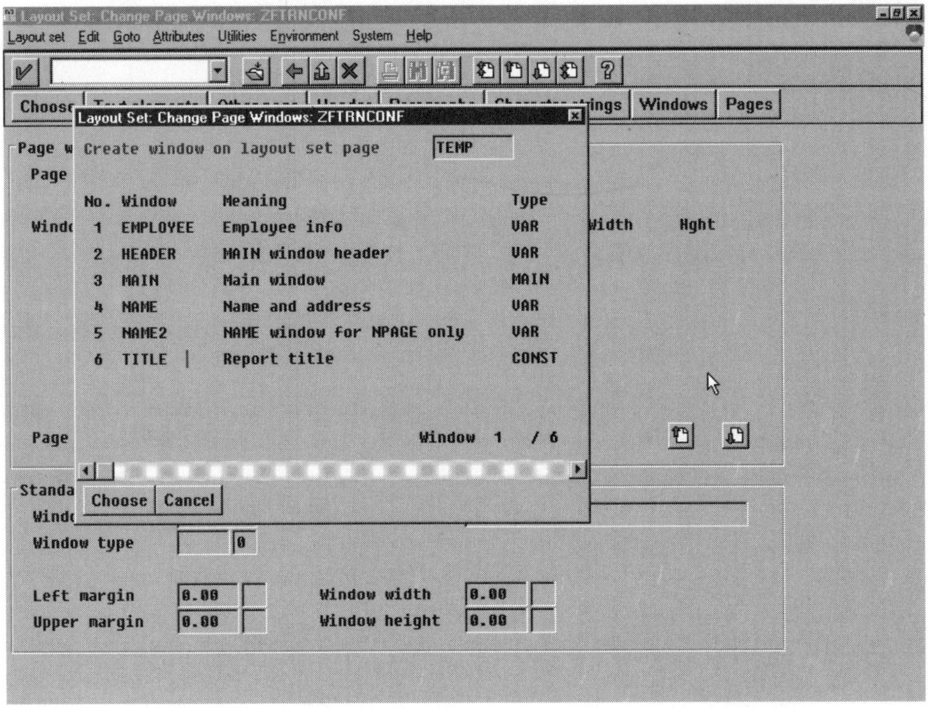

FIGURE 7.13   Select a window to create a Page window definition
Copyright by SAP AG

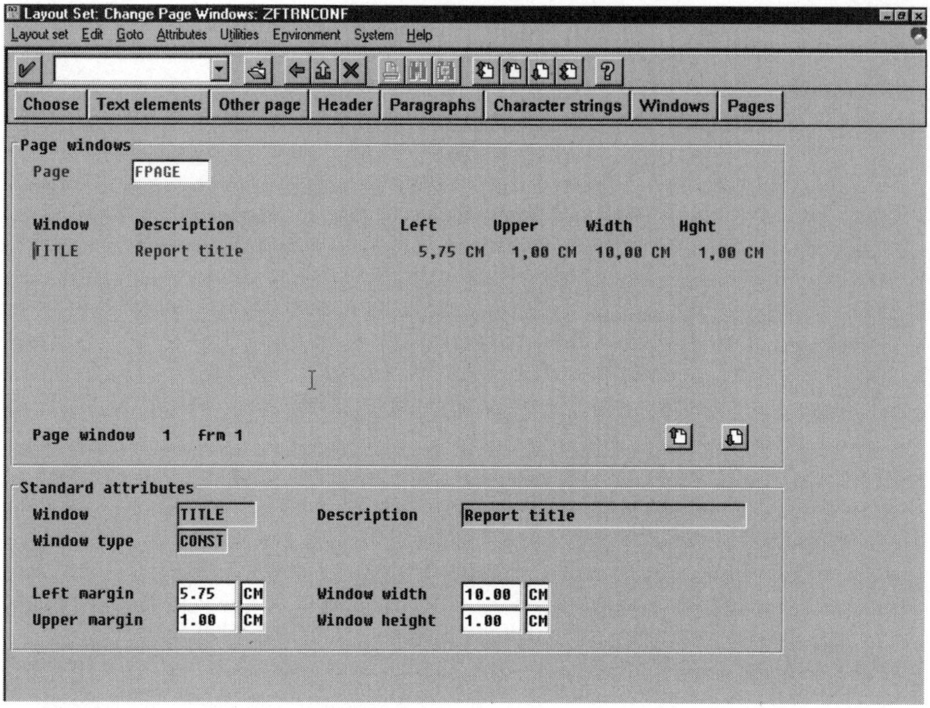

```
Layout Set: Change Page Windows: ZFTRNCONF                          _ □ ×
Layout set  Edit  Goto  Attributes  Utilities  Environment  System  Help

  ✓ [          ] ▼  ❮  ⬅ ⬆ ✕   ▣ ▥ ▤   ❂ ❂ ❂ ❂   ?

 Choose │ Text elements │ Other page │ Header │ Paragraphs │ Character strings │ Windows │ Pages

 ┌─ Page windows ─────────────────────────────────────────────────────────┐
 │  Page       [FPAGE ]                                                     │
 │                                                                         │
 │  Window     Description              Left      Upper    Width     Hght  │
 │  TITLE      Report title            5,75 CM   1,00 CM  10,00 CM  1,00 CM│
 │                                                                         │
 │                           I                                             │
 │                                                                         │
 │  Page window   1   frm 1                              [▣]     [▣]       │
 └─────────────────────────────────────────────────────────────────────────┘
 ┌─ Standard attributes ──────────────────────────────────────────────────┐
 │  Window      [TITLE ]      Description     [Report title            ]   │
 │  Window type [CONST ]                                                   │
 │                                                                         │
 │  Left margin  [5.75 ][CM]   Window width   [10.00][CM]                  │
 │  Upper margin [1.00 ][CM]   Window height  [1.00 ][CM]                  │
 └─────────────────────────────────────────────────────────────────────────┘
```

FIGURE 7.14   Page window for TITLE
     Copyright by SAP AG

Create the other FPAGE Page windows in an identical manner using the following values:

Window height	Left margin	Upper margin	Window width	
NAME	1	3	17	4
EMPLOYEE	1	8	19.5	3
HEADER	1	12	19.5	1
MAIN	1	13.5	19.5	13.4

(All values should be in cm.)

The completed Change Page Windows screen for FPAGE should appear as shown in Figure 7.15.

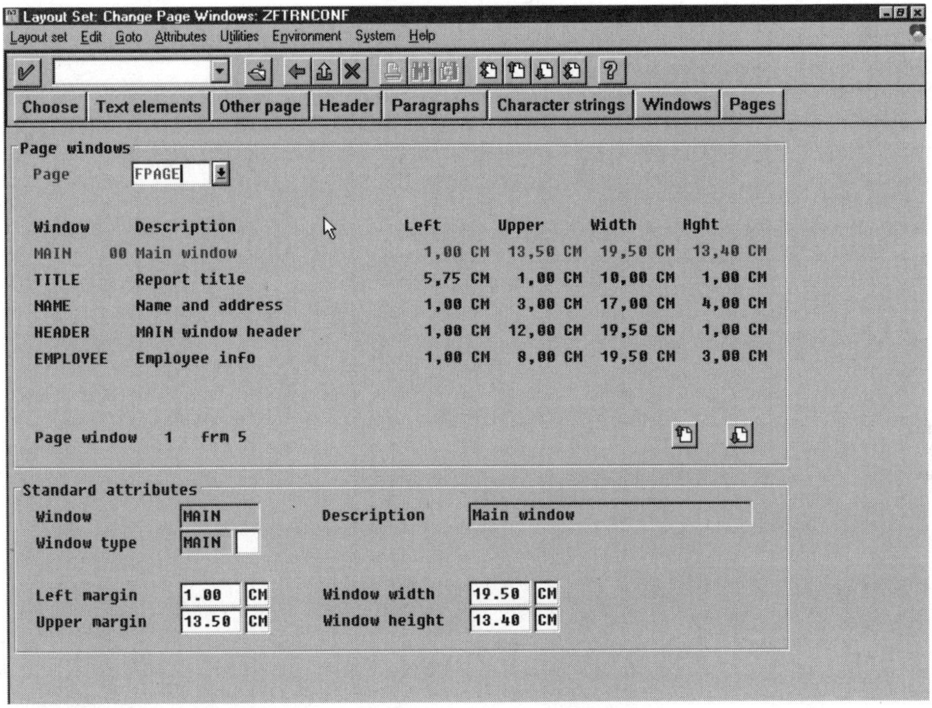

FIGURE 7.15   FPAGE Page windows for ZFTRNCONF
Copyright by SAP AG

So far we have defined where we want the windows and what size they should be for FPAGE. Now we have to do the same thing for NPAGE. To switch pages, position the cursor on the Page field and select the other page from the possible entries. (If the page has not yet been defined, it will not appear.)

We will not use the Employee or Name windows on NPAGE. Instead we will move the Main window up to allow for more detail entries on the page. We will use a new window called NAME2 to replace NAME, which only has the first and last name in it. The layout for NPAGE is shown in Figure 7.16.

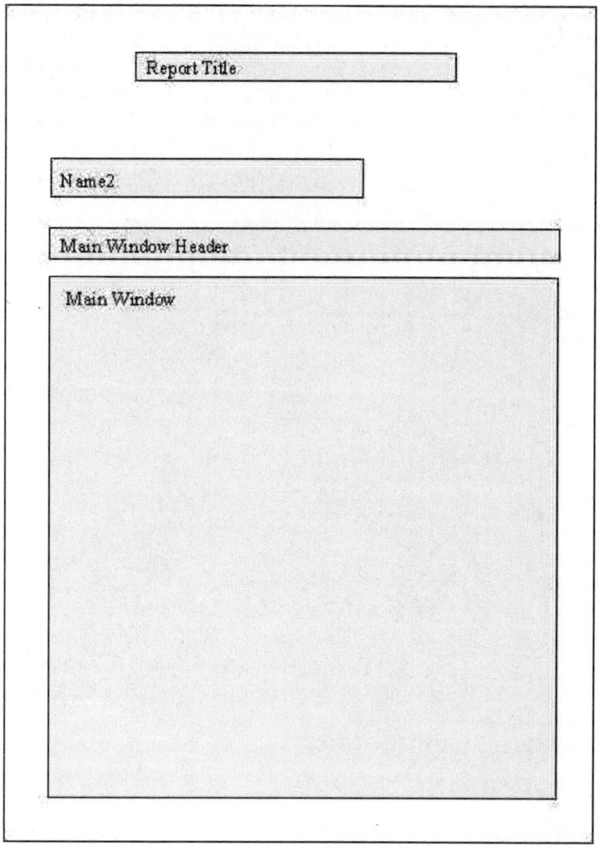

FIGURE 7.16 Layout for subsequent (NPAGE) pages of ZFTRNCONF

Creating the Page windows for NPAGE is a bit easier than creating the Page windows for FPAGE because the values from FPAGE default in as we go. All we have to do is change the values that differ between the two. Use the following values to create the Page windows for NPAGE:

	Left margin	Upper margin	Window width	Window height
NAME2	1	3	17	1
HEADER	1	5	19.5	1
MAIN	1	6.5	19.5	20.4

(All values should be in cm.)

The completed Change Page Windows screen for NPAGE should appear as shown in 7.17.

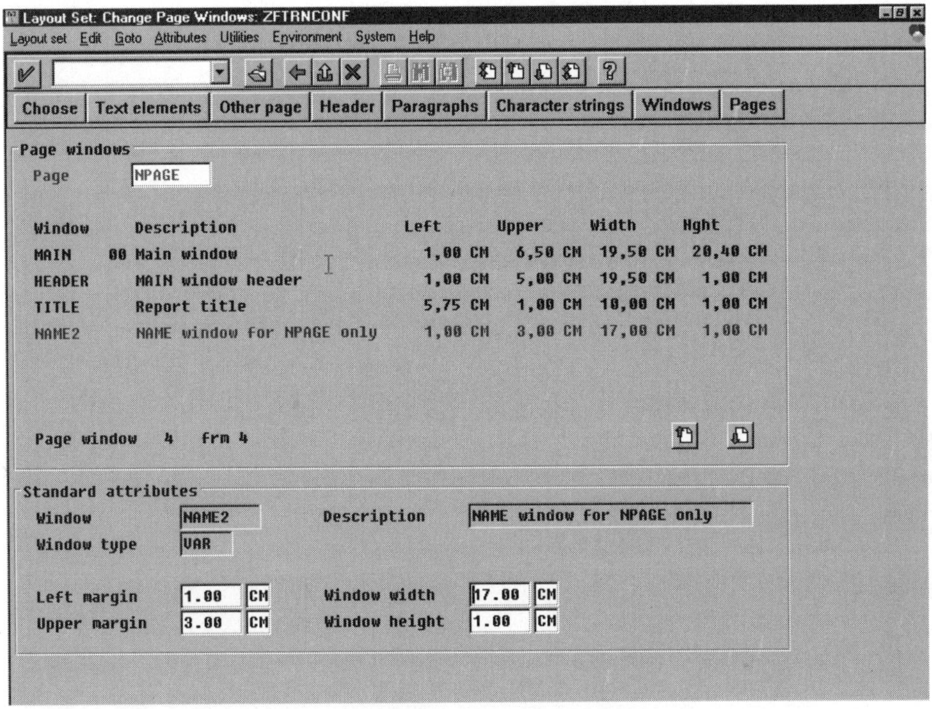

FIGURE 7.17   NPAGE Page windows for ZFTRNCONF
Copyright by SAP AG

Text Elements for ZFTRNCONF

So far, we have created blank windows. To fill the windows we need to create text element(s). We can evoke the Text Editor from the Change Page Window screen or the Change Window screen.

Text Element for TITLE

To create a text element for the Title window, start by selecting the Title page window. Then go to **Edit → Text elements**. Add the lines as shown in Figure 7.18, including the tag column on the left side.

In Figure 7.18 the "/:" in the tag column indicates that what follows is a command, not text. The line BOX FRAME 20 TW INTENSITY 20 means: print a box around the current window. The line thickness of the box should be 20

TW and the inside of the box will be shaded with a 20 percent gradient. The second line prints a blank line using the Default paragraph (*) which is P3. The third line prints the text TRAINING PLAN CONFIRMATION using the Default paragraph.

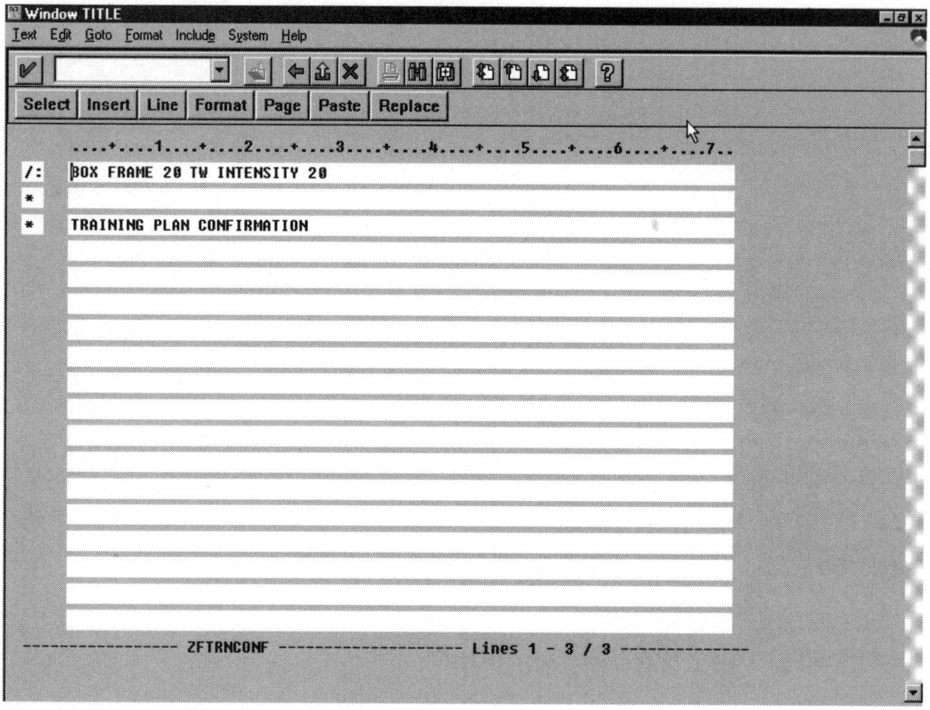

FIGURE 7.18   Text element for TITLE
Copyright by SAP AG

Text Element for NAME

The Name window text element is entirely made up of symbols. There are no static texts or command lines. Enter the text element for the Name window the same way as the others (from the Change Window or Page Window screen and then select **Edit → Text element**). The text element is shown in Figure 7.19.

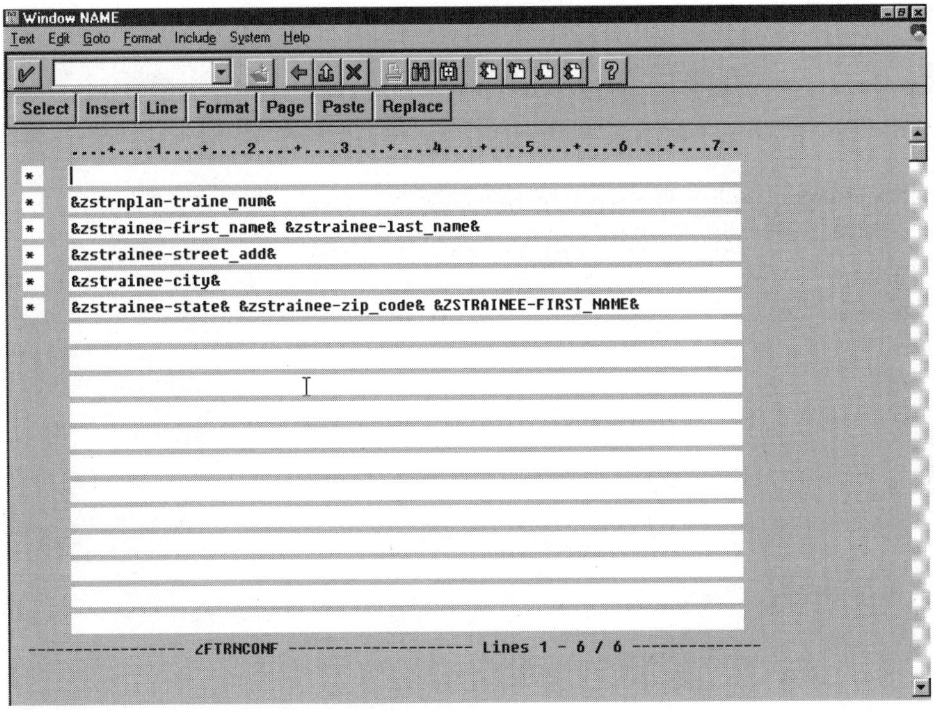

FIGURE 7.19   Text element for NAME
Copyright by SAP AG

Each symbol to be printed in the Main window is surrounded by &. The symbols will print in the order they appear. If there is a space between the symbols then a space will appear when printed. In this case each of the symbols is a field in a structure. These fields were populated by the calling print program ZTRNCNF2.

Text Element for EMPLOYEE

The text element for the Employee window is made up of a combination of symbols and static text (Figure 7.20). All the lines use the default paragraph, P1. The last line has a symbol &zstrainee-work_loc(*)&. The asterisk embedded in the symbol forces it always to use its defined length, regardless of how much of the field is filled up by the value. In this case the field zstrainee-work_loc is 30 characters long, so 30 characters will be used regardless of the entry. Otherwise Work Location: would be right up against Phone: if there were no entry for zstrainee-work_loc.

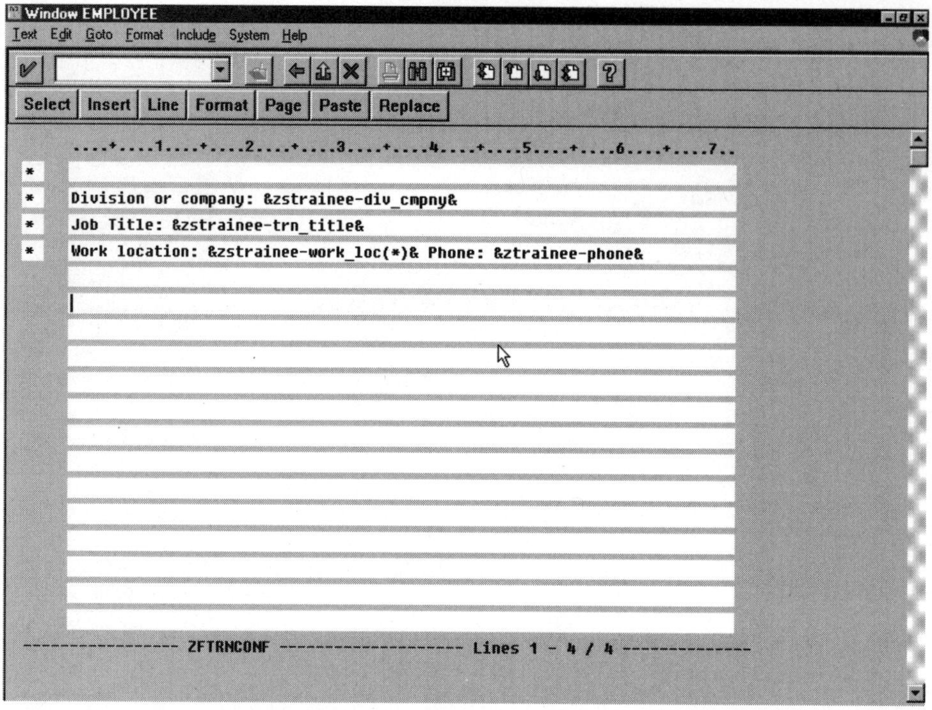

FIGURE 7.20   Text element for Employee
Copyright by SAP AG

Text Element for HEADER

The text element for the Header window is shown in Figure 7.21. In this text element we introduce a series of shaded boxes around all the column headers and then write out the column headers as standard text.

The first line positions the cursor down 2.5 mm before creating the first box so that the column headers appear in the centers of their boxes. The first box is the same size as the window. The second box is slightly shorter in width. The third is shorter yet and so on. Use what ever unit of measure is convenient. I have used millimeters to set the x origin and inches to size the boxes. Trial and error is always necessary here.

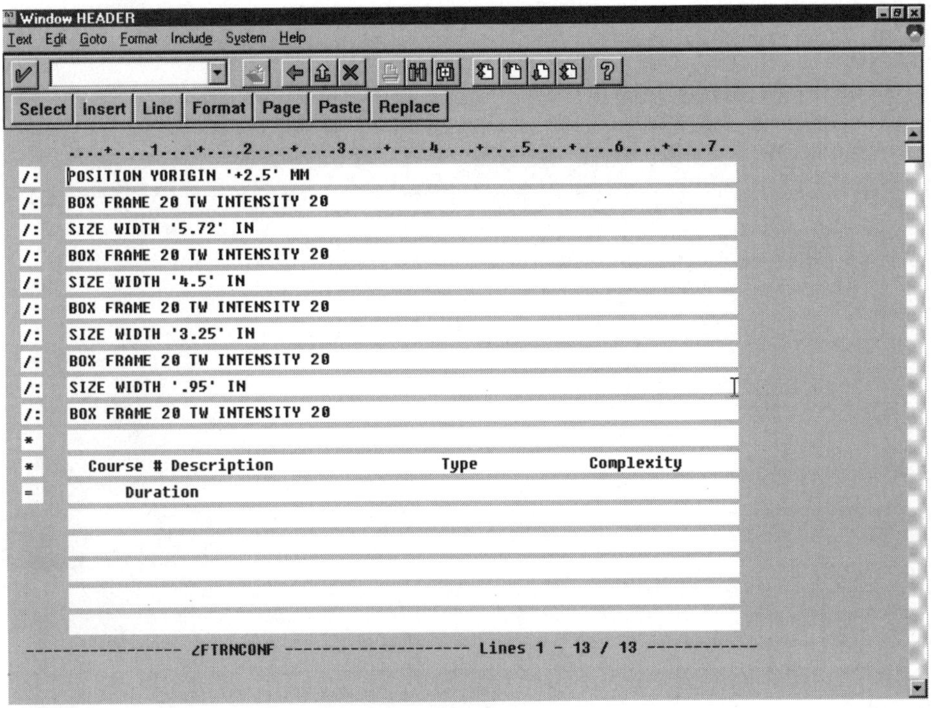

FIGURE 7.21   Text element for HEADER
Copyright by SAP AG

Text Element for NAME2

The text element for NAME2 is similar to that for NAME but uses only the first and last names (Figure 7.22). Notice that the first name symbol (&zstrainee-first_name&), does not have a an asterisk parameter to fix the length of the symbol. This means that the last name will always appear one space to the right of the first name no matter how long or short the first name is.

Character String C1 for MAIN

In the Main window we will make use of a character string. To create the character string select **Goto → Character strings** and then **Edit → Create element**. The process is much like adding a paragraph. Enter a name C1 and a description, then set the font to Courier 10 in the same manner that the paragraph fonts were set. The completed character string definition for C1 is shown in Figure 7.23.

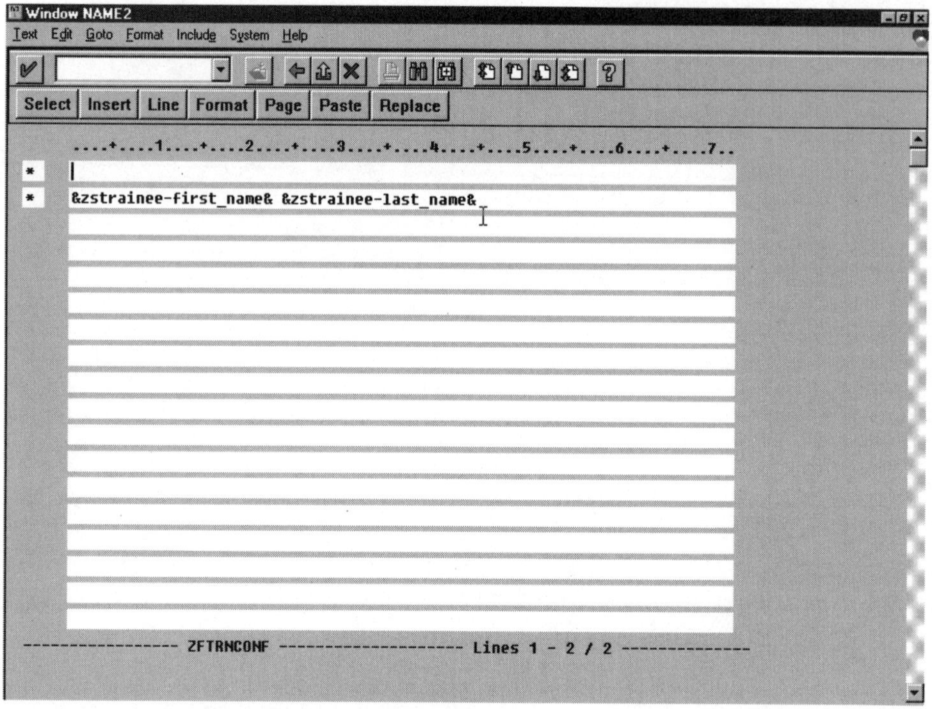

FIGURE 7.22   Text element for NAME2
Copyright by SAP AG

Text Element for the Main Window

The Main window is different from the other windows (Figure 7.24). This is where we typically build our list or body of the report. In our Main window we will print a detail line which holds the course information. Below that, we will print a listing of course offerings. The course offerings will be separated into two columns.

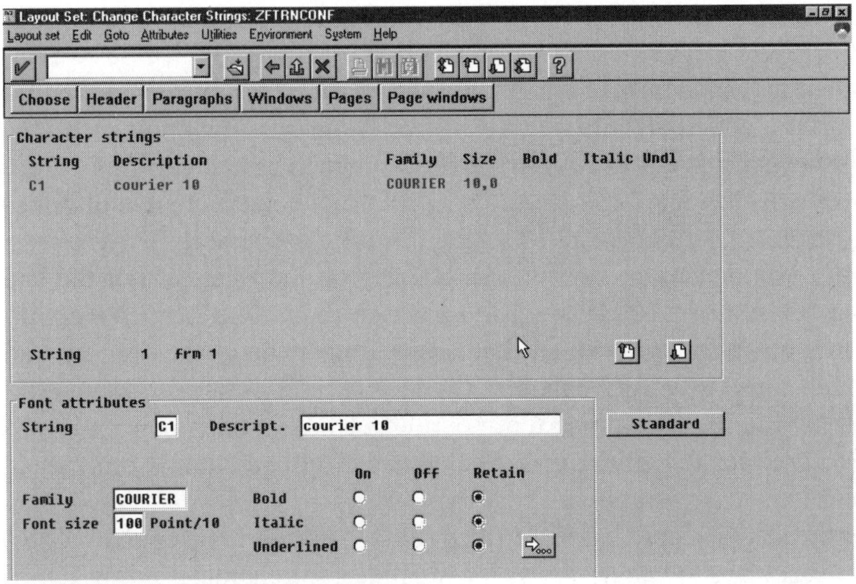

FIGURE 7.23   Character string C1
Copyright by SAP AG

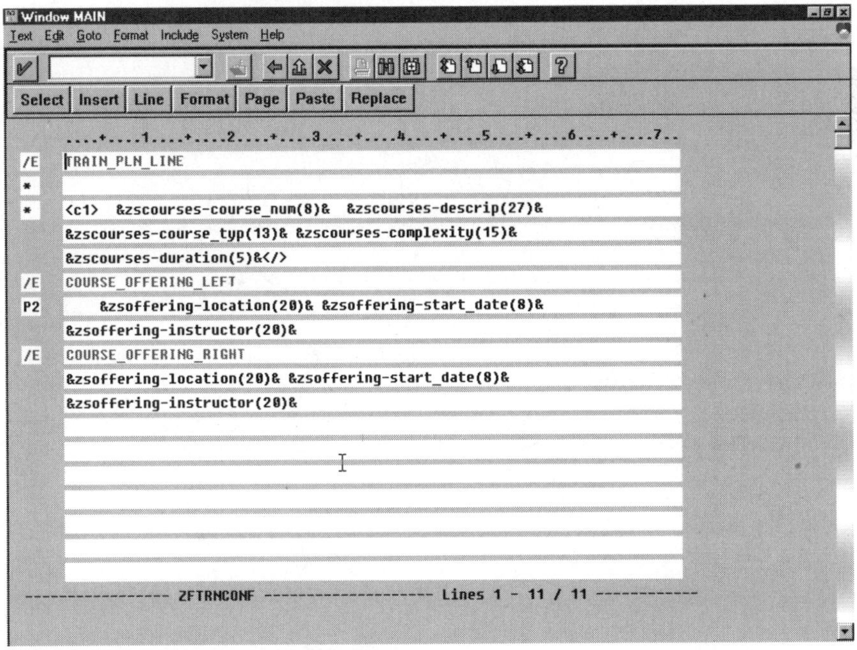

FIGURE 7.24   MAIN window text elements
Copyright by SAP AG

The Main window is separated into three sections: TRAIN_PLN_LINE, COURSE_OFFERING_LEFT and COURSE_OFFERING_RIGHT. These sections are triggered independently of one another when the program runs. When we want to print a course detail line, we call the Main window and specify the Text Element tag called TRAIN_PLN_LINE, in which case everything on the second through fifth lines will print. If we need left-column course offerings we call COURSE_OFFERING_LEFT. After printing a course offering on the left column, we append another course offering on the right side of the line by calling COURSE_OFFERING_RIGHT. Notice that COURSE_OFFERING_ RIGHT does not evoke a new line; that is why it appends to the right instead of beginning a new line when called.

Everything is a fixed length so that nothing gets out of alignment. It is also possible to use tabs to achieve this. The course offering columns print using the smaller font of paragraph P2.

The entire detail record under TRAIN_PLN_LINE is bracketed by <C1> and </>. This turns the character string attributes for character string C1 on and off. C1 is set at Courier 10. Everything between the <C1> and </> will print in Courier 10.

The New Program

Source Code

The source code for the revised report (ZTRNCNF2) follows:

```
 1   *****************************************************
 2   *---------------------------------------------*
 3   * Report   ztrnconf   Calling the layout set
 4   Author: M, Buchanan
 5   *---------------------------------------------*
 6   REPORT ZTRNCONF      NO STANDARD PAGE HEADING
 7                        LINE-SIZE  80
 8                        LINE-COUNT 65(0).
 9   *****************************************************
10   *Tables
11   TABLES:
12   ZCOURSES,     "courses
13   ZOFFERINGS,   "courses offerings
14   ZTRAINEE,     "trainees
```

```
15 ZTRNPLAN,      "training plans
16 ZSCOURSES,     "courses (structure)
17 ZSOFFERING,    "courses offerings (structure)
18 ZSTRAINEE,     "trainees (structure)
19 ZSTRNPLAN.     "training plans (structure)
20
21 DATA: I_TRNPLAN LIKE ZTRNPLAN OCCURS    0 WITH HEADER LINE.
22 DATA: OLD_TRAINE_NUM LIKE ZTRNPLAN-TRAINE_NUM,
23     FORM_STARTED(1) TYPE C,
24     ELEMENT_NAME(21) TYPE C.
25
26 SELECT-OPTIONS P_TRAINE FOR ZTRAINEE-TRAINE_NUM DEFAULT
27     '00000001' TO '00000007'.
28 *---------------------------------------*
29 *select
30
31 SELECT * FROM  ZTRNPLAN
32     WHERE  TRAINE_NUM IN P_TRAINE
33     AND COMPLETED NE 'X'.
34 MOVE-CORRESPONDING ZTRNPLAN TO I_TRNPLAN.
35 APPEND I_TRNPLAN.
36 ENDSELECT.
37
38 *---------------------------------------*
39 *process selection
40
41 CLEAR OLD_TRAINE_NUM.
42 SORT I_TRNPLAN.
43
44 PERFORM OPEN_LAYOUT_SET.   "Open layout set
45 LOOP AT I_TRNPLAN.
46     MOVE I_TRNPLAN TO ZSTRNPLAN.
47     IF I_TRNPLAN-TRAINE_NUM NE OLD_TRAINE_NUM.
48
49         PERFORM NEW_TRAINEE."New trainee - Page
50 ENDIF.
51     PERFORM WRITE_PLAN_ITEM.      "Write course
52     PERFORM WRITE_OFFERINGS.      "Write course offerings
53     MOVE I_TRNPLAN-TRAINE_NUM TO OLD_TRAINE_NUM.
54 ENDLOOP.
55 PERFORM CLOSE_LAYOUT_SET.  "Close layout set
56
57 *---------------------------------------*
58 PERFORMS
59 *---------------------------------------*
```

```
60 *&--------------------------------------*
61 *& Form NEW_TRAINEE
62 *&--------------------------------------*
63
64 FORM NEW_TRAINEE.
65    SELECT SINGLE * FROM ZTRAINEE
66       WHERE TRAINE_NUM = I_TRNPLAN-TRAINE_NUM.
67    MOVE-CORRESPONDING ZTRAINEE TO ZSTRAINEE.
68    IF FORM_STARTED = 'X'.
69       CALL FUNCTION 'CONTROL_FORM'      "Send a new-page
70          EXPORTING                      "command to the
71          COMMAND   = 'new-page FPAGE'   "layout set
72          EXCEPTIONS
73             UNOPENED    = 1
74             UNSTARTED   = 2
75             OTHERS      = 3.
76    ENDIF.
77
78 ENDFORM.
79 *&--------------------------------------*
80 *& Form WRITE_PLAN_ITEM
81 *&--------------------------------------*
82 FORM WRITE_PLAN_ITEM.
83    SELECT SINGLE * FROM  ZCOURSES
84       WHERE COURSE_NUM  = I_TRNPLAN-COURSE_NUM.
85    MOVE-CORRESPONDING ZCOURSES TO ZSCOURSES.
86    CALL FUNCTION 'WRITE_FORM'
87       EXPORTING
88          ELEMENT   = 'TRAIN_PLN_LINE'
89       EXCEPTIONS
90          ELEMENT   = 1
91          FUNCTION  = 2
92          TYPE      = 3
93          UNOPENED  = 4
94          UNSTARTED = 5
95          WINDOW    = 6
96          OTHERS    = 7.
97    FORM_STARTED    = 'X'.
98 ENDFORM.
99
100 *&--------------------------------------*
101 *& Form   WRITE_OFFERINGS
102 *&--------------------------------------*
103 FORM WRITE_OFFERINGS.
104
```

```
105     ELEMENT_NAME = 'COURSE_OFFERING_RIGHT'.
106     SELECT * FROM  ZOFFERINGS
107         WHERE  COURSE_NUM  = I_TRNPLAN-COURSE_NUM
108         AND  START_DATE <= I_TRNPLAN-DATE_REQ.
109         MOVE-CORRESPONDING ZOFFERINGS TO ZSOFFERING.
110     *Toggle left and right
111     IF ELEMENT_NAME = 'COURSE_OFFERING_RIGHT'.
112         ELEMENT_NAME = 'COURSE_OFFERING_LEFT'.
113     ELSE.
114         ELEMENT_NAME = 'COURSE_OFFERING_RIGHT'.
115     ENDIF.
116
117     CALL FUNCTION 'WRITE_FORM'
118         EXPORTING
119             ELEMENT = ELEMENT_NAME     "Print course offerings
120         EXCEPTIONS
121             ELEMENT   = 1
122             FUNCTION  = 2
123             TYPE      = 3
124             UNOPENED  = 4
125             UNSTARTED = 5
126             WINDOW    = 6
127             OTHERS    = 7.
128     ENDSELECT.
129
130 ENDFORM.
131 *&-------------------------------*
132 *& Form  OPEN_LAYOUT_SET
133 *&-------------------------------*
134 FORM OPEN_LAYOUT_SET.
135     CALL FUNCTION 'OPEN_FORM'
136         EXPORTING
137             DEVICE      = 'PRINTER'
138             DIALOG      = 'X'
139             FORM        = 'ZFTRNCONF'
140             LANGUAGE    = 'E'
141         EXCEPTIONS
142             CANCELED    = 1
143             DEVICE      = 2
144             FORM        = 3
145             OPTIONS     = 4
146             UNCLOSED    = 5
147             OTHERS      = 6.
148
149 ENDFORM.
```

```
150 *&- - - - - - - - - - - - - - - - - - - - - - - - - - - - - - - *
151 *& Form CLOSE_LAYOUT_SET
152 *&- - - - - - - - - - - - - - - - - - - - - - - - - - - - - - - *
153 FORM CLOSE_LAYOUT_SET.
154    CALL FUNCTION 'CLOSE_FORM'
155       EXCEPTIONS
156          UNOPENED = 1
157          OTHERS   = 2.
158 ENDFORM.
```

CD-ROM

CE009 ZTRNCNF2

Process Description

Using ZTRNCONF as a basis, program ZTRNCNF2 has been changed to call the new layout set. Essential elements of the program have not changed. The main loop has been revised to open and close the layout set at the beginning and end respectively, and the Write statements have been changed to Function Module calls to evoke different parts of the layout set. As with the other program, some components have been left out for clarity. Normally the errors would be handled more rigorously.

There are other ways to approach this program. This is one approach. We could have used START_FORM and STOP_FORM. We could have added page numbers. The intention here is only to provide an example. The processing steps are as follows:

Step 1. Lines 31–36. Select valid entries from ZTRNPLAN.

Step 2. Line 44. Open layout set ZFTRNCONF.

Step 3. Lines 46–49. Start a new page at FPAGE when a new trainee is encountered in the internal table by sending a NEW-PAGE FPAGE command to the layout set.

Step 4. Line 50. Write the course information on a detail line using the WRITE_FORM function module.

Step 5. Line 51. Write the course offerings information that applies to the course on the line above using the WRITE_FORM function module.

Just before the layout set is called to write a course offering line, there is a toggle that switches the value of ELEMENT_NAME from COURSE_ OFFERING_RIGHT to COURSE_OFFERING_LEFT and vice versa. The ELEMENT_NAME variable is then used as the value for ELEMENT in the function call. This has the effect printing the course offerings information on the left side and the right side repeatedly.

When WRITE_FORM is called, Main is the default window. In our case, we need to only specify the Text Element tag. When the Main window fills, a new page is forced and the other non-Main windows are printed. That is why we see no WRITE_FORM calls for TITLE, NAME, EMPLOYEE and HEADER. The layout set knows that we are starting on FPAGE and it will add all relevant windows to FPAGE before moving on to the next FPAGE or NPAGE.

Tutorial 2 in Review

1. The calling ABAP program must always use OPEN_FORM and CLOSE_FORM.
2. All the component pieces of the layout set must be completed for it to work.
3. Typically the recurring detail lines of the report reside in the Main window.
4. When MAIN is full, SAPscript will begin to fill MAIN on the subsequent page (the subsequent page can be identified as the same page as the current page).

In Brief

Control commands and formatting options are both used to manipulate SAPscript output.

Formatting options are used to qualify symbols in various ways. After interjection of a formatting option, the output of a symbol can be shortened, lengthened, chopped and otherwise rearranged to provide a required output appearance.

Although control commands can also ultimately affect the output of a symbol, their purpose is generally to "control" the output in some manner. Control commands can be used to build logical expressions which direct the output based on the value of the arguments at runtime. Other control commands have specific tasks like "including" other text or "drawing" a box.

Formatting options are always used inside of the ampersands which surround the symbol, i.e. &mysymbol(T)&, while control commands are initiated with /: in the tag column and always begin with a key word like CASE, DEFINE, or SIZE.

The control commands and formatting options are listed below alphabetically:

Control Commands

ADDRESS	Automatic formatting of address information based on destination country.
BOTTOM	Used only in MAIN to print text at the bottom of the window.
BOX	Create a box.
CASE	Use symbols as arguments to create a conditional statement.
DEFINE	Create a new symbol at runtime.
HEX	Hexadecimal values can be passed directly (as is).
IF	Use symbols as arguments to create a conditional statement.
INCLUDE	Include other text (and logos).
NEW-PAGE	Force a new page.
NEW-WINDOW	Force a new window.
PERFORM	Call a subroutine.
POSITION	(For use with BOX) Set the X, Y origin (upper left corner) of the box.
PRINT-CONTROL	Initiate a defined print-control sequence.

PROTECT	Preclude a page break.
RESET	Restart outline numbering sequence.
SET COUNTRY	Set country for use by country-specific fields.
SET DATE MASK	Set date format.
SET SIGN	Put sign on left or right side of the number.
SET TIME MASK	Set time format.
SIZE	(For use with BOX) Set the size of the box.
STYLE	Use a different style.
SUMMING	Adds symbol value to a total.
TOP	Used only in MAIN to print text at the top of the window.

Formatting Options

(<)	Move the sign to the left side of a numeric.
(>)	Move the sign to the right side of a numeric.
' '	Interject a literal prefix or suffix.
(C)	Represent symbol without spaces.
(n)	Define an explicit symbol length.
(.n)	Set the number of decimal places.
+n	Offset n characters to the right.
(En)	Represent a symbol as an exponential number.
(F*f*)	Use a fill character in leading spaces.
(I)	Represent only noninitial values.
(K)	Ignore conversion routines.
(R)	Force right justification.
(S)	The symbol is represented without a sign.
(T)	The symbol is represented without the thousands separator.
(Z)	Ignore leading zeros.

Control Commands

▲ Dynamic values are shown in lowercase italic.

▲ Optional components are shown in brackets.

ADDRESS

Description: This is used to format the address information automatically. Adding address information to a typcial program requires you to write code to handle the P.O. Box field and other elements of the address. (If the P.O. Box field is populated, write "P.O.Box" and then write out the information in the field, otherwise just use the street information.)

The ADDRESS command handles address formatting and takes it a step further by formatting the address based on the destination country.

We usually use symbols passed from the print program for the ADDRESS command, (if the values were literal or constant, we would just write them to the screen as is). The values that we pass for "title", "name", "street" etc., should be like those found in the structures ADRS, ADRS1, ADRS2, and ADRS3 for fields. A Reference field for each value is given in the descriptions which follow the syntax.

Syntax:

```
/ :  ADDRESS [DELIVERY] [TYPE t] [PARAGRAPH a] [PRIORITY p] [LINES l]
/ :  TITLE title
/ :  NAME name1 [,name2[,name3[,name4]]]
/ :  PERSON name [TITLE title]
/ :  DEPARTMENT department
/ :  STREET street
/ :  LOCATION location
/ :  POBOX PO box [CODE zip code] [CITY city]
/ :  POSTCODE zip code
/ :  CITY city1 [,city2]
/ :  REGION region
/ :  COUNTRY country [LANGUAGE language]
/ :  FROMCOUNTRY from country
/ :  ADDRESSNUMBER number
/ :  ENDADDRESS
```

▲ When DELIVERY appears following the key word ADDRESS, the street information is printed instead of the P.O. Box information.

▲ The TYPE parameter changes the type of address format used. Acceptable values are 1, 2, and 3.

▲ The paragraph format used to display the address can be set with PARAGRAPH followed by the name of the paragraph to use (a). The paragraph name should not be in quotes.

▲ With PRIORITY we can tell SAPscript which lines or symbols to leave out if there is insufficient room to print all the lines. It will omit the lines in the order they are listed until there is enough room. The word PRIORITY is followed by any number of the following switches (*p*).

A	title
P	Mandatory blank line 1
Q	Mandatory blank line 2
2	name2
3	name3
4	name4
L	country
S	street
O	city
T	city2
D	department
C	zipcode
N	person
1	location

▲ LINES should be followed by the number of lines (1) that the address should occupy when printed. If LINES are not used in a non-MAIN window, the size of the window is used.

▲ *title* is the name which appears at the top of the address. The format should be like ADRS-ANRED.

▲ *name1* is the name of the recipient. *name2, name3,* and *name4* are all additional name values that can be used if desired. The format of the name values should be like ADRS-NAME1, ADRS-NAME2, ADRS-NAME3, and ADRS-NAME4 respectively.

▲ *person* is the addressee when using types 2 & 3. The value for person should be like ADRS3-NAME_PERS. If this person has a title (Mr., Mrs., Dr. etc.), it is given on the same line by following the person value with "TITLE" and then the value of the title. The value of *title* should be like ADRS-ANRED.

▲ *department* is used in Type 3 addresses and refers to office or business activity. The value should be like ADRS3-DEPARTMENT.

▲ *street* is the street address. Format should be like ADRS-STRAS.

▲ *location* gives additional address information. Value should be like `ADRS1-LOCATION`.

▲ *PO Box* is the Post Office box. Format should be like `ADRS-PFACH`. If a PO Box has a different zip code and or city than the street address, identify them on this line with `CODE` and `CITY`. `CODE` should be followed by a value for the zip code that is like `ADRS-PSTLZ`. `CITY` should be followed by a value for city or town that is like `ADRS-ORT01`.

▲ *postcode* is the Zip code. Format should be like `ADRS-PSTLZ`.

▲ *city* is the town or city name. Two values can be identified. Format should be like `ADRS-ORT01` for each.

▲ *Region* is the county, state or administrative region. Format should be like `ADRS-REGIO` and be populated in the check table T005s.

▲ *country* is the country upon which address format is based. Format of the value is like `ADRS-LAND1`. It must be populated in T005. The language for the country can be explicitly specified on the same line with `LANGUAGE` followed by the language code. The language code should be like `ADRS-SPRAS` and populated in T002.

▲ *from country* is the country of origin. This will affect the way that the receiving country's name is formatted.

▲ *number* is as a key for those countries that have a central address file.

EXAMPLE

```
/* Set up symbols for example
/: DEFINE &S_TITLE& = 'XYZ World'
/: DEFINE &S_NAME1& = 'XYZ Enterprises Inc.'
/: DEFINE &S_NAME2& = 'Commercial Services'
/: DEFINE &S_PERSON& = 'Mary Smith'
/: DEFINE &S_PTITLE& = 'Mrs.'
/: DEFINE &S_DEPRTMNT& = 'Department of Information
   Technology'
/: DEFINE &S_STREET& = '123 Central Blvd'
/: DEFINE &S_LOCATION& = '5th floor'
/* DEFINE &S_POBOX& = '    '
/: DEFINE &S_POBOX& = '456'
/: DEFINE &S_POBOXZIP& = '12345'
/: DEFINE &S_POBXCITY& = 'Hampton'
/: DEFINE &S_ZIPCODE& = '12344'
/: DEFINE &S_CITY1& = 'Hampton'
/: DEFINE &S_CITY2& = 'Hampton Roads'
/: DEFINE &S_REGION& = 'VA'
```

```
/:  DEFINE &S_COUNTRY& = 'US'
/:  DEFINE &S_CTRY_LNG& = 'E'
/:  DEFINE &S_FR_CNTRY& = 'US'
/:  DEFINE &S_NUMBER& = '900001'
/*  Print out address
/:  IF &S_POBOX& NE ' '
/:  ADDRESS TYPE 1 PARAGRAPH P1 PRIORITY 432A LINES 4
/:  ELSE
/:  ADDRESS DELIVERY TYPE 1 PARAGRAPH P1 PRIORITY 432A LINES
    6
/:  ENDIF
/:  TITLE &S_TITLE&
/:  NAME &S_NAME1&, &S_NAME2&
/:  PERSON &S_PERSON& TITLE &S_PTITLE&
/:  DEPARTMENT &S_DEPRTMNT&
/:  STREET &S_STREET&
/:  LOCATION &S_LOCATION&
/:  POBOX &S_POBOX& CODE &S_POBOXZIP& CITY &S_POBXCITY&
/:  POSTCODE &S_ZIPCODE&
/:  CITY &S_CITY1&, &S_CITY2&
/:  REGION &S_REGION&
/:  COUNTRY &S_COUNTRY& LANGUAGE &S_CTRY_LNG&
/:  FROMCOUNTRY &S_FR_CNTRY&
/:  ADDRESSNUMBER &S_NUMBER&
/:  ENDADDRESS
```

Paragraph P1 is Times New 12.

CE010 ADDRESS Command

The values for the ADDRESS command will typically be symbols defined in the print program (usually by populating a structure[s]). In this example, symbols are populated at the top of the script with the DEFINE command so they can be used in the ADDRESS command instead of constants.

The script as listed will produce the following result.

XYZ World
XYZ Enterprises Inc.
PO BOX 456
Hampton VA 12345

A conditional statement before the ADDRESS command will not include the Delivery parameter if the S_POBOX symbol is populated. If S_POBOX is blank the output looks like this:

> XYZ World
> XYZ Enterprises Inc.
> Commercial Services
> 123 Central Blvd
> 5th floor
> Hampton VA 12344

For this output the conditional statement used the following line to initiate the ADDRESS command:

```
ADDRESS DELIVERY TYPE 1 PARAGRAPH P1 PRIORITY 432A LINES 6
```

If the LINES parameter is changed from 6 to 4, lines will be removed in the order that they are shown after the PRIORITY parameter. In this case *name4* will be removed first, but *name4* is not populated so this produces no result. Next *name3* is removed, but this also is not populated and we have still not shortened the total number of lines. When *name2* is removed, this produces five lines, so the next item A in the priority list is reviewed. A refers to the value for title which is removed. With title removed, four lines are left. The result follows:

> XYZ Enterprises Inc.
> 123 Central Blvd
> 5th floor
> Hampton VA 12344

If the value for the TYPE parameter is changed to 2 as shown here:

```
ADDRESS DELIVERY TYPE 2 PARAGRAPH P1 PRIORITY 432A LINES 6
```

The output will be:

> Mrs. Mary Smith
> 123 Central Blvd
> 5th floor
> Hampton VA 12344

Using TYPE 3 in the same line produces the following result:

> Mrs. Mary Smith
> Department of Information Technology
> XYZ Enterprises Inc.
> 123 Central Blvd
> 5th floor
> Hampton VA 12344

BOTTOM

Description: This is used to print text at the bottom of the main window. Everything between BOTTOM and ENDBOTTOM will print at the bottom of the Main window on each page.

Syntax:

```
/:  BOTTOM
/:  ENDBOTTOM
```

▲ The footer will print in each Main window not just the last one. To turn the footer off dynamically under some condition, use the BOTTOM command with no text between BOTTOM and ENDBOTTOM.

EXAMPLE

The following text element is from a Main window. On the first page and subsequent pages the size of MAIN is 10cm x 10cm. The default paragraph is Times New 12.

```
/:  BOTTOM
*    All units are in pounds.
/:  ENDBOTTOM
*    Detail line one
*    Detail line two
*    Detail line three
*    Detail line four
*    Detail line five
*    Detail line six
*    Detail line seven
*    Detail line eight
*    Detail line nine
*    Detail line ten
```

```
*   Detail line eleven
*   Detail line twelve
*   Detail line thirteen
*   Detail line fourteen
```

In this example, ten of the detail lines will fit in the Main window on the first page, then the footer is printed (Figure 8.1). On the second page the remaining four detail lines are printed and the footer again prints at the bottom (Figure 8.2).

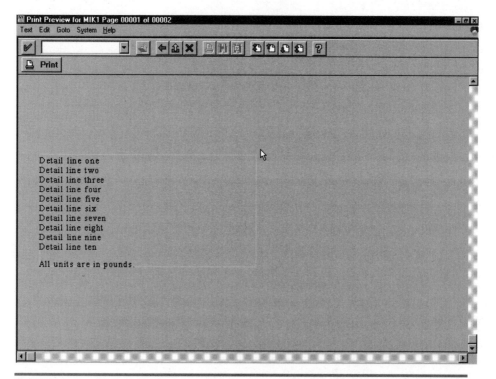

FIGURE 8.1   Main window on the first page using the Bottom command
Copyright by SAP AG

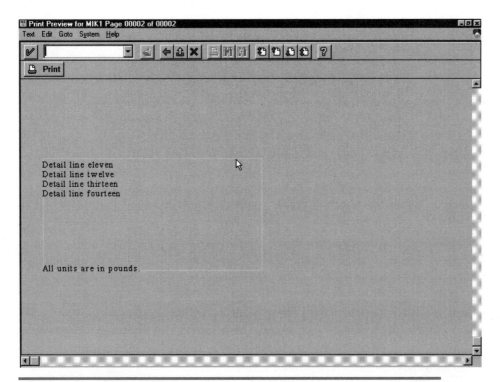

FIGURE 8.2   Main window on the following page using the Bottom command

Copyright by SAP AG

BOX

Description: This is used to create a box. The box can be shaded and sized. The line thickness of the box can also be changed. Boxes are always positioned relative to the uppermost left corner of the window in which the box is written. BOX is used in combination with the commands POSITION and SIZE.

Syntax:

```
/: BOX [XPOS a] [YPOS b] [WIDTH c] [HEIGHT d] [FRAME e]
[INTENSITY f]
```

The values a, b, c, d, e, and f are those of the parameters that precede them. Each of these values except INTENSITY should be followed by a space and a unit of measure. Decimal numbers should be in single quotes. Acceptable units of measure are:

LN	Line (equal to 1/6 in., unless the default lines per inch are changed in the layout set header)
CH	Character (equal to 1/10 in., unless the default characters per inch are changed in the layout set header)
PT	Point (unit of length equal to 1/72 in.)
TW	Twip (unit of length equal to 1/1440 in.)
IN	Inch
MM	Millimeter
CM	Centimeter

▲ XPOS is the (horizontal distance) from the origin that the box should start. If the X origin was not changed with the Position command, it is the upper left corner of the window.

▲ YPOS is the (vertical distance) from the origin that the box should start. If the Y origin was not changed with the Position command, it is the upper left corner of the window.

▲ WIDTH refers to the width of the box. If WIDTH is not used, whatever is put in with the Size command will be used. If SIZE is not used, the default is the window size.

▲ HEIGHT refers to the height of the box. If HEIGHT is not used, whatever is put in with the Size command will be used. If SIZE is not used, the default is the window size.

▲ FRAME is the measure of thickness of the outline of the box. If FRAME is not used there will be no outline. If the value for FRAME is too large, the box will appear black.

▲ If INTENSITY is used, the box will be shaded. The amount of shading depends on the value that follows the parameter. 0 is no shading, 100 is black.

EXAMPLE

```
/: BOX XPOS 2 CM YPOS 1 CM WIDTH 3 CM HEIGHT 2 CM FRAME 10  TW
      INTENSITY 20
```

In this example the box is printed in a window which measures 6 cm x 6 cm. The upper left corner of the box begins 2 cm to the right and 1 cm down from the upper left corner of the window. The box itself is 3 cm wide and 2 cm high. It has a border 10 TW wide and the shading intensity is 10%. The result is shown in Figure 8.3.

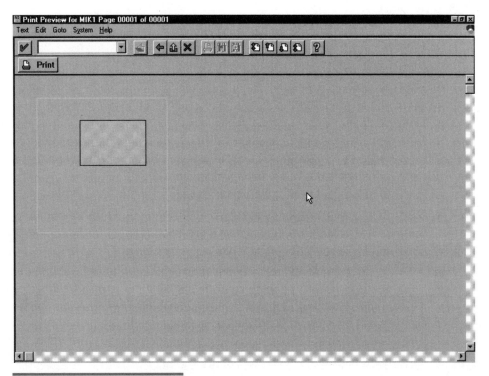

FIGURE 8.3   Box command
Copyright by SAP AG

CASE

Description: This works the same way as the case statement in ABAP, except symbols are used instead of fields (see the DEFINE command for more information on symbols). Lines between the WHEN statements are processed when the value of the first When statement equals the *symbol* value. If there is no match then the lines between WHEN OTHERS and ENDCASE will be processed. WHEN OTHERS is optional; if it is not used and none of the WHEN statements matches the symbol then the whole case statement will be ignored.

Syntax:

/:   CASE   *symbol*

```
    . . .
/:    WHEN    value1
    . . .
/:    WHEN    value2
    . . .
/:    WHEN    value3
    . . .
/:    WHEN    value n ...
[/:    WHEN OTHERS. ]
/:    ENDCASE
```

▲ *Symbol* is any valid symbol at runtime and *value* is a literal of your choice.

▲ Symbols must be surrounded by ampersands.

▲ The case statement must be concluded with the ENDCASE command.

EXAMPLE

The following example shows the case statement used within an IF command.

```
/: IF &VBDKL-LAND1_AG& = 'AR'
/: CASE &VBDKL-LFART(2)&
/: WHEN 'NL'
H1 Country is Argentina, Delivery type is NL
/: WHEN 'FD'
H1 Country is Argentina, Delivery type is FD
/: WHEN 'KB'
H1 Country is Argentina, Delivery type is KB
/: WHEN OTHERS
H1 Delivery type is unknown
/: ENDCASE
/: ENDIF
```

CD-ROM

CASE Statement CE001

In this example we are checking for a specific condition where the country is Argentina and the delivery type is NL, FD, or KB. Depending on the delivery type we print a different message. If the country is not Argentina we print nothing. In this case VBDKL-LAND1_AG is the ship-to country taken from the document header record and VBDKL-LFART(2) is the first two characters of the delivery type, taken from the document header.

DEFINE

Description: The DEFINE command makes it possible to create a new symbol at run time. Typically the symbols will be defined in the calling print program. There are occasions however, when it may be desirable to use pieces of existing symbols to create a new symbol for output.

Syntax:

```
/: DEFINE &new_symbol_name& = 'value'
```

new_symbol_name is the name of the symbol to define.

The value must be surrounded by quotes and can incorporate embedded symbols and format options.

Using := means the new symbol will take on the value immediately. If = is employed, the value is replaced when the new symbol is printed.

EXAMPLE

```
/: DEFINE &TYPEA_NUM& := 'A1B2C3D4E5F6G7H8I9J'
/: DEFINE &TYPEB_NUM& := '123456789'
/: DEFINE &TYPEC_NUM& = '&TYPEA_NUM(10)&-&TYPEB_NUM+2(5)&'
*   &TYPEC_NUM&
```

CE011 DEFINE command

CD-ROM

In this example, substrings of two symbols are concatenated to define a third. The resulting output is the value of TYPEC_NUM:

```
A1B2C3D4E5-34567
```

HEX

Description: HEX and ENDHEX allow a hexadecimal data stream to be passed directly to the printer. Lines between HEX and ENDHEX, with the exception of comment lines, are passed to the printer in their hexadecimal state.

Syntax:

```
/: HEX [TYPE a] [XPOS b] [YPOS c] [HEIGHT d] [LEFT e]
```

▲ TYPE refers to the printer language a. Acceptable values for a are:
POST (Postscript)
PRES (kyocera)
PCL (HP Printer Control Language)
▲ The value b which follows XPOS is horizontal distance from the origin that the hexadecimal value should be placed.
▲ The value c which follows YPOS is the vertical distance from the origin that the hexadecimal value should be placed.
▲ The value d which follows HEIGHT is the height of the space reserved for the hexadecimal value.
▲ The value e which follows LEFT is the distance to indent before beginning the hexadecimal output.

EXAMPLE

```
/* PRINT-CONTROL 'SLAND'
/: HEX TYPE PCL
=   1B266C314F
/: ENDHEX
*   test landscape
```

CE025 HEX command

CD-ROM

The example above will print the line test landscape on a landscape-formatted page. In this case the hex characters used in the HEX command are the same ones used by the SLAND Print Control command. The Print Control command SLAND would have the same effect.

IF

Description: The IF command in SAPscript works like the IF command in ABAP. In its simplest form, IF…ENDIF, the lines between IF and

ENDIF are executed if the conditional statement after IF is true. If the statement after IF is not true, then the lines between IF and ENDIF are skipped.

Another variation of the IF command includes the ELSE statement. If the statement after IF is false, the lines between ELSE and ENDIF will be executed. If another conditional statement is needed, the ELSEIF command can be used.

Syntax:

```
/ :  IF  condition
     ... lines to be executed
/ :  ENDIF
or
/ :  IF  condition
     ...lines to be executed
/ :  ELSE
     ...lines to be executed
/ :  ENDIF
or
/ :  IF  condition
     ...lines to be executed
/ :  ELSEIF condition
     ...lines to be executed
/ :  [ELSE]
     ...lines to be executed
/ :  ENDIF
```

▲ IF statements can be nested one inside the other.

▲ When building the conditional statement the following operators are valid:

= or EQ	< or LT	> or GT
<> or NE	>= or GE	<= or LE

▲ To build logical statements use:

NOT	AND	OR

EXAMPLE

```
/:DEFINE &TEST_CITY& = 'RICH'
/:DEFINE &TEST_REGION& = 'WEST'
/*
/*Example of simple IF test
/:IF &TEST_CITY& = 'RICH'
* The city is Richmond
/:ENDIF
```

```
/*
/*Exaple of two sided test
/:IF &TEST_CITY& = 'RICH' OR &TEST_CITY& = 'PORT'
* This is a city I know
/:ELSE
* This is not a city I know
/:ENDIF
/*
/*Example of nested IF with ELSEIF
/:IF &TEST_CITY& = 'RICH'
/:IF &TEST_REGION& = 'EAST'
* East coast is the correct region for Richmond
/:ELSE
* Richmond is not in the defined Region
/:ENDIF
/:ELSEIF &TEST_CITY& = 'PORT'
/:IF &TEST_REGION& = 'WEST'
* West coast is the correct region for Portland
/:ELSE
* Portland is not in the defined Region
/:ENDIF
/:ENDIF
```

CD-ROM

CE012 IF command

In this example the DEFINE statements can be changed to trigger the different paths of the conditional statement.

INCLUDE

Description: This includes predefined standard text and can be useful if text repeats often and it should be included it in the text. As standard texts are language dependent, it is possible to include standard text of different languages if necessary.

The INCLUDE command is also used to include images. The images are captured as a large hex command embedded within the standard text. The program RSTXLDMC will import a TIFF image (baseline TIFF 6.0) from the workstation and create the standard text. Import the TIFF image and include the standard text created in the text element. Not all TIFF images are baseline

TIFF 6.0, so experiment with different graphical editors to find one that saves the TIFF image in the correct format. A sample baseline TIFF 6.0 is on the CD-ROM and is called `XYZlogo.tif`.

CD-ROM

XYZlogo.tif

Syntax:

```
/: INCLUDE textname [OBJECT a] [ID b] [LANGUAGE c] [PARAGRAPH d]
   [NEW-PARAGRAPH e]
```

▲ The name of the standard text is *textname*.

▲ The OBJECT that the standard text is associated with (a) is a function of the type of text included. Usually this is going to be TEXT. The default value is TEXT.

▲ The ID (b) refers to the text ID, a way of grouping texts that have similar purposes. Custom text IDs can be created in using **Tools →** **Word processing→ Settings**. Normally the text ID is ST for standard text. In creating a custom text ID, there is an option to identify the "default text ID for INCLUDES," if it should be something other than the current text ID. TXT is the standard text ID for layout set text elements and there is no "INCLUDE ID default" assigned to TXT. Therefore, the default value for INCLUDES within a layout set is TXT.

▲ Specify a language key (c) for the text to include after the parameter LANGUAGE. The default value is the language of the current text. If an INCLUDE is issued from a layout set (which is normally the case) the default language will be the language of the current layout set (not necessarily the original language of the layout set).

▲ The PARAGRAPH parameter sets the default paragraph of the included text to d.

▲ NEW-PARAGRAPH does not reset the default paragraph, but reassigns the paragraph name e to the first tag element in the INCLUDE as long as the first line is not a command or comment line. If nothing is provided for the PARAGRAPH parameter then e becomes the new default paragraph for the included text.

All the identification for a standard text can be found in transaction SO10 by displaying the standard text and selecting **Goto → Header**.

NOTE

EXAMPLE
```
/* Print ship quantity in Spanish
/: DEFINE &S_LANG& = 'S'
/*
/* Print ship quantity in English
/* DEFINE &S_LANG& = 'E'
/*
/: INCLUDE ZQTY_LABEL OBJECT TEXT ID ST LANGUAGE &S_LANG&
```

CE013 INClUDE command

CD-ROM

Where ZQTY_LABEL is the name of a standard text that has been created twice with the same name, once using language key E and again using the language key S:

Text name	ZQTY_LABEL
Language	S
Text ID	ST
Text object	TEXT

Contains the following text:
```
* Cantidad Emb
```

and...

Text name	ZQTY_LABEL
Language	E
Text ID	ST
Text object	TEXT

Contains the following text:
```
* Ship Qty
```

The example shown above will produce the text:

Cantidad Emb

If the DEFINE statements are commented the other way so that S_LANG = E, they will produce:

Ship Qty

NOTE

Use **Include → Text** to create INCLUDE statements in the layout set text element.

NEW-PAGE

Description: This forces a new page. If it is used without identifying a page, this command will begin a new page on the page defined as "next page" in the page settings for the current page. Subsequent text will be printed on the new page. If a page is specifically identified just after the key word NEW-PAGE, subsequent text will be printed on the page identified.

NEW-PAGE can only be used in MAIN. If it is used in a non-Main window it is ignored. Typically NEW-PAGE is conditionally issued from the print program by calling the function module CONTROL_FORM.

Syntax:

```
/:  NEW-PAGE   [pagevalue]
```

pagevalue is the name of the page to jump to (optional).

EXAMPLE

```
*   Print this line on FPAGE (First page)
/* Goto the next page (NPAGE) and print the next line.
/:  NEW-PAGE
*   Print this line on NPAGE (subsequent pages)
/* Start another FPAGE and print a line there.
/:  NEW-PAGE FPAGE
*   Print this third line on a new FPAGE
```

CE014 NEW-PAGE command

FPAGE has NPAGE defined as its "next page". NPAGE has NPAGE defined as its "next page". This example is from a Main window. When it is executed as is, three pages will print: the first, on an FPAGE, will have a line that reads:

```
Print this line on FPAGE (First page)
```

The next page will be on an NPAGE and will read:

```
Print this line on NPAGE (subsequent pages)
```

The last page will print on another FPAGE and will read:

```
Print this third line on a new FPAGE
```

NEW-WINDOW

Description: The NEW-WINDOW command is used when columns or labels are created. Multiple Main windows can be created on a page. Each new Main window created automatically gets named with a sequential number. When the first Main is filled up, the next starts filling up and so on. To jump to the next Main window before filling it up, issue the command NEW-WINDOW.

Syntax:

```
/: NEW-WINDOW
```

EXAMPLE

```
*   Line 1
*   Line 2
*   Line 3
*   Line 4
*   Line 5
*   Line 6
/*  Stop at six and print the rest in MAIN 01
/:  NEW-WINDOW
*   Line 7
```

```
*    Line 8
*    Line 9
*    Line 10
*    Line 11
*    Line 12
*    Line 13
*    Line 14
```

CD-ROM

CE015 NEW-WINDOW command

The above example is the text element form MAIN. Two Main windows 5 cm x 5 cm have been set up on the first page. The first window will stop filling at line 6 and print the remainder of lines on the second window (see Figure 8.4).

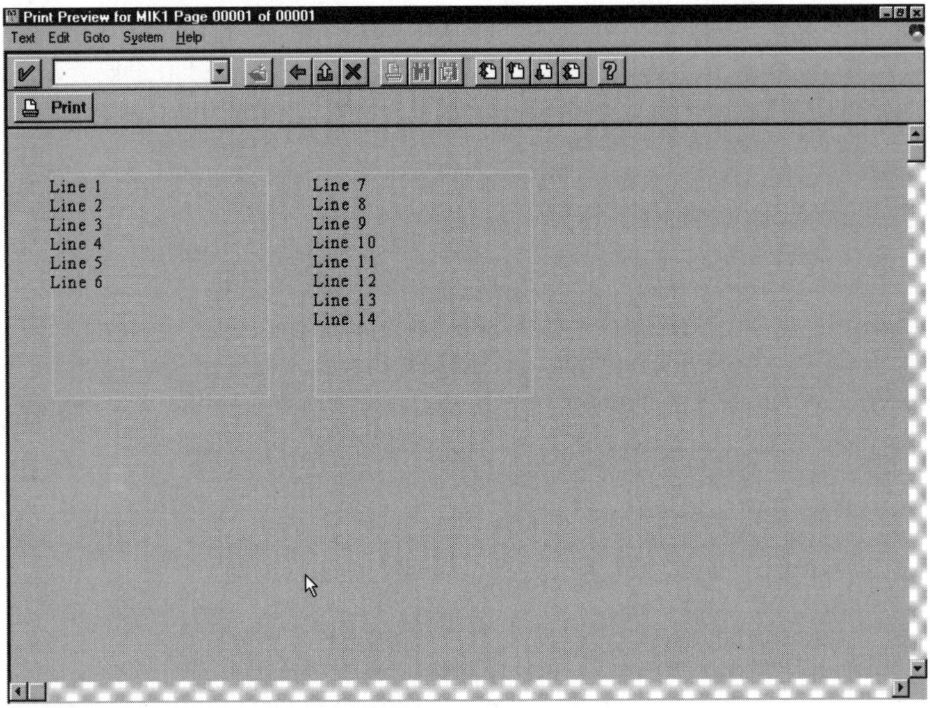

FIGURE 8.4   NEW-WINDOW command
Copyright by SAP AG

PERFORM

Description: This permits calling an ABAP subroutine from the text element as long as the subroutine does not call one of the SAPscript Function modules (Function group STXC).

Syntax:

```
/:  PERFORM    formname   IN PROGRAM prognam
/:  USING &symbol1&
     . . .
/:  CHANGING  &symbol2&
     . . .
/:  ENDFORM
```

▲ The name of the subroutine to call is *formname*.

▲ The name of the program that contains the subroutine is *progname*.

▲ The values are passed to and from the subroutine via internal tables that have a structure like itcsy.

▲ The first of the two internal tables passed to the subroutine contains the names and values of the symbols that followed the key word USING (*symbol1*). The second table contains only the names of the symbols that followed the key word CHANGING (*symbol2*).

▲ The subroutine passes values back to the text element by updating the VALUE fields for the corresponding symbol names in the second of the two tables.

EXAMPLE

This example is provided in two parts. The first is a text element within a non-Main window. The second part is the subroutine that the text element calls.

```
/:  DEFINE &V_COURSE& = '00000002'
/:  DEFINE &DESCRIP& = 'none'
/:  PERFORM GET_COURSE_NAME IN PROGRAM ZTRNCNF3
/:  USING &V_COURSE&
/:  CHANGING &DESCRIP&
/:  ENDPERFORM
*   Course number &V_course& is:
*   &DESCRIP&
```

CE16 PERFORM command

The follow subroutine (GET_COURSE_NAME) is contained in the program ZTRNCNF3.

```
1   FORM GET_COURSE_NAME TABLES INPUT_TAB STRUCTURE ITCSY
2              OUTPUT_TAB STRUCTURE ITCSY.
3   READ TABLE INPUT_TAB WITH KEY 'V_COURSE'.
4   SELECT SINGLE * FROM ZCOURSES
5       WHERE COURSE_NUM = INPUT_TAB-VALUE.
6   IF SY-SUBRC NE 0.
7       MOVE 'not found' TO ZCOURSES-DESCRIP.
8   ENDIF.
9   LOOP AT OUTPUT_TAB WHERE NAME = 'DESCRIP'.
10      MOVE ZCOURSES-DESCRIP TO OUTPUT_TAB-VALUE.
11      MODIFY OUTPUT_TAB.
12  ENDLOOP.
13 ENDFORM.
```

CE017 Subroutine

The example above uses a custom table called ZCOURSES. The structure is provided in the previous chapter. With 'V_COURSE' defined as 00000002, the following output is produced:

```
Course number 00000002 is:
Unix system administration 1
```

POSITION

Description: POSITION is used in combination with the BOX command. The POSITION command precedes the BOX command and repositions the cursor before the box is drawn.

Syntax:

```
/: POSITION  [XORIGIN v1 u1] [YORIGIN v2 u2] [WINDOW] [PAGE]
```

▲ The XORIGIN parameter is followed with the location of the cursor on the horizontal axis, where *v1* is a number and *u1* is a unit of measure.

▲ The YORIGIN parameter is followed with the location of the cursor on the vertical axis, where *v2* is a number and *u2* is a unit of measure.

▲ The XORIGIN and YORIGIN parameters can be used in combination with one another but do not have to be. Positions given are relative to the origin of the current window. Negative numbers can be used.

▲ Numbers with decimal points should be surrounded in single quotes.

▲ The WINDOW parameter means: set the origin to match the upper left coordinate of the window. The WINDOW parameter would not be used in combination with any other parameter.

▲ The PAGE parameter means: set the origin to match the upper left coordinate of the page. The PAGE parameter would not be used in combination with any other parameter.

EXAMPLE

```
/:POSITION PAGE
/: BOX WIDTH 3 CM HEIGHT 2 CM FRAME 10 TW INTENSITY 20
/: POSITION XORIGIN 7 CM YORIGIN '-.5' CM
/: BOX WIDTH 3 CM HEIGHT 2 CM FRAME 10 TW INTENSITY 20
```

CE018 POSITION command

CD-ROM

The text element above produces two windows (Figure 8.5). The first has its origin equal to the current page. The second window's origin is to the right 7 cm and up .5 cm from the origin of the window. The window is shown between the two boxes with a highlighted border.

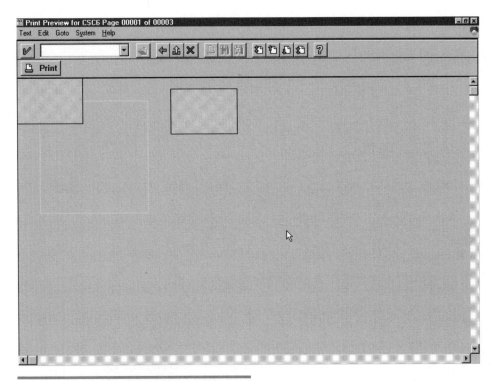

FIGURE 8.5   The POSITION command
Copyright by SAP AG

PRINT CONTROL

Description: This permits passing the Printer Control command directly to the printer.

Syntax:

```
/ :  PERFORM    printcontrol
```

printcontrol is the Print Control command as defined in the Spool Administration menu. To get to the Spool Administration menu follow **Tools → Administration → Spool administration** (transaction SPAD).

The effects of print controls show up only when the work is actually printed.

EXAMPLE

```
/: PRINT-CONTROL 'SLAND'
*    Test landscape
```

The example above will print the phrase `Test landscape` on a landscape-formatted page.

PROTECT

Description: This protects the text bracketed with `PROTECT` and `ENDPROTECT` from a page break.

Syntax:

```
/: PROTECT
   ...
/: ENDPROTECT
```

▲ As a rule, `PROTECT` should always be used with `ENDPROTECT`. If the text will not fit all in one piece on the current page, a new page will be generated and the text will be printed on the new page.

▲ This is only relevant for Main windows. Non-Main windows do not page break when they are filled.

EXAMPLE

The following example is from a Main window defined on multiple pages with a height of 5 cm.

```
*    text line 1
*    text line 2
*    text line 3
*    text line 4
*    text line 6
*    text line 7
*    text line 8
*    text line 9
/: PROTECT
*    These lines
*    should not
*    be separated
*    by
*    a
```

```
*   page
*   break
/:ENDPROTECT
```

CE019 Protect command

CD-ROM

The example above will produce two pages, each with a Main window 5 cm high. The first page (Figure 8.6), contains all the lines up to PROTECT. The rest of the lines will not fit on the same page, so they are printed on the next page (Figure 8.7).

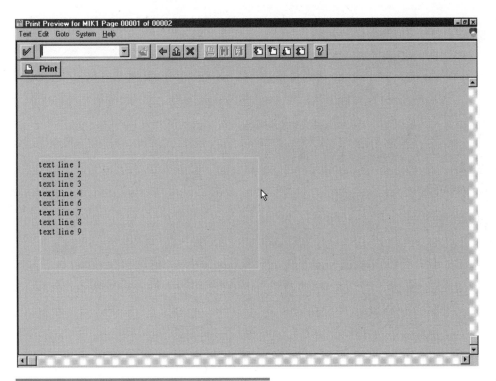

FIGURE 8.6   PROTECT command, page 1
Copyright by SAP AG

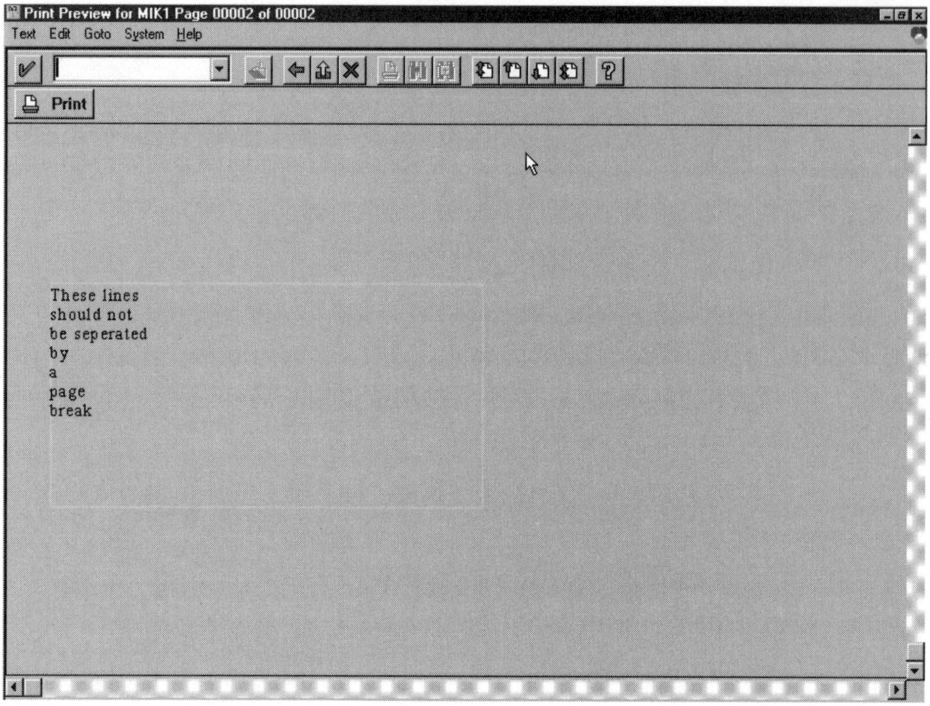

```
Print Preview for MIK1 Page 00002 of 00002
Text  Edit  Goto  System  Help



  Print




        These lines
        should not
        be seperated
        by
        a
        page
        break
```

FIGURE 8.7   PROTECT command page 2
Copyright by SAP AG

RESET

Description: The RESET command resets the outline sequencing back to 1.
Paragraphs can be associated with an outline scheme which is
sequenced at each level. The sequence of a particular level can be
"restarted" by issuing the RESET command.

Syntax:

    /: RESET *parname*

Paragraph name is the type of paragraph (or outline) level to be reset.

EXAMPLE

In Chapter 4 "Building Blocks," an outline was created which looked like
this:

```
a   Title
   aa  chapter 1
       aaa section 1
       aab section 2
       aac section 3
   ab  chapter 2
       aba section 1
       abb section 2
       abc section 3
```

At "chapter 2" the outline is defined to alphabetically increase to the next higher level "ab." If this text element is changed as follows to introduce the RESET command just before the "chapter 2" line, the sequence will start at "aa" again. This change in sequencing affects all dependent levels.

```
AA  Title
BB  chapter 1
CC  section 1
CC  section 2
CC  section 3
/:  RESET BB
BB  chapter 2
CC  section 1
CC  section 2
CC  section 3
```

CE020 RESET command

The text element above which includes the RESET command produces the text shown in Figure 8.8. The sequencing for paragraph type BB is restarted just before "Chapter 2" is printed.

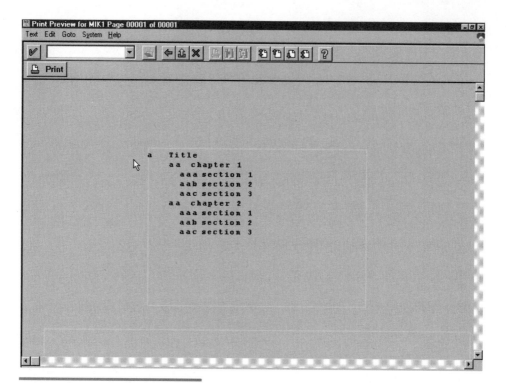

FIGURE 8.8   RESET command
Copyright by SAP AG

SET COUNTRY

Description: Some fields output differently depending on the country key. The country key is set in the user master record but can be changed by using SET COUNTRY.

Syntax:

```
/:  SET COUNTRY    'countrykey'
```

countrykey is the country key to be changed to.

EXAMPLE

The following is an excerpt from the tutorial in Chapter 7. The text element is from the Main window. This particular Text Element tag pair prints identical columns. There is a column on the left with a location, date, and instructor name. The column on the right prints the next course offering with location, date, and instructor name. In this example the original text elements have been altered so that the column on the left uses the country code 'JP' while the column on the right uses 'US'.

```
/E  COURSE_OFFERING_LEFT
/:  SET COUNTRY 'JP'
P2  &zsoffering-location(20)& &zsoffering-start_date(10)&
    &zsoffering-instructor(20)&
/E  COURSE_OFFERING_RIGHT
/:  SET COUNTRY 'US'
    &zsoffering-location(20)& &zsoffering-start_date(10)&
    &zsoffering-instructor(20)&
```

CE021 SET COUNTRY command

Figure 8.9 shows the result of rerunning the corresponding print program ZTRNCONF with the text elements set up as shown above. Notice that the date on the left is formatted with YYYY/MM/DD while the date on the right is MM/DD/YYYY.

SET DATE MASK

Description: Change the date mask.

Syntax:

```
/:  SET DATE MASK        'datemask'
```

▲ *datemask* is the desired date format.
▲ Interject commas, periods, slashes etc. where they are required.
▲ Use the following formats to construct date components:

YY	Two-digit year (99)
YYYY	Four-digit year (1999)
MM	Two-digit month (11)
MMM	Abreviated month (Nov)
MMMM	Name of month written out (November)
DD	Two-digit day (29)
DDD	Abreviated day (Su)
DDDD	Name of day written out (Sunday)

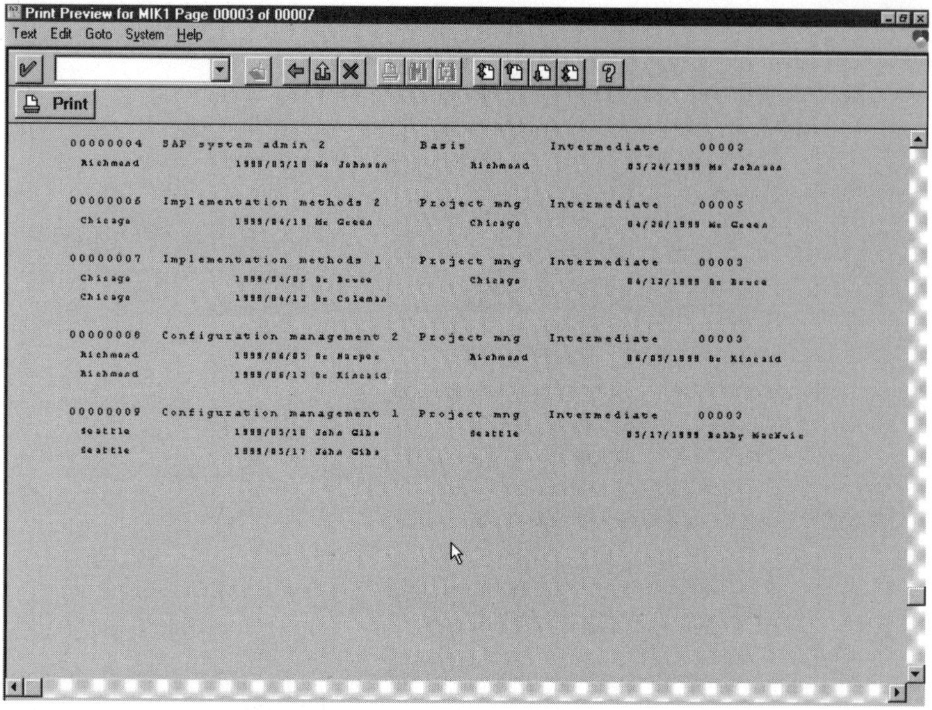

FIGURE 8.9   SET COUNTRY command
Copyright by SAP AG

EXAMPLE

```
*    &SYST-DATUM&
/:   SET DATE MASK = 'DD/MM/YY'
*    &SYST-DATUM&
/:   SET DATE MASK = 'DDD'
*    &SYST-DATUM&
/:   SET DATE MASK = 'DDDD'
*    &SYST-DATUM&
/:   SET DATE MASK = 'MMM'
*    &SYST-DATUM&
/:   SET DATE MASK = 'MMMM'
*    &SYST-DATUM&
/:   SET DATE MASK = 'YYYY'
*    &SYST-DATUM&
/:   SET DATE MASK = 'DDDD, DD MMMM YYYY'
*    Today is &SYST-DATUM&
```

CE022 SET DATE MASK command

The example above produces the text shown in Figure 8.10.

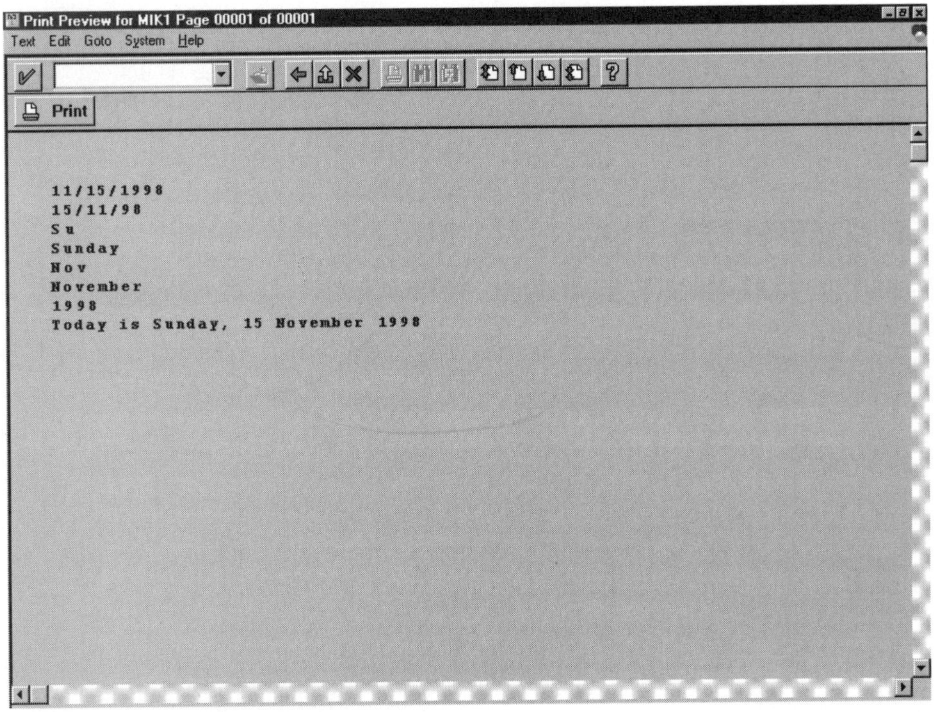

```
Print Preview for MIK1 Page 00001 of 00001                    _ 8 X
Text  Edit  Goto  System  Help

✓           ▼  ◀ ⬆ ✕   🖶  ❓

🖨 Print


    11/15/1998
    15/11/98
    Su
    Sunday
    Nov
    November
    1998
    Today is Sunday, 15 November 1998
```

FIGURE 8.10   SET DATE MASK command
Copyright by SAP AG

SET SIGN

Description: If the symbol uses a sign, it is possible to specify whether to put it on the left or right side of the number.

Syntax:

```
/: SET SIGN  left/right
```

Left/right is either LEFT (if the sign should go on the left side of the number) or RIGHT (if it should go on the right side of the number).

EXAMPLE
```
/:  SET SIGN LEFT
*    &lips-anzsn&
```

LIPSANZSN is a INT4-type field (symbol) passed by the print program. If the value of LIPS-ANZSN is –1003 (for example) this will print out as:

```
- 1,003
```

Without the SET SIGN LEFT the (–) would have appeared to the right of the number.

SET TIME MASK

Description: Change the time format used when the time is rendered.

Syntax:
```
/:  SET TIME MASK 'timemask'
```

▲ *timemask* is the desired time format.
▲ Interject commas, periods, slashes, characters, etc. as required.
▲ Use the following formats to construct time components:
   HH   Two-digit hour (12)
   MM   Two-digit minute (60)
   SS   Two-digit second (60)

EXAMPLE
```
/:  SET TIME MASK = 'The time is HH:MM'
*    &SYST-TIMLO&
```

The time is 11:12 PM. The above text element will produce:
```
The time is 22:12
```

SIZE

Description: This sets the size of a box and is used with the BOX command.

Syntax:
```
/: SIZE [WIDTH n1 u1] [HEIGHT n1 u2] [WINDOW] [PAGE]
```

▲ The key word SIZE must be followed by at least one of the parameters.

▲ WIDTH is followed by a number (*n1*) and a unit of measure (*u1*). The number can be negative.

▲ HEIGHT is followed by a number (*n2*) and a unit of measure (*u2*). The number can be negative. WIDTH and HEIGHT do not both have to be used.

▲ WINDOW sets the dimensions of the box to be equal to the dimensions of the current window.

▲ PAGE sets the dimensions of the box to be equal to the dimensions of the current page.

EXAMPLE
```
/: SIZE WIDTH 1 IN HEIGHT 1 IN
/: BOX FRAME 10 TW INTENSITY 20
/: SIZE WINDOW
/: SIZE WIDTH 1 CM
/: BOX FRAME 10 TW INTENSITY 20
```

CD-ROM

CE023 SIZE command

The text element above produces two boxes (Figure 8.11). The first box is 1 inch wide and 1 inch high. The third line resets the box size to the window size (5 cm wide by 5 cm high). The fourth line only changes the box width to 1 cm. The resulting box size is 1 cm wide by 5 cm high. Both boxes have their origin in the upper left corner of the window. The second box overlays the first.

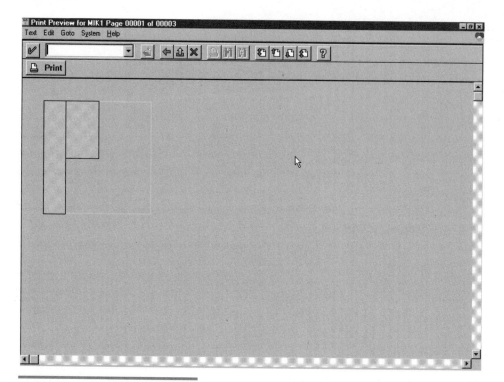

FIGURE 8.11   SIZE command
Copyright by SAP AG

STYLE

Description: Assign a style for the text to use.

Syntax:

/: STYLE *stylename*

▲ *stylename* is the name of valid style.
▲ To view styles select **Format → Style** from the text editor.
▲ To create a style select **Tools → Word processing → Style** from the main menu.

EXAMPLE

/: STYLE DOKU
*   <H>Remit to:</>
*   Company XYZ Inc.

    *   `123 Main Street Richmond, VA 12345`

CD-ROM

CE024 STYLE command

The text above is from a standard text. The style DOKU has a character string H which is set to bold on. The Remit to: line prints in bold. If STYLE DOKU were not present the H character string would not be available. A test print of the standard text is shown in Figure 8.12.

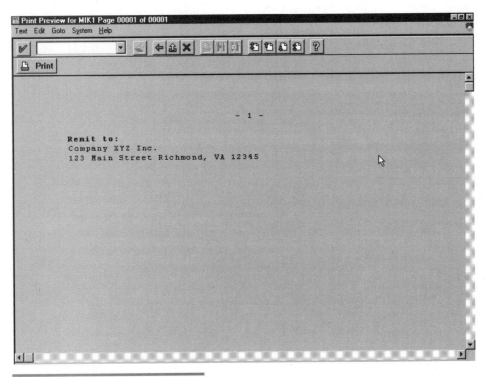

FIGURE 8.12   STYLE command
Copyright by SAP AG

SUMMING

Description: This adds the contents of a symbol to a total. Each time the symbol is printed, its value is added to the "total" symbol.

Syntax:

```
/:  SUMMING    prgymbol    INTO    totsymbol
```

▲ *prgsymbol* and *totsymbol* are numeric program symbols identified in the tables statement of the calling print program.
▲ The symbol being summed is *prgsymbol*.
▲ The total is captured in *totsymbol*.

EXAMPLE

Main window from layout set ZLSSUM:

```
/:  SUMMING &RMCB0-HLAB6& INTO &RMCB0-AGABA&
/E  ITEM_LINE
*   &RMCB0-HLAB6&
/:  BOTTOM
*   These numbers added together equal &RMCB0-AGABA&
/:  ENDBOTTOM
```

CE026 SUMMING MAIN window example

CD-ROM

Print program which calls ZLSSUM:

```
1   REPORT ZLSSUM.
2   TABLES RMCB0.
3   PERFORM OPEN_LAYOUT_SET.
4   MOVE 31 TO RMCB0-HLAB6.
5   PERFORM WRITE_TO_MAIN.
6   MOVE 41 TO RMCB0-HLAB6.
7   PERFORM WRITE_TO_MAIN.
8   MOVE 71 TO RMCB0-HLAB6.
9   PERFORM WRITE_TO_MAIN.
10  PERFORM CLOSE_LAYOUT_SET.
11  *-------------------------------------
12  FORM OPEN_LAYOUT_SET.
13      CALL FUNCTION 'OPEN_FORM'
14          EXPORTING
15              FORM            = 'ZLSSUM'
16              LANGUAGE        = 'E'
17              DEVICE          = 'PRINTER'
18              APPLICTION      = 'TX'
19              DIALOG          = 'X'.
20  ENDFORM.
21  *-------------------------------------
```

```
22 FORM CLOSE_LAYOUT_SET.
23     CALL FUNCTION 'CLOSE_FORM'.
24 ENDFORM.
25 *--------------------------------
26 FORM WRITE_TO_MAIN.
27     CALL FUNCTION 'WRITE_FORM'
28         EXPORTING
29             WINDOW  = 'MAIN'
30             ELEMENT = 'ITEM_LINE'.
31 ENDFORM.
```

CD-ROM

CE027 SUMMING program example

Two DEC type fields from the structure RMCB0 are used here as an example. RMCB0-HLAB6 is populated three times. Each time, the layout set is called and a detail line is printed in the Main window. Each time RMCB0-HLAB6 is used its value at that instant is added to RMCB0-AGABA. When there is no more to print in MAIN, RMCB0-AGABA is printed at the bottom. In this example MAIN is 5 cm by 5 cm and located on the first page (FPAGE). There are no other windows involved. The output is shown in Figure 8.13.

Formatting Options

▲ Formatting options can be combined (7R)
▲ The formatting options are used inside the ampersands
▲ Program examples are shown at the end of the section.

In this section the symbols are shown with ampersands included for clarity.

(<) and (>) Move Sign

Description: This forces the sign to appear on the left (<) or right (>) of the number.

Syntax:

&symbol (>) &

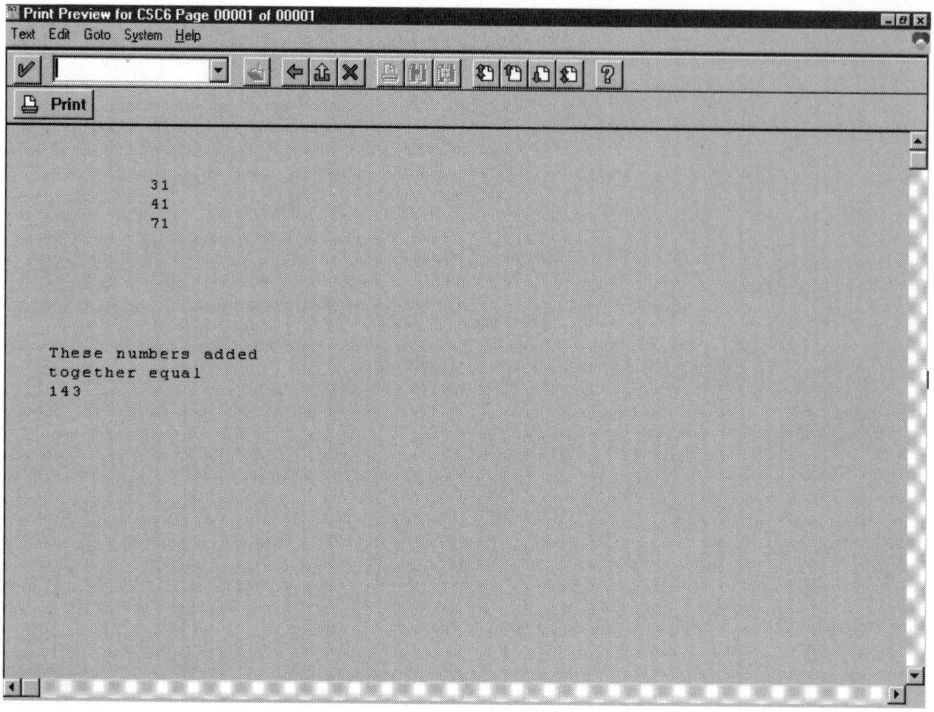

FIGURE 8.13   SUMMING command
Copyright by SAP AG

symbol is a numeric value and we need to force the sign to the right of the number. Use (<) if the sign should appear on the left.

In example 1 of Figure 8.14, &lipsvb-netwr(<)& results in:

```
-312,342.00
```

'text' Interject a Literal

Description: To interject a literal prefix or suffix, put the text inside the ampersands and surround it with single quotes.

Syntax:

    &'my text' *symbol*&   or   &*symbol*' my text'&

my_text is a literal value of choice. The text appears only if the symbol appears.

```
   Print Preview for MIK1 Page 00001 of 00001
   Text Edit Goto System Help

   CURR 15          312,342.00-
   CURR 11       6,526,751.00
   CHAR 25  West side        receiving
   FLTP 16  8.760000000000000E+02
   NUMC 06  000012

   1. Move sign to the left-
              -312,342.00
   2. Interject text-
   The test number is        312,342.00-
   3. Remove spaces-
   West side receiving
   4. Fix length-
   West
   5. Set decimal places-
       6,526,751.0
   6. Offset to the right (3 char)-
   t side       receiving
   7. Exponent (with exponent=3)-
   0.876000000000000E+03
   8. Fill leading spaces-
   xxx6,526,751.00
   9. Don't show anything if value is initial-
              0.00

   10 Right Justification-
```

FIGURE 8.14   Formatting options example
Copyright by SAP AG

In example 2 of Figure 8.14, &'The test number is 'lipsvb-netwr& results in:

```
The test number is      312,342.00-
```

(C) Remove Spaces

Description: Use this option to remove multiple spaces from a text string. If there are two or more spaces between the characters, they are replaced with a single space. Any spaces in the front are removed.

Syntax:

& *symbol*(C)&

symbol is a text string that has multiple spaces.

In example 3 of Figure 8.14, "West side receiving" is replaced with "West side receiving".

(n) Fixed Length

Description: Use this option to fix the length of the output either longer or shorter than what would otherwise have printed. Using asterisk will fix the length at whatever is provided in the data dictionary.

Syntax:

    & *symbol*(n)&

symbol is a character or number and n is the number to use as the fixed length.

In example 4 of Figure 8.14, "West side receiving" is replaced with "West" by using &lipsvb-empst(5)&.

(.n) Set Number of Decimals

Description: The number of decimal places to be used can be fixed with (.n). If n is zero, no decimal will be used.

Syntax:

    & *symbol*(.n)&

n is the number of decimal places to use.

In example 5 of Figure 8.14, &lipsvb-netpr(.1)& results in:

    6,526,751.0

(+n) Offset to Right

Description: To output the symbol starting at n places to the right, use the (+n) formatting option.

Syntax:

    & symbol(+n)&

n is the number of places to offset.

In example 6 of Figure 8.14, "West side receiving" is converted to "t side receiving". The "wes" has been chopped off with &lipsvb-empst+3&.

(En) Format Exponential Number

Description: This is used with fields of type FLTP to format the exponential number.

Syntax:

> & *symbol*(En)&

n is the exponent to use. The decimal place will be adjusted automatically.

In example 7 of Figure 8.14, &lipsvb-UMREF(E3)& results in:

> 0.876000000000000E+03

(Ff) Fill Leading Spaces

Description: This is used to fill leading spaces with the character of choice (*f*).

Syntax:

> & *symbol*(F*f*)&

f is the character with which to fill the spaces.

In example 8 of Figure 8.14, &lipsvb-netpr(Fx)& results in:

> xxx6,526,751.00

(I) Do Not Show Initial Values

Description: If the *symbol* (and any pre or post text) should be ignored when the *symbol* has retained its initial value, use (I).

Syntax:

> & *symbol*(I)&

symbol is any valid symbol.

In example 9 of Figure 8.14, `&lipsvb-KZWI1&` results in:

```
0.00
```

`&lipsvb-KZWI1(I)&` results in:

(K) Ignore Conversion

Description: When special fields like CURR and QUAN are used, the conversion routine can be ignored using the (K) option.

Syntax:

& *symbol*(K)&

symbol derives from a data dictionary field that has a conversion routine associated with it.

(Rn) Force Right Justification

Description: Make symbols justify to the right. An explicit symbol length must be provided.

Syntax:

& *symbol*(Rn)&

n is the explicit length of the symbol.

In example 10 of Figure 8.15, `&lipsvb-posnr(R15)&` is used to force the symbol length to 15 and right justify the value. Result is:

```
000012
```

(S) No Sign

Description: Represent *symbol* without a sign.

Syntax:

& *symbol*(S)&

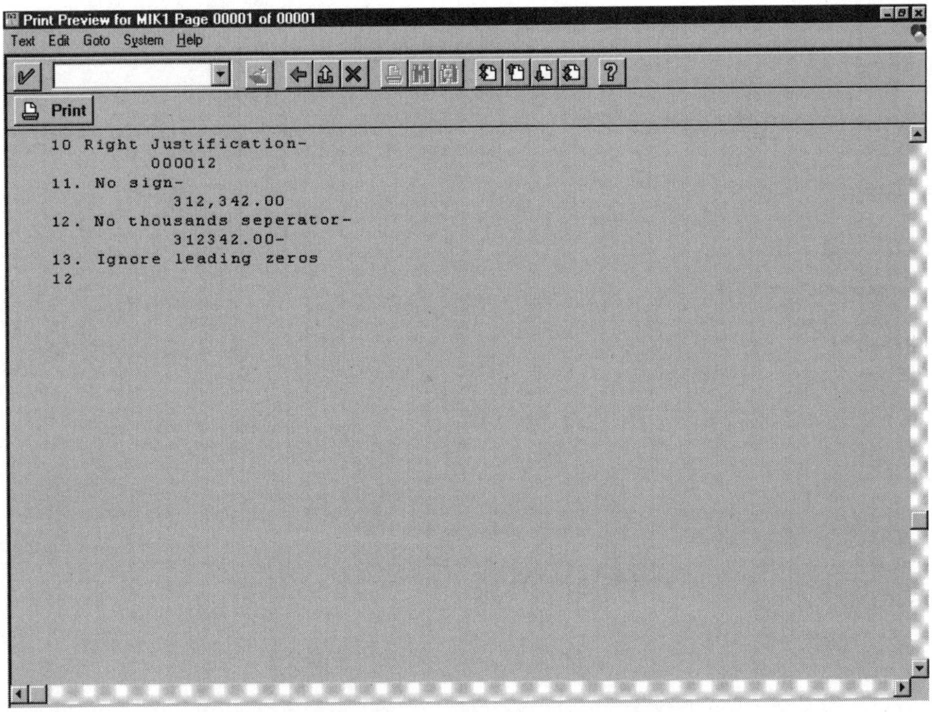

```
Print Preview for MIK1 Page 00001 of 00001
Text  Edit  Goto  System  Help

     10 Right Justification-
            000012
     11. No sign-
            312,342.00
     12. No thousands seperator-
            312342.00-
     13. Ignore leading zeros
     12
```

FIGURE 8.15   Formatting options example continued
Copyright by SAP AG

symbol is a numeric value with a sign.

In example 11 of Figure 8.15, &lipsvb-netwr(S)& is used to remove the trailing sign. The result is:

```
312,342.00
```

(T) No Thousands Separator

Description: Represent the symbol without a thousands separator.

Syntax:
```
& symbol(T)&
```

symbol is a number that has a thousands separator (is greater than 999).

In example 12 of Figure 8.15, &lipsvb-netwr(T)& results in:

```
312342.00-
```

(Z) Ignore Leading Zeros

Description: Leading zeros can be removed with (Z).

Syntax:

& *symbol*(Z)&

symbol has leading zeros.

In example 13 of Figure 8.15, &lipsvb-posnr(Z)& results in:

12

This is the calling print program used to generate the examples above:

```
1   REPORT ZLSFOR.
2   TABLES: LIPSVB.
3   PERFORM OPEN_LAYOUT_SET.
4   MOVE -312342 TO LIPSVB-NETWR.
5   MOVE 6526751 TO LIPSVB-NETPR.
6   MOVE 'West side     receiving' TO LIPSVB-EMPST.
7   MOVE 876 TO LIPSVB-UMREF.
8   MOVE '0012' TO LIPSVB-POSNR.
9   PERFORM WRITE_TO_MAIN.
10  PERFORM CLOSE_LAYOUT_SET.
11  *-------------------------------------
12  FORM OPEN_LAYOUT_SET.
13     CALL FUNCTION 'OPEN_FORM'
14        EXPORTING
15            FORM            = 'ZLSFOR'
16            LANGUAGE        = 'E'
17            DEVICE          = 'PRINTER'
18            APPLICTION      = 'TX'
19            DIALOG          = 'X'.
20  ENDFORM.
21  *-------------------------------------
22  FORM CLOSE_LAYOUT_SET.
23  CALL FUNCTION 'CLOSE_FORM'.
24  ENDFORM.
25  *-------------------------------------
26  FORM WRITE_TO_MAIN.
27  CALL FUNCTION 'WRITE_FORM'
28     EXPORTING
29         WINDOW      = 'W1'.
30  ENDFORM.
```

CD-ROM

CE028 Print program for format options

Here is the text element for window "W1" on the first and only page of the layout set ZLSFOR. The dimensions of window W1 are 20 cm by 20 cm.

```
*    CURR 15 &lipsvb-netwr&
*    CURR 11 &lipsvb-netpr&
*    CHAR 25 &lipsvb-empst&
*    FLTP 16 &lipsvb-UMREF&
*    NUMC 06 &lipsvb-posnr&
*
*    1. Move sign to the left-
*    &lipsvb-netwr(<)&
*    2. Interject text-
*    &'The test number is 'lipsvb-netwr&
*    3. Remove spaces-
*    &lipsvb-empst(C)&
*    4. Fix length-
*    &lipsvb-empst(5)&
*    5. Set decimal places-
*    &lipsvb-netpr(.1)&
*    6. Offset to the right (3 char)-
*    &lipsvb-empst+3&
*    7. Exponent (with exponent=3)-
*    &lipsvb-UMREF(E3)&
*    8. Fill leading spaces-
*    &lipsvb-netpr(Fx)&
*    9. Don't show anything if value is initial-
*    &lipsvb-KZWI1&
*    &lipsvb-KZWI1(I)&
*    10 Right Justification-
*    &lipsvb-posnr(R15)&
*    11. No sign-
*    &lipsvb-netwr(S)&
*    12. No thousands seperator-
*    &lipsvb-netwr(T)&
*    13. Ignore leading zeros
*    &lipsvb-posnr(Z)&
```

CD-ROM

CE029 Window W1 for formatting exp

The output from the print program ZLSFOR and the layout set ZLSFOR are shown here in Figures 8.14 and 8.15.

Command Reference in Review

1. If a command or format option will not work, start off small (or simple), get that to work, and then add on.
2. In many cases the type of field that a program symbol derives from will affect the output.
3. Main windows and non-MAIN windows do not process the same way. Some commands are not relevant in non-Main windows.

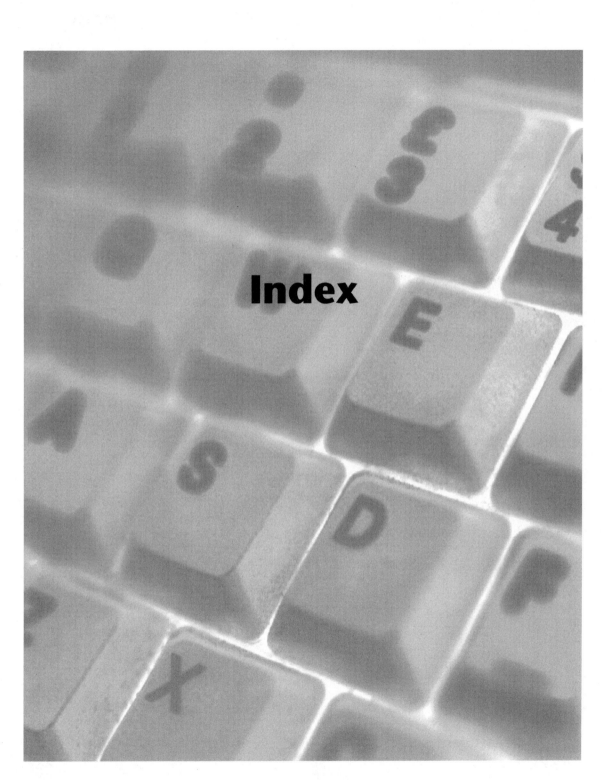

Index

Z

About the Author

MICHAELSON BUCHANAN is an ABAP programmer/analyst with Computer Sciences Corporation's Richmond Operations Center, where he has consulted on multiple SAP development efforts for Fortune 500 clients. Mike has 11 years' experience in the evaluation, proliferation, maintenance, and development of automated system solutions. He resides in Chester, Virginia.

SOFTWARE AND INFORMATION LICENSE

The software and information on this diskette (collectively referred to as the "Product") are the property of The McGraw-Hill Companies, Inc. ("McGraw-Hill") and are protected by both United States copyright law and international copyright treaty provision. You must treat this Product just like a book, except that you may copy it into a computer to be used and you may make archival copies of the Products for the sole purpose of backing up our software and protecting your investment from loss.

By saying "just like a book," McGraw-Hill means, for example, that the Product may be used by any number of people and may be freely moved from one computer location to another, so long as there is no possibility of the Product (or any part of the Product) being used at one location or on one computer while it is being used at another. Just as a book cannot be read by two different people in two different places at the same time, neither can the Product be used by two different people in two different places at the same time (unless, of course, McGraw-Hill's rights are being violated).

McGraw-Hill reserves the right to alter or modify the contents of the Product at any time.

This agreement is effective until terminated. The Agreement will terminate automatically without notice if you fail to comply with any provisions of this Agreement. In the event of termination by reason of your breach, you will destroy or erase all copies of the Product installed on any computer system or made for backup purposes and shall expunge the Product from your data storage facilities.

LIMITED WARRANTY

McGraw-Hill warrants the physical diskette(s) enclosed herein to be free of defects in materials and workmanship for a period of sixty days from the purchase date. If McGraw-Hill receives written notification within the warranty period of defects in material or workmanship, and such notification is determined by McGraw-Hill to be correct, McGraw-Hill will replace the defective diskette(s). Send request to:

Customer Service
McGraw-Hill
Gahanna Industrial Park
860 Taylor Station Road
Blacklick, OH 43004-9615

The entire and exclusive liability and remedy for breach of this Limited Warranty shall be limited to replacement of defective diskette(s) and shall not include or extend to any claim for or right to cover any other damages, including but not limited to, loss of profit, data, or use of the software, or special, incidental, or consequential damages or other similar claims, even if McGraw-Hill has been specifically advised as to the possibility of such damages. In no event will McGraw-Hill's liability for any damages to you or any other person ever exceed the lower of suggested list price or actual price paid for the license to use the Product, regardless of any form of the claim.

THE McGRAW-HILL COMPANIES, INC. SPECIFICALLY DISCLAIMS ALL OTHER WARRANTIES, EXPRESS OR IMPLIED, INCLUDING BUT NOT LIMITED TO, ANY IMPLIED WARRANT OF MERCHANTABILITY OR FITNESS FOR A PARTICULAR PURPOSE. Specifically, McGraw-Hill makes no representation or warranty that the Product is fit for any particular purpose and any implied warranty of merchantability is limited to the sixty day duration of the Limited Warranty covering the physical diskette(s) only (and not the software or information) and is otherwise expressly and specifically disclaimed.

This Limited Warranty gives you specific legal rights, you may have others which may vary from state to state. Some states do not allow the exclusion of incidental or consequential damages, or the limitation on how long an implied warranty lasts, so some of the above may not apply to you.

This Agreement constitutes the entire agreement between the parties relating to use of the Product. The terms of any purchase order shall have no effect on the terms of this Agreement. Failure of McGraw-Hill to insist at any time on strict compliance with this Agreement shall not constitute a waiver of any rights under this Agreement. This Agreement shall be construed and governed in accordance with the laws of New York. If any provision of this Agreement is held to be contrary to law, that provision will be enforced to the maximum extent permissible and the remaining provisions will remain in force and effect.